ONLY THE GOALKEEPER TO BEAT

Francis Hodgson

ONLY THE GOALKEEPER TO BEAT

MACMILLAN

First published 1998 by Macmillan

an imprint of Macmillan Publishers Ltd
25 Eccleston Place, London SW1W 9NF
and Basingstoke

Associated companies throughout the world

ISBN 0 333 68693 4

1 3 5 7 9 8 6 4 2

A CIP catalogue record for this book is available from
the British Library.

Phototypeset by Intype London Limited
Printed by Mackays of Chatham plc, Chatham, Kent

Contents

Introduction

Christmas Day 1937, and Sam Bartram, goalkeeper, was having another day at the office.

Soon after the kick-off [fog] began to thicken rapidly at the far end, travelling past Vic Woodley in the Chelsea goal and rolling steadily towards me. The referee stopped the game, and then, as visibility became clearer, restarted it. We were on top at this time, and I saw fewer and fewer figures as we attacked steadily.

I paced up and down my goal-line, happy in the knowledge that Chelsea were being pinned in their own half. 'The boys must be giving the Pensioners the hammer,' I thought smugly, as I stamped my feet for warmth. Quite obviously, however, we were not getting the ball into the net, for no players were coming back to line up, as they would have done following a goal. Time passed, and I made several advances towards the edge of the penalty area, peering through the murk which was getting thicker every minute. Still I could see nothing. The Chelsea defence was clearly being run off its feet.

After a long time a figure loomed out of the curtain of fog in front of me. It was a policeman, and he gaped at me incredulously. 'What on earth are you doing here?' he gasped. 'The game was stopped a quarter of an hour ago. The field's completely empty.'

And when I groped my way to the dressing-room the rest of the Charlton team, already out of the bath, were convulsed with laughter.[1]

What on earth are you doing here? It's the basic question, the one every goalkeeper asks several times a game. Keeping goal can be a genuinely horrible activity. You get embarrassed, hurt, blamed, defeated. If your team wins, you're a passenger; by definition, if you lose, you let in goals which you could or should have prevented. You're an alien, a wacko, the obvious butt of obvious jokes. What on earth are you doing here? Picking yourself up in the wet mud of a January goal-mouth. You just know there are more agreeable ways to spend a Sunday morning.

I am a goalkeeper. A good bad one, although certainly not a bad good one. That is to say I've never played at anything like good-football standard, but I'm a pretty good goalkeeper at the lucky-if-eleven-men-turn-up, park-pitch and has-somebody-remembered-to-bring-a-ball level at which I play. Nothing glorious: I've never played serious football, but I am a goalkeeper all the same. I think like a goalkeeper, and have done since I was tiny, six or seven years old.

It started as the obvious way to be different from the others. Then it became a kind of gamble: if I could get good at this stuff, this horrible, painful, melancholic stuff, then I could perhaps sometimes earn the feeling that I could do something nobody else could do. Then quite suddenly I could no longer say I was a footballer. It wasn't that I played in goal last week, or took my quarter-hour turn the week before. I was a goalkeeper. Not by a miracle of training or a natural gift uncovered. Just that I grew, and have kept, a goalkeeper's mind. And that, let me tell you, is not just a footballer's mind with gloves on. That fine goalkeeper John Burridge, now long since retired, but still willing to play for anybody anywhere, a man so obsessed with getting it right that he once imitated Peter Shilton's perm, is alleged still (in his forties) to watch *Match of the Day* in his goalkeeping kit, with a washing-up bowl for the ball, and to fling himself around in front of the television in anticipation of every goalkeeping move he sees. I don't do that, but I do watch as a goalkeeper. What on earth are you doing here? has been a part of my life for years. That's what I mean when I say I am a goalkeeper. It's a question worth trying to answer.

Football, the simplest and best ball game in the world, almost collapses under the elaborate mythology that sits over it like too much hat on a slim girl at Ascot. Between player myth, club myth, national myth, manager myth, even commentator myth and stadium myth, the simple little game struggles terribly for breath. If half a dozen small boys are kicking a ball about in a car park, just playing football, you can be sure that at least one of them calls himself Shearer, one is imitating a commentator, and all of them are convinced that the garage doors that clatter and ring as the ball pounds against them are perfectly ideal replacements for the Kop or the North Bank or the Shed, temporarily unavailable for play. But the natural home of football myth is the crowd, where lying for the greater glory of the game is an art form and the simplest emotion echoes like something from Homer. Your new (perfectly average) striker beat a defender last Saturday and scored a simple goal? Before you reached the pub it was five men that he beat and Georgie Best never did it better. You were mildly disappointed to lose a game you had a chance of winning? Gutted is the word. Hyperbole hangs around football like a bad smell.

In the centre of all that exaggeration and to-do, in conversation and in dreams, are the goals. The myth of the goal is the central myth in football, the heaviest and most burdensome, the one which gives the whole circus its reason for being. Ask anybody in football what they like about it and the answer will centre on goals. In the endless round of trite interviews they have to give to club programmes, professional forwards quite alarmingly often claim that scoring a goal is 'better than sex', and somehow nobody picks them up on it. The British, seen by the rest of the world as a race of reserved persons unable and unwilling vividly to express emotion, quite routinely celebrate goals by kissing strangers and leaping uncontrollably about. Even a dull goal on a dull day leads to this collective epilepsy, this short-circuit of the brain. A quietened crowd starts to sing again after a goal, there is more movement and the sense of being alive is increased. It is hardly an overstatement that a good goal sustains twenty or thirty thousand people for the whole of the week, providing a galvanic increase in heart-rate and energy levels that neither job nor family can supply. People feel so much better after goals they get hooked on them. And while some enjoy other things about football, there is no doubt that goals are what we pay our money to see; a great deal of money.

So there we all are, in our stadium, keenly looking forward to our goals. We deserve them, we've paid for them in money and in hours of no-goals. Goals are status symbols in our lives, theoretically meaningless, but practically important. It takes a minimum of effort to get a new car or the latest piece of gadgetry, but it takes none at all to claim goals. Once attached to a team, you can feel improved simply by considering its goals your own. There is nothing in modern society more collective than football support. Even family is disguised in embarrassed phrases designed to conceal the closeness of the tie: 'the old lady' or 'her indoors', 'the folks'. But football supporters unhesitatingly, nauseatingly bang in the first person plural. We scored. We stuffed them. We belong. If the hard practical fact is that goals are the way the score is kept in football, like points in tennis, the emotional story goes much further. Nobody has ever heard even the most devoted tennis fan claim a match point saved or a game won with that collective 'we'. In football it is the norm.

There is only one man on each team whose specific role is to prevent goals. All that desire, all that concentrated longing can be frustrated by the goalkeeper. More than that: he *must* frustrate it. The better he is at what he does the more regularly will he dash the expected taste of goal-frenzy on the lips of the crowd – in a word that reeks of an older attitude to competition than the one we have now, the goalkeeper is a spoilsport. He starts as a negative presence. His whole job is to negate. He is there to do his utmost to prevent the very thing that everybody else present wants to occur. The most basic triumph of goalkeeping is the nil-all draw, the outcome everybody loves to hate. For a goalkeeper to have a good game necessarily means that half the people present have had a less good one than they might have had, had he been off-form or out-classed.

So the goalkeeper is responsible for leaving people wanting more. But he is also responsible for a great deal else. The last line of defence, indeed, with all that can imply of heroism and its antithesis. People depend on the goalkeeper in a way they depend on no other player. He can save them embarrassment and ridicule, in the professional game can frequently be the difference between the bonus for a win and another bad week. The whole picture of the goalkeeper as the unflappable 'captain of the defence' is familiar enough. Every crowd, every player is happy enough to rely heavily on the goalkeeper. The confusion comes from the plain fact that everybody gets used to relying on the man they don't really want to perform: by relying on the goalkeeper we are relying on the spoilsport. Whatever happens, the better he does, the more the game will lack its core. To earn one's reputation by eliminating the thrilling euphoria of the goal, magnified and multiplied many times beyond its real worth by generations of mythology, is a terrible thing. To deprive team-mates and spectators of all that, no wonder the goalkeeper is regarded from the outset as not entirely trustworthy. We want goals desperately. Ours, preferably, but any goals at all are better than none.

Here is the original reason for the general mistrust of goalkeepers which finds its most consistent expression in such phrases as 'You've Got to be Crazy' and 'Goalkeepers are Different'. The first was chosen as the title of a book by Bob Wilson, and the second for one by Brian Glanville, two of the very few experts to have turned their minds and their typewriters to this exotic sub-branch within the straightforward sport of football. It is not that goalkeepers are crazy, but that they are locked in a crazy relationship with the rest of the game. Fundamental to their sides' success, they are committed against the very thing their team-mates are devoted to. If you believe in football it is axiomatic that you believe in the surge of elation that comes with goals. And the goalkeeper, by an inescapable logic, believes in something else. The goalkeeper may indeed be different. At root, he is an anti-footballer. By being devoted to the prevention of goals he is set against the core of football.

Lots of games have specialized positions, and people often try to compare goalkeeping to one of the others. Every goalkeeper must be familiar with the assumption made in conversation that once the season is over he becomes a wicket-keeper at cricket. In point of fact, very few do both, for wicket-keeping has very little to do with goalkeeping beyond the pleasant symmetry of their names. The wicket-keeper is in an attacking position even though he takes the ball. The player who most resembles the goalkeeper in cricket is the batsman. He is the one whose 'life' can be ended every time he comes into action, and he is the one who will find that several hours of brilliance are undone in the most public way by a single gesture. A wicket-keeper, after all, cannot be out every ball. A goalkeeper may remain on the field, but every ball he receives is a chance of disaster. Unlike a batsman, he accumulates no points as he stays there. On the contrary, his job is to accumulate the absence of points. All sportsmen collect superlatives: best time, highest average, greatest distance. Only goalkeepers collect nothingness. A perfect performance in goal is marked by a zero, the full round circle with which we denote emptiness. Nil. Sure, the goalkeeper is different.

For a forward to be the hero of the day, he needs to score a goal; any goal, often scored off his arse or his ear. The opposite applies to a goalkeeper, whose success is measured not merely by things done right, but also by the absence of things done wrong. To save virtually everything a superior team can throw his way as they breeze past inadequate cover at will is not enough. Every goalkeeper knows that for him a great performance is normally blown by any lapse. In the goals it becomes critically clear that the notion of collective responsibility, the very idea of the *team*, is fickle in the extreme: *we* scored, *we* won, *we* made it through to the quarter-final but *he*, differentiated from the rest of us, let in a goal. Small wonder that goalkeepers don't always think like the rest of the team.

Among the things goalkeepers routinely do, there are several that have parallels elsewhere. But the whole extraordinary package is unique. For example, most sportsmen get into a rhythm of one kind or another, with an opponent or with themselves. To rally in racquet games or to pace oneself in laps is a tremendous help. To establish a rhythm and to learn how to up it and break it if need be is something almost every sportsman gets to know. Not goalkeepers. Nothing that they do happens in a regular pattern. Goalkeepers are part of a defence, but the word is the wrong one. In reality they are attacked. All the choices are their opponents'. For unpredictability, the nearest equivalent is slip-fielding, where the ball, coming by definition from a mistimed shot, is never delivered in a rhythmic way the fielder can get used to. Even the best close fielders have records that compare poorly with the minimum needed by a goalkeeper. To hold two hard chances out of three in the slips is thought pretty good. It wouldn't hold your place as a goalkeeper.

Great goalkeeping has everything that we look for in sportsmen: reflexes and timing, great strength and speed, high drama and perfect bodily movement. For competition, for courage, there is nothing we admire in sport that isn't somewhere in goalkeeping. In every team there is a goalkeeper, and often a spare who might play outfield but be able to take a spell in goal when needed. That makes an awful lot of goalkeepers in the country. Yet because the essence of keeping goal is to treasure the absence of something, and something which everybody else badly wants to happen, this most athletic part of football remains the least appreciated. Goalkeeping can be brutal, but can also be more graceful than anything else to be found on a sports field. It can be the desperate floundering of unhappy losers in deeply appropriate mud, but it can also be the scientific and physical overwhelming of long odds against him by a nonpareil. At the very highest level, goalkeeping gets more attention now than it ever has before, and the two or three best known goalkeepers are sports stars comparable in profile to any other. But goalkeeping remains an unknown and largely unloved activity. The goalkeeper is there to carry the blame, to be laughed at, and to look decorative as he gets beaten by the kind of over-emphatic goal all players love (but usually fail) to score. It isn't fair, it isn't right. But these are still clearly the attitudes that goalkeepers have to put up with. At least part of the point of this book is to make the other case.

Many of my own prejudices will become perfectly clear as we go along. But here, just to get started, are a few that might as well be out in the open once and for all. In the first place, I don't believe that goals are particularly important in football. I know that games are won and lost by them, but I don't (unless I happen to be playing) care about them that much. As a spectator, I tend to enjoy rather small things. To see somebody trap the ball neatly, swerve away from a defender, and give a thoughtful and efficient pass to move the game on is often more of a pleasure than to watch some routine goal work again against a foolish defence. I like the quick-changing patterns of football, and I like the way those movements express thought. I like skill, and care less for all those allegedly British virtues of 'good engines' and 'covering every blade of grass' and 'giving a hundred and ten per cent'. I think fandom, in its simple sense of attaching oneself to a team, is absurd. Nobody in their right mind would become a 'supporter' of a particular theatre company, and refuse to go to the better one nearby when the chosen company was playing. I think grown men singing that some wretched outfit of miserable no-hopers are the 'finest team the world has ever seen' are simply sad. I have zero memory for results, league tables and so on, and frequently can't remember who I watched playing a week or two ago. I can think of nothing worse than hoarding programmes, fanzines, autographs or other football impedimenta. I would no more try to visit all the League grounds than I would try to visit all the motorway service areas in the country. I like playing football, watching it and reading about it in equal measure. Above all I think goalkeepers have got a rough deal over the years, and I often find that there is an enormous amount of pleasure to be had from watching them. That's why I'm here. I've never been pearl-diving, or down the Cresta Run – there are lots of things I don't know. But I've never found any sporting activity to compare with goalkeeping.

If you try to play football with a toddler you will find he is not very enthusiastic about the kicking part of the business. Proud dads do it the whole time, even though it is not very surprising that a child who can hardly stand on two legs is a little hesitant to get into the full performance. But what he will invariably do is lurch forwards and try to get his hands on the ball. It's fun – you can check this by scrutinizing the grimacing and giggling that results. If successfully accomplished, it also prevents him having to run and fetch the ball from thirty yards behind him. Right there is the basic goalkeeping skill: using hands to stop the ball, and saving oneself from unwanted cross-country running by doing so. The toddler will discover, as he marches boldly up the ladder of experience, that goal nets are a luxury without which he will have to do for years. To make a save is to save oneself from that ignominious jog to recover the ball. The better you save the ones in the goal frame, the more you are entitled to make the full-back go to fetch the ones which went wide of it.

Catching things seems a pretty basic pleasure. Dogs and dolphins like to try it. Children catch snowflakes or leaves, given the right time of year, just because that is what you do to things dropping around you. It happens to be a pleasure which is essentially banned in the rules of football, and everybody knows that doing anything is more fun when it is not allowed. At that level, goalkeeping is the simplest and most obviously satisfying part of a very simple game. There is nothing difficult about identifying a successful goalkeeping gesture: the ball which looked likely to pass through the goal did not.

'Just get something on the ball, lad.' It sounds absurd, yet that is often what goalkeeping comes down to. But for every situation, and specifically for every goalkeeper, there is a different solution to the fundamental problem. A goalkeeper must stop the goal. How he does it is a lifetime's work. To save one goal every so often is easy enough; I've before now saved with my nose – that's what happens if you're slow to get your hands up to a fast volley from close in. The ball bounces well out of the penalty area. Through the streaming tears I have seen players evenly divided between those who saw what had happened and thought for the tenth or the twentieth time they were glad they didn't keep goal, and those who hadn't and who overestimated my speed of reaction as a result. It isn't difficult to save with your nose, provided, of course, that you have learnt not to duck as any sensible person would. But keeping goal is not about occasional saves. The only standard is an extraordinary one: to be any good, the goalkeeper must aim, must *expect* to save everything. He doesn't collect few-goals or only-good-goals. He collects the absence of goals. No goals. Any goal is a defeat.

The goal, let me remind you, is huge. Eight yards long – twenty-four feet – and eight feet high. When Bob Beamon long-jumped twenty-nine feet, people talked about jumping to the moon. It was unthinkable. To cover a goal against every eventuality, at the kinds of speeds necessary in football, should be impossible. A hundred and ninety-two square feet of goal – it's a vast area, bigger than a barn door, bigger than the back end of a bus. It's impossible to miss, far bigger than most living-room walls. Get your kid brother to stand in front of the living-room wall and kick a ball (of rolled-up socks, if you value your furniture) at him. He won't stop it hitting the wall once in twenty, once in thirty times. Quite quickly he'll start to use the word 'unfair' at you. It *is* unfair, manifestly, grotesquely unfair.

Hockey goals are tiny, ice hockey goals even smaller. If you stand on the goal-line in the middle of the goal either top corner is fourteen and a half feet away from your heels. That's a lot more than twice your height, an insane distance to be expected to reach accurately in a hurry. If you haven't done it for a while, wander on to your local pitch when nobody's looking and simply stand in the goal. It's enormous. There are plenty of middle-aged men who can hardly touch the crossbar at all. People hang the netting up before games standing on ladders, or chairs, or each other. Say you're six feet tall; with your arms above your head, that's eight feet. From the centre of the goal to the foot of a post is twelve feet; you're four feet short if you lie down and try and reach the thing. You've got to dive! Or run and then fall over. Or crawl a bit on your belly. All the dimensions are ridiculous. There's nothing bigger than a goal. It contains all the hopes and dreams of all the people in the world, apart from the tiny handful who don't like football. So just stand there a while and stop people scoring in it, will you?

The goal isn't the whole story, either. The six-yard box is meant to be wholly dominated by the goalkeeper. More dimensions. Let's see. Six yards from either post, plus the length of the goal: twenty yards long! You could graze a horse on it. It's a prairie. How are you supposed to dominate that without artillery?

Wait a second. The penalty area is the goalkeeper's domain, not just the six-yard box, and we know, because that's what it's sometimes called, the eighteen-yard box. Eighteen yards forward from the posts, and eighteen yards out from them towards the corner flags. Add the width of the goal. Eighteen yards by forty-four. It's monstrous. It's not even worth thinking about. It's simply too big.

Outfield players, as we know, do a certain amount of running around. They have to roam. But when it matters, they send the ball across vast distances. They roam to be in a position to do things later. But for goalkeepers it's the opposite. The goalkeeper can be expected to be in any part of his massive acreage at any moment. Wherever the ball can be sent, he must be able to reach. And later is no good. In the horizontal plan, on the elegant graph of the penalty area, that can be improbable enough. In elevation, in front of the plane defined by the goalposts and crossbar, it's absurd, against nature.

Anybody who can do this stuff is doing something so unlikely that it's understandable to want to know more. To that extent, great goalkeeping is not so far removed from any other sport at the highest level. There are lots of athletic achievements which are just so far beyond mortal comprehension that they fascinate only by the acknowledgement of impossibility. Nobody who has skied thinks they can race downhill, for example. If you weren't put off just by imagining how ridiculous you'd look in a skin-tight suit with your backside sticking out, you'd certainly stop when you got to the starting-gate and looked down the precipice beneath you. You'd want a rope, or better, a chair-lift going steadily down. Or take that business gymnasts go in for, of hanging by their arms from two rings suspended in space. They stretch out into a crucifix position, and you might conceivably think: 'Yeah, but if I spent as many thousands of hours in a gym as they do, I could do that.' But then they put some leverage on those arms already at full stretch to pull themselves elegantly into the same position upside down. You should have shut up by now. When they start doing perfectly smooth press-ups in that position, unsupported by anything beyond their own appalling muscularity, you have to acknowledge that this is not something you can begin to copy. It's out of reach. You can allow yourself to be impressed. Just try holding your little basket of groceries at arm's length while you hang around the checkout queue at the supermarket to see how it feels.

Great goalkeeping is as comprehensively out of the reach of most of us as anything in sport. Even good goalkeeping is a rare and admirable combination of unlikely qualities. Yet we persist in pretending that anybody can do it. It's ordinary. It's what the player who can't run is supposed to do. Ten players agree to make a football team and place an extra, the one who 'can't play football', in goal. The idea that goalkeeping is an unathletic sinecure for fatties, people with glasses, and people who can't kick needs to be scotched right here. There are some of those in goal up and down the country. But keeping goal is a sporting activity measured only by perfection. It is a fact that goalkeepers simply cannot afford to make the kind of mistakes that outfield players routinely make. For some other sportsmen, a certain kind of success is measured in percentages: first serves in, for example, or batting averages. Football doesn't (yet) get too hung up on such things, and outfield players get away with an awful lot of errors. Goalkeepers do not. An error looks like an error and is ruthlessly marked down to you, in goal. The percentage is a hundred or you're slated. Not for doing something easy, like serving a tennis ball, as and when you want, but for doing something practically impossible, on a cue chosen by somebody hell-bent on preventing you do it.

A tremendous amount of nonsense is talked about goalkeeping. I'm not just talking about saloon-bar nonsense, or the wittering gibberish that passes for knowledge. The most basic facts about goalkeeping are forgotten, and the most elementary equity in commenting about it more often than not abandoned by football writers, by commentators, by television pundits. The most basic fact of all is simply this, that the goalkeeper is by far the most important player in the team. He can make more difference to a game or to a season than any other player. His form to all practical purposes defines the form of the rest of the team. Goalkeeping is not some obscure extra tacked on to make football more complicated. It is the heart and soul of football.

The most common nonsense about goalkeeping is the simplest and most offensive of all. Many people enjoy reading about a football game they have already seen. You go to a game on a Saturday afternoon, and it is no small pleasure to compare your impressions to those of the journalists on the Sunday morning. It is not about news, but about analysis. You want accuracy on the bits you missed, explanations of details you may not have understood. It happens often after you have seen a game on television, too. You want to compare what you saw, in slow motion and from several different angles, to the way a good reporter tells it having seen just once, the old-fashioned way. Time and time again the goalkeeping simply doesn't get mentioned. Or gets mentioned formulaically, grudgingly. You know, because you saw it, that a goalkeeper did such-and-such a thing. But what you get from your admired and respected correspondent is all from the other point of view.

Think of a piece of standard commentary: it is normal to hear a move, described with mounting excitement, culminate in a frenetic 'Great shot!' You expect a goal, you even glance at the netting to see the billow which would prove that you missed what went before. But there has been a save, unmentioned or perhaps reluctantly acknowledged as the reason for the audible disappointment in the commentator's voice. The obsession with goals and with scoring means that great goalkeeping is usually passed over in silence: so much so that it is not rare to see a saved penalty ascribed to the forward as a miss. This is absurd, not merely because it leaves an important part of the game unappreciated and undescribed. It fosters the cult of the goal to an extent which puts an impossible strain on the game. If you can't appreciate fine goalkeeping, I argue, what chance have you of understanding the other subtleties in which the game is so very rich?

There are many pressures in football already pushing towards a results-above-all attitude. Many of these are the result of its prodigious commercial success, but they need sensibly to be resisted. Look only at basketball, which always seems to finish 110–111, and where practically nothing takes place that is not part of a scoring move. It has become, in chess parlance, a game with neither opening gambits nor middle game. The short word for it is dull, even though the individual athleticism of some of the people who play it is breathtaking. Nobody would want football to go that way, but it will if fine and honourable things other than goals are allowed to go misunderstood and unreported. It happens often that some player is withdrawn from an advanced role into a more central one. His scoring record goes down, even though he has done precisely what a coach wanted him to do in the pursuit of some deliberate tactic. The comment most often heard is that he is having a bad season. There is no mention of the change of tactic, little thought given to anything a player might contribute to teams except goals.

That attitude leads to a particular kind of madness which is by no means confined to the replica-shirted purblind. From team-building to the administration of the rules, in every corner of football, goals are overvalued and the rest struggles to be noticed. How often would a team have been immeasurably improved by the signing of a goalkeeper for half the money wasted on another forward? It happens all the time. The constant whispers about future rule changes almost invariably solidify into something which makes scoring goals easier, in sad acknowledgement of our diminishing tolerance for the less obvious parts of the game. In a period when television increasingly controls football, and television itself is terrified of the short attention spans and zapper-happy faithlessness of its audience, even football has to conform to the new need for exaggerated drama. It used to be that a 'move' in football was as meticulously appreciated as the development of a sonata. The sheer beauty of the thing when well done is astonishing: the probing for weakness, the overmatching of one side's strength to the other's deficiency, the changes in tempo and direction leading to a sudden visible moment that makes all the difference. It is wrong to think that all this is summed up in the last gesture. Edited highlights very often start too late in the move and go on too long after it. We get the shot, perhaps a couple of passes before it if we're lucky, the goal, and endless triumphal celebrations afterwards. It's as though we're not to be trusted with the real game, but need to be spoon-fed with the bright and glossy bits that decorate it. But I don't want to live mainly on maraschino cherries; I want the whole cake.

Plumb in the centre of all these swirling attitudes to football, framed square in the goals, is the goalkeeper. If you regard him merely as somebody who delays or prevents the yelling exhilaration that is all you want from football, he is a nuisance. You'd rather he didn't do his stuff quite so well, although you naturally never admit it when he is your own. We're not so very far from abolishing goalkeeping altogether, if we go down that line: sure, you can position a last man, but he can't use his hands. Lots more goals, plenty of obvious 'action', and a product that television might find even harder to resist. You think it far-fetched, but the back-pass rule has already said, in effect, that he can no longer use his hands in certain critical circumstances. That, too, was unthinkable only a few years ago. There is a long tradition of making it harder for goalkeepers, all based on a wish for more goals. They tend to cope remarkably well with each successive hurdle, but we need to address the attitude as much as the individual rules. And my attitude is this: a football goal is a vast enough target. To miss it, or to hit it feebly enough that a single athlete exposed in the middle of it is able to reach your attempt, is pathetic. It is easy to score goals and very hard indeed to save them.

Goalkeepers have reached a standard of excellence in what they do, far superior to outfield players. They have had to, and have responded magnificently to the demands the game has placed upon them. We need to redress the balance. We need to applaud goalkeepers for what they do. Before we can do that we need to make some effort to understand.

1. Fossil Footballers

In the beginning, everybody was a goalkeeper. The peculiarity of football as it evolved into something we might now recognize was the increasing restriction on the use of the hands. As James Walvin put it in his *The People's Game*: 'Crudely stated, the football game which emerged in the third quarter of the nineteenth century as "soccer" was in origin the game as played at Eton, Harrow, Westminster, Charterhouse and later in other schools, where handling was allowed but where it was forbidden to catch the ball and run with it.'[1] Earlier football, the splendidly unruly Shrove Tuesday and other games which set village against village (and boot against head), had certainly been a handling game, whichever idiosyncratic set of rules operated. The fundamental principles of football until the Victorian public-school men (with their mania for codification) got hold of it were really only two: to propel the ball in opposite directions at a target, and to prevent the others from so doing by every means possible.

These means inevitably included violence. The splenetically puritan Philip Stubbes, no friend of football, who famously described the game as 'a frendly kinde of fyghte', gave a plain idea of some early football skills:

> Whosever scapeth away the best goes not scotfree, but is either sore wounded, craised, and bruseed, so as he dyeth of it or else scapeth very hardly. And no mervaile! for they have the sleights to meet one betwixt two, to dash him against the hart with their elbowes, to hit him under the short ribbes with their gripped fists, and with their knees to catch him upon the hip and pick him upon his neck, with a hundered such murthering devices: and hereof groweth envie, malice, rancour, cholar, hatred, displeasure, enmitie and what not els, and sometimes murther, fighting, brawling, contortion, quarrel, kicking, homicide, and great effusion of blood, as experience dayly teacheth.[2]

Clearly, it was not a game for wallflowers. The 'short ribbes' tingle merely reading it.

Football is one of those activities that makes its first appearances in history mainly through attempts either to disparage it or to crush it. There are plenty of authoritarian instructions that it should cease, and not a few coroners' reports that deal with it. Occasionally, a more benign view is glimpsed, as in these lines by Alexander Barclay of 1514:

> *The sturdie plowman, lustie, strong and bolde*
> *O'ercometh the winter with driving the foote ball,*
> *Forgetting labour and many a grevous fall.*

As one writer put it, commenting on these lines, he made it sound very agreeable in an unsophisticated sort of way:

> *. . . in the winter, when men kill the fat swine,*
> *They get the bladder and blow it great and thin,*
> *With many beans and peasen put within.*
> *It ratleth, soundeth, and shineth clear and fayre.*
> *When it is thrown up and cast in the ayre,*
> *Each one contendeth and hath a great delite*
> *With foote and hande the bladder for to smite.*[3]

'Foote and hande'. There's the point. As long as handling was part of the game, football implied violence. Most early authorities see something closer to the kind of mayhem Stubbes objected to than the genteel business described by Barclay, and there is no doubt that football was about as chaotic a way of letting one's hair down as society could stand. It was something of a Saturnalia, with normal behavioural restrictions lifted for the day. And those boys certainly knew how to have a good time: there are many early accounts of football-related deaths, dutifully dredged up by historians chronicle-surfing on Mondays with half their minds still stuck on Saturday afternoon. Henry de Ellington, son of William, was killed in a game on Trinity Sunday, 1280 when he ran into David le Keu and impaled himself by accident on his knife.[4] This puts into perspective the modern linesman, ritually running his hand over an oncoming substitute's studs to check that they have no sharp edges to cause injury. Pope John XXII found it necessary to hear evidence in a parallel case, before absolving a Norfolk canon who had accidentally killed a fellow player in a similar manner in 1322.[5] The chorus of objections to football (to cite only one of many, the Lord Mayor of London issued in 1314 a proclamation on behalf of the king calling for order during the forthcoming royal absence on his Scottish campaign, splendidly forbidding *rageries de grosses pelotes de pee*, which translates as 'large skin ball uproars'[6]) makes it clear that the administrators were a little slow to impose order on the game, including a ban on the wearing of knives while playing.

Gore and sport have been associated for a long time, and are not necessarily separated yet. Early football was a bloody activity, even if only occasionally murderous. It seems to have been largely confined to 'special' days, either feast days or days of particular importance in a local calendar, and usually to have had rich tribal and caste honours at stake. There are recorded games between bachelors and married men, between the apprentices of rival guilds, and always between neighbouring towns, villages, and parishes. Almost any rivalry that can split a community used to burst into football. Many still do. The ferocious and frequently fatal skirmishes between 'town' and 'gown', for example, in those places where a large student body aroused the powerful and righteous envy of a less favoured population, lasted until comparatively recently. Football seems to have gained a certain measure of support as a social safety-valve: it looks like an activity that had to be sanctioned because it could not be stopped. As long as it took place only on high days, and as long as the mayhem was kept under some kind of tolerable limits, it was probably preferable to the same degree of violence unformalized and running free.

In Siena every year, there is still run a lunatic medieval horse-race around the steep-sided shell-shaped main square. The Palio has to some extent been damaged by tourism, and no doubt a proportion of the razzmatazz is closer to Disney than to Dante. But it is also true that to belong to the winning parish (each horse, ridden unsaddled, represents one of the town parishes) confers a warm feeling through the year which may or may not result in material advantage, but which will certainly be triumphantly shoved under the noses of less fortunate burghers until the next time the Palio is run. A great deal of money is spent getting the best horses and on the best preparation for them. Rumours of cheating are so common that one looks for the fire under all the smoke. Horses are ceremonially blessed in church before they run, and so are jockeys, banner-wavers, marching bands, and everybody else who can claim to be involved. The micro-local patriotism is fierce, and closely reproduces the atmosphere of early football. Modern football derbies can often justifiably be treated with cynicism. It doesn't take a very imaginative TV executive to claim some ancient local rivalry to spice up an otherwise ordinary fixture, and in the age of jet travel the true rivalries are just as likely to be several hundred miles apart as across the hill. Yet the spirit of the derby match, of truly local pride and resentment being at stake, is as old as football itself and fundamental to it.

Some have called early football a form of stylized warfare, like jousting, and found evidence in the tales of vanquished opponents' (often Danes') heads being used as the ball. There is something to this: all games are a codification of adversarial energies that could easily be more damaging if they were not given the roughly controlled outlet of the game. In the nineteenth century it was fashionable to seek Roman or even Greek or Phoenician roots for football, as though something which had been so enthusiastically taken up by public schools devoted to the classical curriculum had itself to be authenticated by a classical lineage. It is certainly probable that miserable Roman soldiers booted things around in a more or less organized way, once they had discovered just how northern and how Atlantic their British posting was to be, and indeed we have evidence that they did. But from there to seeing in their *harpastum* and their *ludus pilae* recognizable and traceable ancestors of our football seems an awfully long jump.

Looking for the ancestral origins of football is a little like looking for the beginnings of cinema: you can certainly find vague precursors, or those culs-de-sac which might nearly have led to the present version had something been slightly different. But the actual history is glorious enough as it is. After all, if what we want from our sport is long lines we can always take up dog-fighting or ratting. Indeed, to turn to the pages of the earliest sporting publications, *Bell's Life* and *The Sporting Magazine* and their rivals, which date essentially from the Regency, is to be struck by how easily they switch from ex-aristocratic sports like riding to hounds to 'low' ones like wrestling. Time and again we see that once a particular sport has acquired a certain popularity it acquires a purportedly glorious history to go with it. That history is likely, understandably enough, to reach back further than is strictly justifiable.

Football has been no different. By the early years of this century, people interested in football found themselves looking back over forty or fifty years of pretty impressive activity, and wishing that their passion were slightly more respectable. Phoenician and ancient Chinese and medieval and Renaissance football are all very well in themselves, no doubt, but they also provide a welcome pedigree for a sport so mongrelly rooted in the demotic and the popular. Imagine writing about football in the 1940s, for example. Your neighbour on the sports desk felt no compunction in beating you about the head with the superior moral and aesthetic virtues of cricket. The 'muddied oafs' stuff was taken for granted, and an utterly spurious equation of cricketing skill with personal worth had entered the language. How galling to hear all the not-quite-cricket, straight-bat nonsense from a game that mistook its dotage for its prime and has since all but died. There was a time, which lasted too long, when any sport was more snob-approved than football. 'Popular', as so often in England, meant 'too popular for our sort of people, dear'.

The key to the popularization of the sport lies in the speed and extent of the changes brought about by industrialization, and in particular the rise of the middle classes. If you read Pierce Egan, author not only of the first history of boxing but also of *Life in London*, one of the greatest bestsellers never to make its author's fortune, you will be struck by how his (Regency) London contains sporting aristocrats and slum dwellers and almost nobody in between. Both share a passion for sport, and Egan's great set-piece accounts, of the prize fights at Moulsey Hurst, of pedestrian contests and sporting dinners, are remarkable for a kind of alliance in sport between the gaudiest damasks and the plainest fustian. It becomes clear that Egan is describing an explosion in the interest in sport by people who had been previously barred from all but traditional, and occasional, sporting outlets. His prizefighters are backed by dukes, often the royal dukes, even when prizefighting is illegal, and huge crowds, as big as modern football crowds, traipse out from the cities to the chosen field to watch and wager. The recently migrated urban populations, severed from the traditional pancake-racing or hurling of their original rural communities, took to sport in huge numbers.

By doing so, they presented an enormous threat to order. Sport was always accompanied by gambling and by drink, whether on the racecourse or around the prize-ring. There had been major political disturbances under cover of sporting rendezvous, notably against the Enclosures Acts, and by the late eighteenth century and the early nineteenth it always seemed likely that worse was just around the corner. From the French revolution, through the long and nationally exhausting wars, through the succession of political crises at home and abroad that included the Reform Bill and the year of revolutions in 1848, it looked as though catastrophic social breakdown was imminent. Any large assemblage of excited crowds could turn into the start of such a crisis at unpredictably short notice, and as the Victorian demography of a vastly expanded middle class looking for social certainty and stability began to settle down, so the occupants of that new class began to be anxious that sport itself might threaten them more seriously.

By the time Dickens, in his early book *The Pickwick Papers*, looked back at a vanished era of coaches and canals, the old sporting alliance had thoroughly broken down. Think of Victorian menswear, and the only colour is black: the extraordinary union of dukes and dustmen was vanishing. Large numbers of new participants in sport, clerks and factory workers with a Saturday afternoon to get some air into their lungs are usually identified as the primary reason for the explosion in organized sport, and they certainly were. But organization meant control, too, and we should not forget how determined the Victorian desire for social stability could be. Football did not really spread as a grandson of the Ashbourne game or any other folk-football. Those are better placed somewhere in its prehistory, as activities of a related type that might have become dominant in other circumstances. Football in one form or another had existed everywhere. It spread as the most successful mass-participation sport in an age of mass participation in all activities, under the permanent threat of social disorder.

The first impulse to this new expansion of football came from a very specific problem in social control. It was found necessary to invent a social glue in schools to replace the fellow feeling of class and locality which had been removed by the new industrial mobility. Towards the end of the first half of the nineteenth century pupils at the great schools had little in common beyond their aspirations. They were subjected to a stifling classical curriculum and their tendencies to violent outburst were becoming a threat to the orderly imposition of the new morality they were there to learn. A system of recreation which they themselves would accept, and which promoted only acceptable levels of damage to limb, was badly needed. Football was ideal. It had all of the muscularity and a certain amount of Christianity could be imposed upon it. Most boys had played some version of it somewhere, and it was simple enough that they could quickly learn the new variant of their school.

The trouble was its roughness. Handling versions of football did an enormous amount of damage to the participants. Whatever the local rules imposed by the shape of a cloister or the number of players, the scrimmaging was more dangerous than schools intent on recruiting larger numbers of pupils could tolerate. So limits had to be imposed, and the first we get to hear about are either the simple restriction on the number of players, or regulations beginning to limit the use of the hands.

With the suddenness of the right idea at the right time, we see an explosion of interest in making this basically enjoyable activity more workable. In Sheffield, at Cambridge, but above all in the public schools and in the regiments such as the Royal Engineers, largely officered by ex-public school students, there is a flurry of law-making energy. Its intentions are clear: eliminate danger, and increase excitement. Thus, increase popularity.

Achieve uniformity and so allow competition, and through competition arrive at the possibility of improving performance. The history of this development is tolerably well known, and easily read.[7] It worked like a dream; football clubs mushroomed, and both playing and spectating spread rapidly. By the time the Football Association was formed in 1863, the debate about regulation had already crystallized around those points which would affect the popularity of the emerging game.

In the fifth meeting of the FA, on 1 December 1863, at the height of the argument as to whether 'hacking' and 'handling' were to be included in the rules under discussion, the secretary-elect E.C. Morley of the Barnes club, said this:

> I agree with Mr Alcock in thinking that these two rules affect everything so materially that I am strongly of the opinion that it would be well if we went into consideration of them at once. Hacking and running [Morley implied running while controlling the ball with the hand] so affect every rule – the length of the ground, the tape, the width of the goalposts and, indeed, everything connected with the game, that they must be looked upon and dealt with as most vital points. If we have 'hacking', no one who has arrived at the years of discretion will play at football, and it will be entirely relinquished to schoolboys.[8]

Mr Morley used a telling phrase: he was looking for players 'for the most part men in business, and to whom it is of importance to take care of themselves'. He quite specifically foresaw a disinclination to join the new association if it meant going home every Saturday with a broken shin or worse. Mr Campbell's rejoinder, in the same meeting, is famous: 'Be that as it may, Sir, I think that if you do away with it you will do away with all the courage and pluck of the game, and I will be bound to bring over a lot of Frenchmen who would beat you with a week's practice.'

Hacking and handling: kicking men as well as the ball, and propelling the ball by hand as well as by foot. Together they represented the older version of football, the unimproved version. In the end, the FA excluded its proposed rules 9 and 10:

9. A player may be entitled to run with the ball towards his adversaries' goal if he makes a fair catch, or catches the ball on the first bound; but in the case of a fair catch, if he makes his mark, he shall not run.

10. If any player shall run with the ball towards his adversaries' goal, any player on the opposite side shall be at liberty to charge, hold, trip or hack him, or wrest the ball from him; but no player shall be held and hacked at the same time.

Football turned away from the brutalities of hacking, and with it from the game-slowing business of handling the ball all over the field, and left those to the various other codes which survived around the world. It left them on the principle that it is so hard to control the ball effectively without one's hands that the ball would pass faster around the field from man to man, and the play would be more fluid, more unpredictable, and more entertaining to watch as a result. The worldwide expansion of football is the only vindication needed; football avoided siege warfare in favour of something immeasurably lighter and faster, commando skirmishing or light cavalry charges, and it worked.

It did not, of course, abandon its muscular roots without a backward glance. Two stories about the Honourable Arthur (later Lord) Kinnaird, the Scottish landowner who played in nine Cup Finals between 1873 and 1883 – three for the Wanderers, and six for the Old Etonians – and later became the President of the Football Association for more than thirty years (the game's nearest equivalent to W.G. Grace), show how it was done. Sir Francis Marindin, himself a distinguished footballing pioneer, is alleged to have heard Kinnaird's mother worrying one day about what he got up to. 'I am afraid,' she told him, 'that one of these days Arthur will come home with a broken leg.' 'Never fear, dear madam,' said Marindin, 'it will not be his own.' In a match between Kinnaird's Old Etonians and the Old Harrovians, Kinnaird was approached by the equally distinguished C.W. Alcock (who first put forward the idea of a cup competition), complaining of contusions. 'Look here, Kinnaird, are we going to play the game, or are we going to have hacking?' 'Oh,' said Kinnaird, doubtless fingering his bright red and aristocratically full beard-and-whiskers combination, 'let us have hacking, by all means.'

Kinnaird would have been just as happy playing rugby or some early version of American football; he was a clubbable sort of cove, and the details of the sport seem to have mattered less to him than all the things that went with it, of good fellowship, and good leadership and enthusiasm, a certain kind of hearty effort. And, of course, he had to be happy with an inexact form of the game we know today: football did not spring fully armed from the forehead of Zeus. It evolved quickly, and under the very determined guidance of people who had little truck with rebels who wanted a less playable and watchable system, but it did take a while to settle, during which time it might have become something very different.

In his *Century of Soccer*, Terence Delaney reconstructed an imaginary game of the 1860s:

> The pitch is about the same size as a modern one, with its width and length marked out by flags, but no halfway line is drawn; there is no centre circle, no goal area and no penalty area. The goalposts stand eight feet apart, but there is no crossbar. If it is towards the end of the 1860s, say 1867, there may be a tape instead of the bar, eight feet from the ground, but before that a goal was scored simply by kicking the ball between the posts, and it made no difference how high the ball was when it passed between them . . . When the game begins, the play is almost as strange to us as the costume. The players line up, if it is about 1863, with nine forwards and two 'behinds' – a back and a half-back. By 1865 there was a goalkeeper – in the same dress as the other players – a 'goal-cover', a back, and eight forwards; by 1870, there were seven forwards and two half-backs; by 1875, two backs, two half-backs and six forwards. It was not until 1883 that one saw the familiar arrangement [Delaney was writing in 1963] of two backs, three half-backs and five forwards . . . The first thing we notice, as an attack begins, is the apparent selfishness –

or is it perhaps shortsightedness? – of even the most skilful players. A forward with the ball begins to run, holding it, and however many of the other eight forwards on his side seem to be in good positions, he goes on holding it, dribbling and swerving with considerable ingenuity until it simply is not possible to go further or beat another man. Then, when he loses it, it may be fastened upon by another of his own side 'backing up', but that man in turn holds on as long as he can.

This is 'the dribbling game', the great pride of the early forwards . . . The old style dribbling forwards were exciting to see and, at their best, far from simple-minded . . .

So, watching this old match with our modern eyes, we accept the dribbling – but what seems stranger to us is that the players use their hands. We realize that we are seeing the game at the stage when Rugby and Association have still not really parted in fact, whatever the laws may say. It is true that the players do not run with the ball in their hands, nor do they throw passes to one another; but a man with the ball at his feet that bounces too high for him, will pat it down with his hand to bring it under control; or a back, perhaps, running in to meet a high one, will catch it in his arms, a 'fair catch', strike his heel into the ground, and call for a 'mark' – and this entitles him to a free kick. The throw-ins are strange to us, too. When the ball goes out beyond the line of flags, we see opposing players chasing it; the first to reach it touches down, as in Rugby, and claims the throw, which he takes with one hand, but he must throw in at right angles to the line, and the ball must bounce before it can be played. Goal-kicks, we notice, are taken from the goal-line, but only if one of the defending side has succeeded in touching down, and then from a point on the line opposite the touchdown. If one of the attacking side touches the ball first, after it has crossed the goal-line, a free kick at goal is given, fifteen yards out from where the ball was touched – almost as good as a modern penalty, if the touch was made near the post, because all the defenders must stand behind their goal-line until the kick is taken. When a goal is scored, to our surprise, the players change ends, and do so after every goal. The offside rule seems strict to us; when the ball is kicked, it cannot be played by any man on the same side who is nearer to the opponents' goal, until one of the other side has played it. In effect, this means that a forward pass is not possible.[9]

The similarities to other codes of football which survive today are striking, but the idea that concerns us most is that at this early stage, when few clubs played by the same rules, and looking for fixtures meant looking for an agreed set of rules to abide by, football included widespread handling by any player, although not in any circumstances. That was the residue of all pre-existing football, and it is by the withering of that aspect of the game that football came to be recognizably what we play today.

So the modern goalkeeper is a relic of the football that was played before the game was organized into the present-day form. For all that he seems so strictly up-to-the-minute, with his gloves made of sticky high-technology materials, and brand-new rules applied to him alone, the goalkeeper is a fossil within the game. He can do one specific thing, that is use his hands, which is prohibited to all other players. Yet it is not a new privilege accorded to him to deal with some newly emerged aspect of the game. It is, critically, something which every player used to be licensed to do and is no longer. The right to handle has been removed from the bulk of footballers and vested in one super-handler.

This is the first reason for the general suspicion under which goalkeepers act. They live in a separate cage marked out on the pitch, and they wear identifiably different clothes, like prisoners in their suits of arrows. But difference alone does not explain the wary, slightly contemptuous attitude that goalkeepers meet. Their history does, and their very presence on the field is a reminder of the way football used to be. All the slick modernity of the ten outfield players contrasts with the ponderous Victorian stolidity of the 'immobile' guardsman at the back. Outfield players, without ever openly regretting their own lost permission to handle the ball, somehow know this, and feel a strong sense of superiority over the less evolved footballer behind them. He has to be included in their formation, but it is nowhere said that he should be accorded the same kind of respect they accord each other. It is as though ten Association players always had to play with one Gaelic, or one Australian Rules, or one gridiron player. Welcome, stranger, and what is it exactly that you're doing here?

From the moment the goalkeeper was separately identified, when his team-mates were barred from doing what he alone remained entitled to do, he was put under the constant obligation of justifying his inclusion in what had become *their* game. However far back we dig, the goalkeeper always seems to have been met with this doubtful, if not contemptuous, welcome. The official laws of the game make no mention of goalkeeping until

1871, incredibly late. There is no doubt at all that he had been there before. But he used to wear the same uniform as his team-mates, and his job was perhaps only slightly different to that of the other defenders. Goalkeepers narrowly missed being called the full-behind, the goalkeeper in organized football developing from one of the defence dropping ever more steadily back and specializing there, until he just got stuck there. But the very slowness of the legislators turning their attention to the goalkeeper is instructive. When all players were proto-footballers there was no need to single out one among them for particular attention. It is only as the goalkeeper got left behind, playing his older football while the successive newnesses grew around him, that he began to look dated and to need his own rules.

Here is an early, and not untypically sweeping, attitude to goalkeeping:

> The goals were about twenty yards wide; the ball, to score a goal, had to pass at any height between two trees at either end, and had to hit the rails or pass over them. The small boys, the duffers, and the funk-sticks were the goalkeepers, twelve or fifteen at each end, and were spread out across this wide space; if any fellow who was playing out showed any sign of 'funk' or failed to play up, he was packed off into goal at once, not for that day, but as a lasting degradation. On the other hand, if any goalkeeper made a good save of a goal, he was called for immediately to play out, and thenceforth he played out always.[10]

That was at Westminster School in the 1840s, well before football had spread beyond the schools in any kind of organized way. The contempt is palpable: the 'lasting degradation' redeemable only by heroism, the hideous assumption that duffers and goalkeepers were immediately equivalent are pretty bad. But that word 'funk-sticks' is horrible. It sticks in my craw, unreasonably, beyond placation. W.R. Moon, the glorious goalkeeper for the Corinthians in the 1880s, and the sporter of one of the finest waxed moustaches ever seen on a football field, went to Westminster before becoming a thoroughly upstanding-looking solicitor. Did he get called a funk-stick? Not twice would be my guess, because Moon, for all his sportsmanship, was a muscular goalkeeper, well able, in modern jargon, to 'look after himself'. Indeed he formed for the Corinthians a famously physical defensive partnership with the ferociously beefy full-back brothers A.M. and P.M. Walters (predictably known as the Meridiem Brothers).

The plain fact of goalkeepers being regarded with hostility is nothing new. Like any other minority they have to be three or four times better at what they do than their colleagues to get the same recognition. Goalkeeping is underrated as a physical, athletic activity ('Anybody can go in goal'), but it is also hugely undervalued in other ways. The goalkeeper is generally not quite a full member of the team, he costs less than outfield players and he gets less than his fair proportion of awards. He is routinely snubbed, even officially and publicly. Before Euro 96 the sportswear company Nike produced posters in the heroic mould of the Italian defender Paolo Maldini, confidently (but wrongly) anticipating him to star in the tournament. The slogan read:

'Italy's goalkeeper. Easiest job in Europe'. There he was, formally announced as an extra tacked on to the team. To be regarded simply as a burly nutter who can't kick is the norm; to be constantly vilified, often collectively over a period that spans generations, is not rare; to make jokes about Scottish goalkeepers is the automatic privilege of every lout in football; to mouth huge generalizations about 'continental' goalkeepers (a strange continent, this, which stretches according to whim from Colombia to Korea) is the reflex of every Englishman who ever sees a game from outside his own league pyramid. The Premier League has been filled with quite excellent foreign goalkeepers over the last few years, but even that revolution does not stop the Pavlovian reaction. Otherness, craziness, these are the standard qualities goalkeepers are supposed to have.

But if football has been steadily evolving away from a game in which two teams of players originally indistinguishable from goalkeepers played each other, then some of this near contempt, this heavy-handed teasing and exclusion of goalkeepers from all that is considered most shared in the team, begins to be understandable. If goalkeeping is fossil-football, and a modernizing tendency would do away with it if it could, the problem becomes not of identifying goalkeepers as weirdly different, but of acknowledging the way they have kept up with the successive developments of a game eager to leave them behind. For there is a distinction to be underlined: the *definition* of the goalkeeper, the handling relic in a team which has long since agreed that the game is more fluid without handling, is archaic; but the *role* he plays in the game is inseparable from its full modernity. To handle the ball is to control the lovely balance in the tempo of the game, which is fast enough for drama but slow enough for development. And by being allowed to handle the ball goalkeepers manage to make goals rare enough to uphold the value of a scoring system which without them would suffer from a terrible inflation. For a goal to be worth even a fraction of the emotional value we ascribe to it, it has to be hard-won. That is what modern goalkeepers do, within their old-fashioned definition. Only the goalkeeper retains the right 'with foote and hande the bladder for to smite'. It *is* a relic, but a relic which by surviving has given sense to the whole game.

2. Forget Him or Foul Him

The pitch did not always have the inevitability that it has now. Until 1902 the six-yard box was kidney-shaped; it was defined by two six-yard arcs of circles drawn from the foot of each post, in such a way as to include anything in one or the other or both. It looked like the upper part of a heart as drawn on a playing card, and was every bit as emotive. It must have looked wonderful from high in the stands, and had the great advantage of giving a clear indication to the goalkeeper of the centre of the goal. It is often stated to be against the rules for goalkeepers to mark the centre of the six-yard line with a scraped stud-mark, as many nowadays do; in fact the rules make no mention of such a practice, but nonetheless to have it ready-marked by the groundsman must have made life a fraction easier. The halfway line itself, so obvious now, was insisted upon, in the words of an FA *Memorandum for the Guidance of Umpires and Referees* of 1887, because 'the Committee does not consider a goalkeeper to be in *defence* of his goal when he is in his opponents' half of the ground, therefore a goalkeeper is prohibited from using his hands in his opponents' half'. This was a reference to the very first official mention of the goalkeeper, in 1871, who 'shall be at liberty to use his hands for the protection of his goal'.[1]

The penalty area used to stretch all the way across the field, originally twelve yards out when penalty kicks were taken from the point along the line nearest to the place where the offence had been committed. The eighteen-yard line was the line behind which players had to stand until a penalty had been taken, in conformity with the then general six-yard clear territory given at free kicks and throws-in. That, too, was changed only in 1902.

The 'D', the arc of the circle which stretches upfield beyond the leading edge of the penalty area (ten yards away from the penalty spot, designed to keep players at the right distance until a penalty had been taken, in a manner exactly parallel to the centre circle, intended to ensure a correct kick-off), did not appear until 1937. The pitch looks somehow naked without it in old photographs, and yet that 'D' is the strangest marking on the pitch. The area it encloses is not part of the penalty area; fouls by defenders within it do not give rise to penalties, nor does it extend the zone in which goalkeepers may handle the ball. It is a marking which only applies to penalties; it may not come into play for weeks at a time. It is a patch of quicksand or perhaps a minefield on the pitch. Any time it is to be used for its true purpose it means that there is immediate and urgent danger of a goal – that's what a penalty is. In open play, any time it is crossed by the player with the ball, because it lies where it does, there is a substantial increase in tension; terrible things can happen from the 'D'. Defenders are frightened of it. It is the one place where an unsophisticated booting of the ball away, anywhere, is almost always a better option than trying to play the ball carefully to a colleague. For attackers, it is *the* place to get into, either oneself as a player, or the ball, despatched there with intent to do damage. It is an enemy bridgehead too close, much too close, for comfort. It is vaguely eye-shaped, malevolent and evil. Bad things happen around the 'D'. Other games have markings, but I know of none where they carry such a burden. It is as though every football pitch had leached a little of the tension from every game it had supported and collected it right there, in a nasty little saucer, between eighteen and twenty-two yards in front of goal. And the saucer opens towards the goalkeeper; he cannot but be aware of it.

There is a rhythm to the markings on a football pitch which seems to contradict the piecemeal development that produced them. In the midfield, on a full-sized pitch, there are wide plains with no marks at all. In a match, these are the places where tension is low. People talk about games won and lost in the middle third, and they can be. But whatever is developed there has to be delivered closer to the goals. The halfway line is a milestone worth crossing as you turn defence into attack, and players do take notice as it is left behind, but it is a neutral line. It stretches amply across the field, and is emphasized by a full round circle. Nothing could better express the balance of forces: if play is there, both sides have an even chance. But as you approach a goal, the rhythm picks up: edge of 'D', edge of area, penalty spot, edge of six-yard line, and then the only line that really matters, the goal-line, between the posts.

The pattern is like those lines on the approach to major roundabouts that are spaced more tightly as you get closer, to give the uncomfortable illusion of acceleration, to force you to slow down. The football field mirrors the way that play funnels towards the goal. The lines are irregular, the 'D' gives them a dramatic stutter even as they accelerate: four yards from 'D' to front of penalty area, then six to the penalty spot, six again to the inner box, and another six to the goal. In other directions, the effect is similar: maybe twenty yards from corner flag to penalty area, then twelve, then the six to the foot of the post. On the diagonals, it is even more obvious: corner of area, then a pause, then corner of six-yard box and it's all too suddenly too close. The rush of momentum is palpable as everything draws towards goal. If you knew nothing whatever about football and were taken to a ground and asked to look down on an empty pitch, you would know, for certain, that preliminary gambits give way to the real stuff as the game crosses those lines of increasing tension on the way to the gallows structure at the very end. It is the most fantastic stage; nobody could have designed it so perfectly.

Only one player is confined by this spider's web of tension lines. Every player has a zone in which he conducts the majority of his business, but it doesn't necessarily confine him. Switching positions is a normal tactical part of the game: the left-winger finds himself for a period on the right, or the wide-back becomes an attacker. It was so even before Total Football, the blistering interchangeability invented by the German national side and perfected by the Dutch in the 1970s. Willy Meisl, himself a goalkeeper, dreamed up something similar years before and called it the Whirl,[2] and even before then, when players were expected to get a role and stick to it, outfield players would have been foolish to restrict themselves by the lines on the field. Not so the goalkeeper. He must stay in his penalty area or cease to be what he is. Outside it, he is another ordinary outfield player.

It does happen, of course, and perhaps much more today than it used to, now that goalkeepers have willingly taken on the role of 'sweeper'. But the instant he crosses that line, he loses his magical powers. Inside his cage, he is the natural focus of the whole game as it increases in concentration towards him. Outside it, he can be useful, in an ordinary sort of way, but is more likely to be a fish out of water. Watch a goalkeeper on a wet day, collecting the ball as he slides forward on hip and elbow. As he nears the line beyond which he is no longer a goalkeeper he will writhe and twist and wriggle and turn to keep his hands and the ball in the penalty area. He is desperate to stay on his territory. An inch beyond, and Samson has had his hair shorn. Or cast your minds back to Naples, in 1990, and the Colombian goalkeeper Rene Higuita, at least forty yards out of his goal in extra time, trying insanely to dribble past the veteran Cameroonian star Roger Milla. Milla, in Pete

Davies's words, 'was on to him like a shark, round him, and racing to the empty goal with this huge grin on his face'.[3] Higuita, out of his box and out of his mind for a second, had put Colombia out of the World Cup. Goalkeepers belong in their penalty areas like no other player belongs anywhere in particular.

Then there are the nets. They are so much part of the game that they have passed into the language: 'sticking it into the back of the net' is football-speak for scoring a goal, and worse, 'picking it out of the back of the net' is the completion of the goalkeeper's defeat by ritual humiliation. Why, incidentally, is it always the *back* of the net? Surely the back of the net is what spectators throw toilet rolls at. Nobody except in parody refers to the net as the onion-bag. We know what they look like. Square- or hexagonal-meshed, they should hang loosely enough that once in, a ball should stay in. English goals often have curling brackets at the top corners to keep the nets back from the goal-line; elsewhere a stick outside the net, attached to it and pulling away from the goal is more common. Nets can be painted in stripes, which show up better on television than they do in the real world, and on park pitches they are often endearingly threadbare. Occasionally some Roy-of-the-Rovers with a ferocious shot will break one, but they are made of polypropylene cord and only really break if they have been exposed to too much ultra-violet light from the sun. They have the advantage of saving goalkeepers from that lugubrious trudge halfway into the next county to recover a blasted goal; a trudge during which black thoughts are apt to fester, but which occasionally serves as a convenient way of turning one's red-faced embarrassment away from carping team-mates. All in all, nets are a useful adjunct to the game, pleasantly accepted for their original purpose of preventing dispute as to whether the ball had passed within or without the frame of the goal.

When a well-struck ball hits the net it makes a peculiarly unpleasant noise. The knots at each junction in the mesh collide with the spinning edges of the panels in the ball to make a whirring, fizzing sound which goalkeepers most often hear in the fraction of a second before yodelling jubilation wipes out all other audible effects. It is a sound which hardly carries, and many outfield players have never noticed it. But to a goalkeeper, who may in training hear it many, many times in an afternoon, it is a minutely compressed death-rattle. Culpable or not, goalkeepers feel bad enough about letting goals in without that. Conceding trickling goals which barely make it over the goal-line is a terrible thing, often worse than not being able to stop the cannon ball shots. But at least if it trickles it won't make that little buzzing reminder, that finger nail down the blackboard.

As a matter of fact, goal nets very nearly missed becoming part of the standard equipment of the game. They were invented in 1890 by the City Engineer of Liverpool, J.A. Brodie, 'who was afterwards engaged by the Indian Government for the laying out of Delhi, the capital of that part of the Empire'.[4] He was careful to patent his invention before beginning to manufacture them. They were first used in January 1891 in the North v. South match at Nottingham. J.J. Bentley, the secretary of Bolton Wanderers, and one of the prime movers of the Football League, approved the new invention and used nets in a game between Bolton and Nottingham Forest. But the FA had some trouble negotiating an agreement regarding his patent rights with Brodie. According to the minutes of an FA meeting on 4 February 1891, 'the Council approve the use of nets as under Mr Brodie's patent, but cannot take any steps to amend the rule so as to make their use compulsory until some satisfactory arrangement can be made with the patentee as to prices to be charged to clubs'.

Satisfaction was evidently obtained, because the nets were installed at the Oval in time for the 1892 Cup Final, the last to be played there. And Mr Brodie didn't sell his genius for nothing. An advertisement from early this century read: Brodie's Patent Goal Nets, Complete with Back Poles and Galvanised Steel Head Lines, in Tarred Super Strong Laid Hemp for 137/6 per pair. This was not cheap, at a time when 'Pure Wool Goalkeepers' Sweaters, Scarlet, Royal, Green, Amber or White' were 13/6 each and 'Goalkeepers' Gloves, Rubber Back and Front, on Stout Cape Leather (Youth or Men's)' were 10/6 a pair. If Brodie had been really smart, he would have insisted on some infinitesimal payment every time one of his nets was billowed by the ball. Simon Inglis once calculated that just under 401,000 goals were scored in the first hundred years of League football.[5] There are ninety-two clubs in the League, but something like thirty thousand clubs in the country altogether. Brodie should have put himself on a royalty.

The goalkeeper is like the central receiver in a radar, positioned so that everything, wherever it starts and at whatever angle, comes eventually through him. Strange then that the busiest man on the field should spend so little of his time in actual contact with the ball. Goal-keepers spend a lot of time standing on the escarpment of their own penalty area gazing across the valley of the midfield at the rival plateau opposite, like high-ranking officers watching a battle from a withdrawn position. They spend a lot of time jigging about, keeping loose, doing miniature exercises, keeping themselves on red alert. They pace about like neurotic tigers too long in a zoo. In winter they run, lazily, backwards and forwards for much of the game; twenty yards along the six-yard line, ten from the penalty spot to the 'D', perhaps a few exposed yards upfield. All the while, even when their own side has a corner, even when they are winning comfortably, when nothing very bad is likely to happen to them for a while, they are thinking their one characteristic thought.

'What if?' is the goalkeeper's refrain. It starts sensibly enough; it is impossible to keep goal without constantly weighing little percentages. The goalkeeper has to reduce the risk of things happening. If the forward really can beat me from that unlikely position, all right. Fair play to him. But there is no way he is going to be able to better his chances, because I've seen to that chance and this risk and those probabilities. Guard the near post without leaving the far one uncovered. We've all seen it go wrong, but that is what goalkeepers are balancing all the time. Advance to smother a shot, and risk being chipped. Reckon a cross is too far to reach, yet feel exposed on the line. The basic options are straightforward. At the crisis point, close to goal and with all to play for, many of the imponderables have already been ruled out. But as an attacking move develops nothing is impossible. The goalkeeping mantra becomes an absurd chattering list of remote threats: What if the ball holds up in that puddle? What if the wind catches the ball? What if the opponents finally notice that our midfield is slower than theirs? What if a divot, a dog, a shoelace?

It can get quite wearing, this constant rewriting of the immediate future as a series of changing likelihoods from right now. And it is not lunacy, or paranoia. Every goalkeeper knows that the unlikeliest happenings are just common enough that you have to take them into account. Pele missed his fifty-yard lob by a whisker. That was in a World Cup game. Nayim succeeded in doing it to David Seaman many years later, in a European final. Then soon after that the young Manchester United midfielder David Beckham did it to the unfortunate goalkeeper for Wimbledon, Neil Sullivan, in a League game. These things are just not rare enough that you can afford to discount them. On amateur pitches, smaller than professional grounds and rougher, exposed to every wind and with vicious slopes one way or another, a lob from halfway is not surprising at all. It hasn't happened to every amateur goalkeeper, but there is none who has not at some stage been seriously alarmed that he would be next. So the 'What if?' keeps churning, and the goalkeeper stays jumpy, and once in a while 'What if?' turns into 'Shit! why me?'

So the goalkeeper, who lives in the most exposed part of the ground and wears his own clothes when everybody else wears a uniform, is obviously the star of the drama, yet much of what he does is invisible. He worries, he works out chances. His nerves jangle and twitch, and his perpetual companions are unlikelihood and unforeseeability. He's busy, all right. He's an actuary, stalking the freakish mischance that makes all the difference.

Footballers with an eye for the perpetually changing strong and weak places on the field are credited with 'vision'. It is a compliment. To have vision means to be able to unlock a defence – or bolt one up – by a movement that lesser-sighted players would have missed. 'Vision' means an ability to read the game faster or further ahead than the norm. Great players all have it to a marked degree; it is one of the footballer's two senses. (The other is 'touch', which simply means that when you kick a ball it does what you intend and not some hideous compromise between your intention and its own.) By reason of the constant chafing of the 'What if?', goalkeepers are good at reading the game. Obscure tactical shifts, of position or of role, make a great deal of visible sense to the goalkeeper. Not simply because he has the leisure to 'see the whole pitch' (it's surprising how often goalkeepers are assumed to be spectators, with nothing better to do than watch the ebb and flow of a game with which they have no concern), but vitally because the variations will all have to be factored into his kaleidoscopic equations of risk. Yet no goalkeeper is ever, ever complimented on his 'vision'. It is almost a grammatical rule of football. Credit should be given where it is due: to make any stop at all, the goalkeeper needs to have understood with clarity and speed the way the game was evolving in the moments before. What he does seems negative – he prevents a goal – but that should not disbar him from the standard marks of respect that other footballers can earn. You may laugh at football-speak, with its hoary lexicon of cod psychology and its clichés on walking-frames, but the language of football is very revealing.

Team games are very old-fashioned, now. At their core is a notion, now less willingly accepted, that the cohesion of the group is more important than the achievement of its individual members. In point of fact, the altruistic side of British team games was always more visible in principle than in practice. Think only of W.G. Grace refusing to accept his dismissal from the wicket with the words 'These people have paid good money to watch me bat.' No doubt Grace behaved as though he were larger than cricket, like any number of commercial superstars in all sports since. In football there is the story of Arthur Kinnaird, no less, in goal in a Cup Final, and responsible for an own goal, using all his clout to persuade the FA to rewrite the score in the official records to avoid the shame.[6] The team ethos has taken a tremendous battering from the every-man-for-himself attitudes encouraged by nearly twenty years of Thatcherism in the UK and its equivalents abroad. New sports look more Californian than Victorian, all to do with personal achievement, fairly generally contemptuous of rules and rule-making bodies, and to a quite astonishing extent dependent on the consumer virtues of buying expensive quantities of gear.

A gym used to be a stinking room inhabited by boxers and a handful of people, like policemen, who needed to be fit for professional reasons. Now look at it. New sport is all about one's self, one's own experience. Yet team games at their finest have something which no individual activity can match. Teams can do things which none of their individual members would dare to think he could do. At its least inspiring, this phenomenon is simply good drill. A fine, well-trained rowing eight will continue rowing at a punishing rate and with every sinew stretched into the stroke long after every single oarsman would have given up if the choice had been his alone. But at its best it makes teams catch fire. It's as much a phenomenon of imagination as of athletic prowess. It depends on every member of the team being utterly confident in all the others. It needs the right mood, an extraordinary combination of enjoying the game *as* a game, and wanting to win it as a contest. It looks like virtuosity, but may well be the result of no conscious decision or sequence of decisions. It can happen to modest outfits from time to time, and nobody can honestly say why. The great football teams have days like this perhaps several times a season, and you can be sure that clever and determined men have worked very hard to make sure that it happens often; your Real Madrids and your Brazils and even your Liverpools, all great teams on paper, have surprised even themselves by passages of play so close to perfection that all they could do was give thanks.

The hope of seeing such a game is the real reason to go to football matches. Goals which come at the end of such incandescent sequences are really worth watching. Nobody *needs* to know a lot about football, but nothing is more pleasing than knowing enough, just enough, to recognize these occasional moments of team perfection when they happen. Neville Cardus once wrote that cricket made aesthetes of men who had never heard the word and would be frightened of it if they ever did. He knew what he was talking about, since he had struggled so very hard to make an aesthete of himself, but he would have chosen a better example in football. Cricket is a curious concatenation of individual acts of prowess. There is almost no genuine team action in cricket, unless it be such comparatively minor business as the backing up of the bowler or wicket-keeper when he is to receive a throw from the deep outfield. Certainly the three principal acts in cricket – bowling, batting, and fielding – are done alone, against one's own standards, and in such a way that the rest of the team cannot help once each moment of play has begun. Whereas a soccer team, when it catches fire, is so much greater than the sum of its parts even the players themselves are not certain what is happening. They seem able to do anything at will, starting by slowing time until it is their servant not their enemy. The ball becomes a willing helper, team-mates seem to glide into the right positions to be most helpful, the opposition grow leaden-footed and numb-minded. Nobody who has seen it will deny that it is the most exhilarating spectacle, a mystery built on good habits in the right circumstances.

At the root of such teamwork, which is impossible without the most heady confidence of each player in each other, is the goalkeeper. No such transcendent football can take place without an excellent goalkeeper, in full confidence, at the peak of his form. This seems mad, since great flowing moves of football can patently happen without the goalkeeper's involvement. But it is true. Given a minimum level of ability, the great passages of football are rooted in confidence. Sequences *can* look perfect when only a handful of players are involved – think of Diego Maradona, who could play quite divine football alone, almost at will. His second goal against England in Mexico in 1986, when he left Terry Fenwick for dead, is one example among many. It didn't atone for the disgrace of the Hand of God goal that he had just scored, but it came as close as anything ever could. Platini could do this, and many others. But for the whole team to play beyond themselves is different. It is not to do with responding to the hunger or determination of one man, still less a question of having the game made easier by one man's help. When football clicks into that higher mode, it signals its own collective sense of perfection. The spectators see it, and the opposing team have to be very special indeed not to fear it. There are days – and they can do as much for the soul as a Beethoven sonata – when football teams cease to play a muddy game for bonuses and points, but somehow make a living sculpture, a dance and a drama that can grab us by the throat and make even the most prosaic come over all emotional. Without rock-certain confidence in themselves, it cannot happen. Indeed those moments are often the direct expression of confidence itself, just as trembling fingers and sweaty palms are the expression of nerves. And confidence, in football teams, always comes from the goalkeeper first.

You can see why. A dodgy goalkeeper is an accident waiting to happen. Watch schoolkids in goal, and everything is a surprise to them. When they catch something, they look relieved. One of the hardest things that goalkeepers ever do is learn to defeat that relief. They learn to expect success, even against the odds that they routinely face. Until they do, their team-mates can never be sure that they are free to do the much easier things they have to do without their effort being wasted by an accident in defence. Outfield players mistrust goalkeepers for many reasons, but one is that goalkeepers' mistakes are so very visible, and their successes (with spectacular exceptions) so very discreet. Outfield players certainly don't feel that they share in goalkeepers' mistakes – goalkeeping is alien enough that it becomes easy to shift the blame – but they do share in their successes. A goalkeeper who gives off the aura of a Panzer division, who feels that nothing can beat him, actually becomes harder to beat. And he transmits that to his team. Peter Shilton based his game on enormous physical effort. He was always the most determined at training, even to the point of hanging from door-frames as a young lad to increase his reach a fraction. By the time he was a senior goalkeeper he had built up an enormous confidence to go with his agility and strength and stamina, a confidence that certainly contained a share of arrogance. It became his habit to yell his defenders further forward, away from himself. He wanted space in which to do his stuff, and he got it. He automatically created a potentially attacking formation, merely by insisting that his end of the deal was sewn up from the outset. And if, as happened from time to time, a mistake or a piece of ill fortune left even him beyond recovery, the confidence cut to seconds the time for his peace of mind to return and business to be back as usual. How could you not play better in front of such an attitude? More importantly, how could you be short of confidence?

It has always been noticeable that uninspired and uninspiring critics of the game value goalkeeping less than talented ones. Good goalkeeping is discreet, and it takes quite subtle antennae to notice it. Few players really understand in detail what the goalkeeper contributes to the game. Goalkeeping provides an occasional relief or a stock joke, and that's about it. Yet it is so obvious: to strengthen a side, improve the goalkeeping. Get coaching for the ones you have, concentrate more on training routines centred around them. If you play the kind of football where people buy and sell players, decide how much to spend, find the very best goalkeeper available, and then spend more than you had intended. Goalkeepers are incredibly cheap, still. As Alan Hansen, himself a world-class defender, and one of the more illuminating television 'pundits' in British football, never tires of saying, the goalkeeper is the most important man in the team. It's blinding: goalkeepers win matches. The vast majority of football games are won and lost by a single goal. Good goalkeepers, let alone great ones, can be counted on to make one save of an otherwise certain goal every game. Indeed, British managers used to talk about 'certain-goal' saves, which had a lack of logic, but we knew what they meant. No forward, not even the most deadly, ever averages a goal a game for any substantial period. To average a goal in two is thought pretty astonishing. Yet any first-class goalkeeper will earn his side at least one a game, week after week and season after season. And he will do all the other things he does as well, as a bonus.

It happens from time to time – since I have a lobe in my brain that says 'goalkeepers get a raw deal; goalkeepers can do no wrong' – that I watch a game on television and see clearly that the goalkeeper was the star. The commentators normally don't notice; on the contrary, they act all disappointed at being deprived of more goals. The producers decide that it's more important to show slow-motion sequences of something else, like the deputy manager's coaching assistant in charge of bootlaces having a bit of a tantrum. The post-match interview more often than not contains some implicit devaluation on the goalkeeper. ('The boys deserved a draw.' Deserved? When their goalkeeper made six of the saves of the season? What do you mean deserved? They deserved to give all their wages to him.) Then I buy the paper the next day, and the report contains not a single mention of the goalkeeper. This is because football reporters work in a fairly formulaic way. They note times of goals and bookings, they either question or loftily approve a referee's decision, and they quote a few lines from the obligatory press conference after the match. Goalkeepers don't really figure in the scheme, and often get left out altogether.

It is not just that goalkeepers routinely get a bad press; they by no means always do. They can be lauded to the skies. But the analysis and the criticism of what goalkeepers do is very much devalued by fundamental assumptions about them which are not justified. So, for example, if you assume that a goalkeeper should have little to do when his team are dominant, it is natural to see a busy goalkeeper as a sign of his team being overrun. It can be so, and many great goalkeeping performances have kept an otherwise losing team in a match, or won it outright. But it need not be so. Nobody thinks that a busy midfield is a sign of anything except the particular shape of that particular game, and the same should be true of goalkeepers. The goalkeeper is a player, he can and should be involved in the game without a presumption of crisis. He can be fundamental to attacking football, and that is very rarely acknowledged. Some teams have thrived on the huge forward clearances in which some goalkeepers specialize, and others have used accurate throws from the goalkeeper as the swiftest way of switching the direction of play. You cannot appreciate these parts of the goalkeeper's performance if you think of him only as an eccentric who doesn't object to the humiliation of watching goals fly past him. Goalkeeping remains a mystery more through the prejudices of football-watchers than through any intrinsic quality. It shouldn't be so. There is every likelihood that on any given football field, the finest athletes, the most luxuriantly skilled technicians, and the players with the fullest understanding of the strategies of the game will be the two goalkeepers.

It is not just outsiders, writing or talking about the game, who give goalkeeping a rough ride. Goalkeeping is hard enough to do. Yet the history of goalkeeping is in part the history of administrators making it harder. The only aspect of football which is under constant legislative attention, goalkeepers routinely find that as they collectively learn to master their craft, the rules (or the guidelines to referees which interpret the rules) change to make it just that little less likely that they will be able to do their job. Each time, goalkeepers learn new habits. A few years after each revision, goalkeeping looks impregnable again, and the administrators are looking for another difficulty to heap in their way.

Remarkably few rules have been made to alter outfield play since the game settled down. The throw-in was fixed as a two-handed affair in 1882, to prevent the disproportionate advantage that a one-armed bomb used to give from the fairly trivial accident of the ball passing over the sideline. Corner kicks were established in 1872, and a few lesser details have been added from time to time. Of the two really vital rule changes since the game has had its recognizable form – the introduction of substitutes and the refinement of the offside rule – both have been of inestimable advantage to outfield players. The attentions of football legislators have been less kindly to goalkeepers. When, in 1910, in a match between Third Lanark and Motherwell both goalkeepers scored, it was obvious that they were contributing fully to their respective teams. Too fully, apparently, for it was that incident which prompted the change in rules to restrict goalkeepers to handling the ball in their penalty area. The negative tone was set.

The goal-kick used to be what it ought to be, a defensive free kick which gave undisputed possession of the ball to one side. It was standard practice for the full-back to flick the ball gently into the goalkeeper's hands for him to initiate whatever move was most advantageous. It was hardly an evil in the game – it wasted little time, and was a perfectly sensible way to get play moving after a brief stop. It was outlawed by insisting that after a goal-kick the ball should leave the penalty area before any player next touched it, and the rule remains framed that way today. But if the goal-kick is no more than a particular kind of indirect free kick, there is no logical reason for more restrictions to be placed upon it than on any other, except perhaps that the defending side have an advantage in that their opponents are held at a greater distance than normal from the kick. Goal-kicks have become very dull. Although it can still happen that a goal-kick is taken short, to a wide-placed defender, it more usually gets the familiar mortar-launch upfield, with all the ungainly headed duels that invariably follow. Would it not be a good idea to remove the artificial distinctions of the goal-kick and treat it like any other free kick? Attacking players would be allowed the normal ten yards from the ball, which would force goalkeepers to look for more variety in their use of the ball. It would be likely to go short more often, thus promoting movement through the entire team. The obvious danger resulting from an ill-taken kick would oblige goalkeepers to treat them with thought and care, and so to become in that instance more like their defending colleagues and less a machine for clearing the defensive lines as brutally as possible.

Nobody changed the rule applied to goal-kicks with intent to be difficult to goalkeepers. It was felt that a little glitch in the game needed to be ironed out, and it duly was. The same has happened many times. Goalkeepers used to be able to carry the ball around their penalty areas only if they bounced it on the ground every four strides. We all remember the marvellous stuttery rhythm of a goalkeeper giving his team a little time to re-form and to catch their breath before he delivered the ball to them; pitter-patter bounce, repeated to the edge of the area, or into the middle from a position out on the flanks. It was thinking time for the fans and recovery time for the players. Utterly harmless, although it could be used to waste time in the dying moments of a game. These days the goalkeeper must release the ball from his hands after the fourth stride. The Arsenal goalkeeper John Lukic invented the way to deal with that when he developed the habit of rolling the ball to himself, often many yards ahead of the area, and then kicking from there. His successor at Arsenal, David Seaman, acquired the habit, and most British goalkeepers now do it as a matter of course. It takes far more time than was ever wasted under the old regulation, and results in just the same ugly few moments of the ball flying out of control between straining heads in the midfield, only that much further forward. The rule change has not eliminated the ill it was aimed at, and may have exacerbated it. Deprive goalkeepers of the ball, runs the unspoken message, and it will spend more time with proper players, which is not the way to run the game.

The change in the rules relating to back-passes is much worse. Passing back to the goalkeeper used, in the pompous moral code of the game, to be considered unmanly. So much so that good critics almost invariably felt called upon to defend it from the storm of catcalls and abuse from the terraces that inevitably greeted it. As Gil Merrick, goalkeeper of Birmingham and England, put it, 'Though I have found that crowds as a rule don't seem to like passing back tactics because of the obvious safety-first element – one always get those shouts of "windy" and so on – I rate the pass-back as a most valuable form of defence play.'[7] It was a perfectly legitimate thing to do, and it worked, but it was outlawed. Or at least made a great deal more difficult. It is still legitimate to pass the ball back to the goalkeeper; it is hard to imagine how it might sensibly be proscribed altogether while still considering the goalkeeper a full member of his eleven. But the goalkeeper is no longer allowed to collect with his hands a ball deliberately returned to him by the foot of one of his own side.

It is a shocking rule, a frontal attack on the role of the goalkeeper. Here is a player entitled to use his hands in the defence of his goal, suddenly no longer allowed to use them in one instance. Goalkeepers have coped, as they always do. Professionals are barely hindered at all, and even Sunday football has failed to become a succession of ten-all scorelines as defenders unable to turn while harried by a forward have hesitated and been lost.

Goalkeepers now collect the ball with foot or chest only marginally less safely than they used to catch it, and the game goes on. They 'waste' just as much time as they always did, when the circumstances are right. (Why is it a 'waste' of time to think for a few moments? If an outfield player tries to gain the same heartbeat to collect himself and see what is going on around him, he is complimented for that peculiar football skill, his ability to 'put his foot on the ball'.) Quite apart from the burden on referees of deciding which sliced, spinning pass was a deliberate back-pass and which was not, and the impossible business of second-guessing goalkeepers when another player just touched the ball on his way to him, it is utterly absurd to deprive a skilled player of the chance to use his skills properly. It is arbitrary and runs against the fundamental principle of the game that players should try to do their very best to play. Do your best, says the law, by all means. But you did it so well that we've decided to make it a little tougher. Imagine drafting a rule to prevent volleyed goals. Only a minority of players ever score them, because it is not an easy thing to do. But the whole football world would be appalled, and the rule could not be written. But goalkeeping is different. It is somehow fair to mess it about, on the assumption that a goalkeeper isn't really a footballer.

The rationale for such attacks is never far away. More goals! cry the clubs, anxious that without them their customers might find it more exciting to watch topless snooker on television. More goals! cry the American advertisers, lukewarm about football as ever (it's so *boring* that all your soccer games end in a tie).

The administrators try to deliver more goals, cravenly, even at the cost of diminishing one of the positions on the field. The suggestions that floated around before the World Cup went to the United States in 1994 were terrifying in their contempt for the game. There is no doubt that they were taken seriously, too. If the absurd decision to send the world's major football competition to a country which had no serious football league could be taken in the pursuit of all those dollars, then nothing was impossible. Play to be divided into quarters, not halves, to allow more time for advertisements in the telecasts; kicks-in to replace throws-in; bigger goals. Abolish draws one way or another. At one unbelievable point there was even discussion about playing with two balls on the field at once. More goals, you see. The short attention spans of American viewers, and their advertisers' mistrust of anything which was not artificially 'exciting', came within an ace of ruining the game. Complaisant administrators fell over themselves to fall in with these unjustifiable 'needs'. Experiments were tried in advance, in lesser leagues in lesser countries (like Britain), and a season or two were spoilt so that a report might be written in time for the competition.

It is an old, old story, and it isn't over yet. The goalkeeper will soon not be allowed to collect by hand a throw-in from his own side. It's not even certain that the changed back-pass rule, which came out of this rush to seduce American television and happens to have survived, is such a bad thing. It's just that bringing in such changes for any reason other than the clear and necessary good of the game as a whole has got to be a bad idea.

It's too easy, when cosmetic change is sought, to pick the goalkeeper as the obvious butt, and to assume that by stacking the odds endlessly against him more goals will be scored. They may be, although goalkeepers show an enduring ability to adapt to each new rule change, but there is only one natural conclusion. Football with ten men and no goalkeeper is the spectre that looms in the fog.

One of the 'standard' things that goalkeepers learn to do is the smothering dive at the feet of a forward. Several fine goalkeepers have made a substantial part of their reputation by doing it, among them Bert Trautmann and Bob Wilson. It is a difficult, risky, and very brave thing to do. If done right, a solid part of the goalkeeper, his braced hands, or his chest or his hip, will be on the goal-side of the ball while the forward's foot is on the further side. It is inevitable that if done wrong the forward will score. And it is just as certain that if done right, the forward will fall over. No doubt goalkeepers can commit fouls in such a situation; they can clatter into the forward with no heed for the ball. At less risk to their own health, they can clip the forward's feet or ankles with a swept hand and up-end him as they lie on the ground. But when the manoeuvre is carried out with the most scrupulous integrity, with all the courage and timing it requires, it looks very like a foul. With a forward whose slightest inclination is to dramatize his fall, let alone with one intent on 'diving' theatrically for the notice of the top tier of the stand, it is hard for the referee to resist the surmise that there must have been a hideous foul.

In recent years, most directives from FIFA have had the clear aim of protecting players and protecting creative play. Defenders can assassinate a game of football and the goalkeeper's dive to feet can look very like that. Nobody would say that goalkeepers should be allowed to get away with doing it wrong. But nowadays we have to be absolutely certain that referees can tell a good one from a bad, because the price has become awfully high. Goalkeepers do their work in the penalty area and the goalkeeper, in the nature of things, is the last defender. Fouls adjudged to be deliberately made by the last man when the opponent is otherwise clear on goal now result in an automatic sending-off. So if a goalkeeper is deemed to have fouled in these circumstances, which look so like a foul even when perfectly done, he is likely to concede a penalty, and therefore almost surely a goal. He will be sent from the field of play, another substantial disadvantage to his side. He will accumulate 'disciplinary points' which may well result in a period of suspension at a later date, as well as a fine from his club's internal disciplinary system. This is an awful lot of punishments for the same offence, too many when you consider that a goalkeeper would hardly be worth including in the side if he weren't certain to try to make such saves when occasion demanded.

All goalkeepers used to know that they could get hurt, badly hurt, diving at feet. Now they have to factor a whole sequence of consequences into the equation. Typically, the more important the competition and the later the stage in it, the more is at stake. Nobody wants to be banned from the later rounds of a major football competition. Yet goalkeepers can hardly not try to prevent the goal. In such circumstances, we need absolute certainty that referees get the decisions right. We need to know that they can tell the difference between a perfectly legal, a brave and effective action, and the same one become illegal by a fraction of a second or a handful of inches.

Goalkeepers do have very great disadvantages heaped on them by the administrators and the legislators, anxious as they ever are to let more goals advertise the excitement of the game. The usual pattern has been for changes in the law or its interpretation to happen in response to a perceived good to be aimed at, and not in response to a perceived ill to be abolished. Goalkeepers, in other words, have consistently been the subject of alterations which might in somebody's view make the game better to watch or to sell, rather than (as happens in the case of most outfield changes) make it more correctly played. But in one critical department, the opposite happened. It used to be common, at least in the British version of the game, for the goalkeeper to be 'charged'. Now 'charging' was a very emotive subject. It was an older part of the game which, like 'hacking' before it, was supposed to demonstrate manliness. A legitimate charge, shoulder to shoulder, is one which the player on the receiving end has every chance to brace himself to receive. It does no great damage. Crowds liked it as a demonstration of earnest physical commitment to the cause; it is easy for the less gifted spectator to feel that he himself could at least give and take buffets in the interest of his team, and sharply to notice deficiencies in that department of players less eager to do so than he himself imagines he would be.

'Charging' goes with the knickerbockers and handlebar moustaches of Edwardian public-school men, and it goes with the 'better-than-work' attitudes of players drawn from the industrial working class who might otherwise have been down the pit. Crowds still love unskilled loyalists, and most of those can 'charge' until midnight, if required. But if you charge an outfield player who is not using his hands to deal with the ball, he is able to protect himself with an angled upper arm. It is a very grey area; the whole business of hampering another player, tugging him back by shirt or arm and obstructing him, is decidedly murky. My own feeling is that almost all pictures published in newspapers show a foul being committed. Aerial duel? One is clearly levering himself up with an arm across the shoulder. Run on goal? The attacker is holding the defender away with an outstretched arm, or the defender is tugging the attacker's arm to delay him and disturb his balance. Midfield battle? The ball has gone, and the studs are only just about to hit the shin. But these concern players equally equipped, equally banned from using their arms to the ball and therefore free to use them to each other (within limits enlarged by referees' understandable, indeed laudable, desire to keep the game flowing). But come into close contact of this kind with a goalkeeper, whose arms are likely to be away from his body, and you can hurt him very easily. If his hands are high, an elbow or the point of a shoulder in the ribcage or the stomach will do a lot of damage. If he has dropped his hands low, perhaps to collect a ball at waist height, his head is lowered and exposed.

At its most brutal, and its most brutal was terrible to see, charging the goalkeeper was simply a question of waiting until he was in such a position and doing him the maximum possible harm. Charles Buchan, the Sunderland and Arsenal inside-right, once recalled 'Harry Hampton, that terror of goalkeepers, the bustling, charging Aston Villa centre-forward, who once won an international for England by charging the Scottish goalkeeper over the goal-line with the ball in his arms'.[8] In an amazing match in the Cup in the mid-1950s between Fulham and Newcastle, when Fulham drew back in little more than five minutes from 3–1 down to lead 4–3, Newcastle's equalizing goal came when Fulham goalkeeper Ian Black caught a centre from Bobbie Mitchell and was charged over the line by Newcastle centre-forward Vic Keeble. Keeble was apparently something of a specialist, like the brutal little Arsenal and Wales forward Trevor Ford. Charging was a monstrosity, a left-over from the football of pre-industrial England. Kenneth Wolstenholme, in a chatty book about his experience as a commentator, said: 'What about charging the goalkeeper? Well, I was all for it until I saw how the continentals have improved by not charging."[9] Nobody can really have enjoyed it, except the handful of forwards too slow to score by more elegant methods, and the bloodthirsty rump which attends football matches when there is no bear-baiting or cock-fighting scheduled that day.

Not the most violent of these episodes, by any means,

but certainly the most shameful, occurred in the 1958 Cup Final, that most public arena of them all, in the year of the Munich disaster. Manchester United, their team hastily rebuilt on the ruins of the one destroyed in the wreckage of an aircraft on an icy runway in Munich (twenty-three people died, including eight of the great team known as the Busby Babes), had managed to reach the final on a tide of emotional support. For United to have won that final would have been fitting, a tribute to those who had died, and understandably enough the majority wanted it to happen. There can rarely have been less popular opponents in a final than Bolton Wanderers, unfortunate to have made it that year. Bolton scored early through Nat Lofthouse, and United were never really in the final. And then in the fifty-fifth minute, Lofthouse grossly fouled Harry Gregg in the United goal. It was described as 'bundling' him over the line, and as a 'competitive challenge'. It was nothing of the sort. It was deliberate foul play, reckless and dangerous. The surprise is not that the 'goal' was allowed to stand, but that Lofthouse was not sent off and banned for months as a result. Gregg was badly dazed, possibly concussed, as was predictable, and spent many minutes effectively out of the game. He had a damaged back and a black eye.

Lofthouse, by then nearing the end of his career, had always been a physical player. He was known as the 'Lion of Vienna' for a combination of aggression and courage that had never left him since a famous performance in that city in 1952 (he ran much of the length of the field to score, fouling the goalkeeper as he did so).

His scoring record was high-class, yet he was never really a high-class player. Strong, tough, and limited; good for morale and bad for opposing goalkeepers. People tolerated his play for his goals, and there is a long and uninspiring tradition of moderate but muscular centre-forwards in British football to show that people always have. Lofthouse should have been reviled for what he did to Gregg, and for making such fouls a part of his game. In 1957, the very year before, the pre-Munich Manchester United's final had been blighted by a very similar foul, by Aston Villa's Northern Ireland international Peter McParland. He had quite recklessly run full tilt into Gregg's predecessor in the United goal, Ray Wood, smashing his cheek-bone and knocking him out. Wood heroically returned to the field (no substitutes were allowed at the time) as a make-weight winger, and Jackie Blanchflower went in goal, but there can be no doubt that McParland had quite illegally swung the game away from the favourites, United. By the time Lofthouse came to the repeat performance in 1958, United were a much diminished team, and we can see that they had little chance of winning the final. But they were illegally deprived of what chance they had.

These were disgusting fouls. Neither carried much risk of injury to the forward, and in each case, if the intention was not actually to inflict hideous injury on the goalkeeper, at least it was utterly predictable that such an injury might result. Astonishingly, neither player was cautioned at the time. The culture of 'putting oneself about', of 'letting the goalie know you're there', had been allowed to go too far, as so often happens. Ray

Wood and Harry Gregg had to take the pain as well as the goals, the disappointment for the losses as well as the anger for the way they had been brought about. In the climate of the time, when apologists for a British game which had already been exposed as weak in the face of the best foreign opposition looked to its excessive physical brutality as a secret ingredient which lesser nations could not match, Wood and Gregg became the losers in a revolting contest of spurious 'manliness'. Let me be clear: both McParland and Lofthouse could have avoided their collisions. Both must have been aware of the kinds of consequence which would result from following through. Both are vastly diminished as players and perhaps also as men by the fact that they did not restrain themselves.

Those incidents, like many others, remain in the collective memory of goalkeepers. In those cases, the goalkeepers remained unprotected by the referees from serious foul play, with serious consequences. Those collisions were not accidents; they were quite specifically intended to scare the goalkeepers, at the very least, and if they got hurt in the process, so much the better. Now we hear a lot about how goalkeepers are *too* protected, although some of the skulduggery that goes in the six-yard box makes it seem very questionable. But protecting the goalkeeper has for many years been on the legislative agenda, and rightly so. It is far better that a handful of possible goals should go unscored every season than that the assaults on Wood and Gregg should ever be repeated.

They are, of course. It happens all the time. But fans and managers, all understandably desperate for a goal, should understand that there is something gallantly sporting about that forward who in the last fraction of a second of his race against the goalkeeper understands that he is beaten, and swerves round or jumps over him. It happens at very close quarters. The referee will do his best, but he can't tell. Often only those two players will really know whether the forward left his foot or his elbow in the goalkeeper's ribs or his face, or whether he pulled away at the last moment. Goalkeepers know when they have been hit in a fair, accidental collision, and when they have been hit late. They certainly know that they can get hurt in genuinely unavoidable accidents, when it would be unfair to ask the forward to back away from a good chance to score. But far too many thugs have got away with the other; it becomes a part of the goalkeeper's make-up to expect it. The protection that referees can give them is welcome, but no goalkeeper believes he can rely on that alone.

In that one important respect, of getting slightly more protection than they used to, goalkeepers have benefited from changes in the laws of football that are applied. It is the exception. Goalkeeping has had to evolve to catch up with rule changes, as perceived defects in the game have been identified. The trouble, of course, is that defects tend to be identified for very precise reasons of interest. Clubs have traditionally wanted too much football for their own players' good, for the gate receipts. FIFA has wanted for the last twenty years to make inroads into the last great untapped market for football, the United States. The handful of large clubs which expect to be part of it want to institute a pan-European

Super League, as the senior British clubs want to make either an all-British League or an all-British Cup. The drift, at least until the pendulum swings back the other way, is towards ever more competitions, ever more matches, and ever more goals. We accept grudgingly that the goalkeeper's person should get some protection. But his role in the game gets none.

3. Graciously Tolerated, Hardly Appreciated

On the exceptional occasions when a game of football is so unbalanced that one of the two teams could hardly win whatever they did, one goalkeeper has an easy afternoon. After equipping himself, he warms his muscles and waits for his nerves to settle. As he gets changed again, quietly thankful that he has neither bruises nor humiliations to add to his collections, he will find a peculiar absence. His team-mates will not have noticed that he has had a holiday. They will see nothing unusual. It has been an easy game, but they have still had to run about a bit, still had to do what they always do, and they assume that the same has been true for the goalkeeper. For them it is normal service. A little heart–lung workout, some shouting, occasional touches of the ball. On such a really dominant day, they will be pleased because some fancy trick they have tried will have worked: 'Did you see my killer through-ball?' 'I scored with my left foot.' They cannot see that the goalkeeper has had a rare day. Because the majority of outfield players think that goalkeepers have a day like that every day. They really do.

There is a certain usual level of joshing, about how goalkeepers never have to run, never 'do any work', and in most teams it does no harm. But far beyond that is the assumption that goalkeeping is easy, that any fool could do it. If anything, outfield players think that their goalkeeper hitches an agreeable ride on their coat-tails, that by graciously allowing him to stand around chatting to the spectators, they are allowing a supernumerary to share in their tremendous athletic glory. At park-football standard, pub-team football, it is a universal attitude. Any outfield player takes for granted that he can criticize any goalkeeper, even if it is perfectly clear that the mistake was his own, a few seconds earlier.

We know that when a goal is scored the celebrations are likely to be euphoric. In recent years there has been a tendency for players to have routines ready, choreographed and practised, each more absurd than the next. A handful are funny. When Jürgen Klinsmann, the captain of Germany, improbably came to Tottenham Hotspur, he had a reputation for 'diving' in search of penalty kicks. He gave an interview with flippers and a snorkel, and when his first goal duly arrived a posse of Tottenham players flung themselves into elaborate belly-flops in unison. It was funny and it went a long way to defuse the xenophobic and specifically anti-German nonsense which could easily have got out of hand. Klinsmann insisted on driving an old Volkswagen Beetle and showed rare grace in his dealings with the often graceless world of British football; his goal celebration was calculated, and it worked. But the vast majority of these little rituals are pretty witless and vain. Older fans regret that goals are no longer celebrated by a muted handshake and nothing more. Rugby players still do this after scoring their tries, but there seems little hope of a return. Soccer players, for twenty or thirty years now, have at the very minimum made great heaps of embracing bodies after every goal, and the fans love it; that is how the fans themselves feel, and they want their players to be seen to care. George Best and Denis Law used to raise one arrogant arm to acknowledge themselves and their prowess. Charlie George famously flung himself on the ground and waited for his team-mates to pick him up. Now we have everything from silly walks to dance routines to miniature bits of stage musical. One rather po-faced school of thought maintains that these rituals should be banned, and it can be argued that some of them are likely (and calculated) to upset crowds. But why ban them? The time they take should ruthlessly be added to the game, and a few late goals scored in 'time-allowed-for-celebrations' would quickly see them toned down.

The goalkeeper is 'beaten' every time a goal is scored. Of course he has done everything possible to prevent it, and it has still been scored. As he gets ready to restart play, attention is on him, and however little the goal was due to error on his part there is an inescapable feeling that he has failed. The goal has been conceded by his entire side, not just the goalkeeper, but nobody thinks that way on the instant. The goal celebration adds insult to injury, a triumphalist little offence that somehow gets divorced from the quality of the goal that led to it. By all means celebrate a great goal, but why claim all that credit for getting in the way of a misdirected pass, or for slicing your own kick? The answer heard every week is as true as such platitudes tend to be: 'They all count.' They do, indeed. But there is no reason for it to be rubbed more vigorously in the goalkeeper's face than anyone else's.

It would be nice to see a goalkeeper get up from a save to draw attention to the abyss that separates his great skill from the miserable goal-hanging poaching that is the best the unsuccessful forward can muster by a little dance of contempt and scorn. Well, dream on! It could never take, because a goal is permanent and a save is not. A goal, once gained, is a part of the score of a game, and cannot be wiped away. A save, even a string of saves, is a negative (no-goal-yet) and can disappear at the next instant. There is only one exception. Goalkeepers who have won penalty competitions to decide drawn games have become used to clenched-fist salutes and even victorious arms in the air. Even in the matter of celebration goalkeepers are constrained. When Gordon Banks made *that* save, against Pele's header in Guadalajara in June 1970, the only save most people recall with the same clarity that they routinely reserve for eight or ten or a dozen goals a season, the save of everybody's century, his hair was tousled by Alan Mullery as he untangled himself from the post. Thanks, Alan. Don't get all emotional, will you? Bobby Moore, who knew what he had just seen, stood and applauded. It must have felt good to get a public round of applause from Bobby Moore (and a later, private compliment from Pele himself), but it hardly compares with the minute or so of centre-stage full-on adulation that all forwards routinely claim for every goal.

Nobody could be surprised if goalkeepers had developed a sense of embattlement. They are embattled. Unsung, undervalued, picked on by the game's administration and taken for granted by their colleagues, their lot is like the policeman's, not a happy one. Yet they are in large measure responsible for football having become the way it is. It isn't difficult to score a goal; how can it be when the target is so huge? Yet the standards of defending, at every level of the game, and of goalkeeping in particular, are so consistently good that we regard those playground scores as funny aberrations. 'Ah, yes,' says the manager of every big favoured club in the Premier League, coming up against some lesser fry his men are expected to roll over without problem, 'there are no easy games any more.' In cup competitions, domestic and international, the same refrain has become loud. Austria are going to play the Faeroe Islands in the European championships? A walk-over, surely? A goalkeeper with a woolly bobble hat which had brought him so much luck he wouldn't discard it plays the game of his life to upset the odds and it isn't a great performance by him. Or it's a bit of that and a bit of 'no easy games any more'. It should be easy to stuff a lesser team, it should be easy to score ten or twelve times in a match. But it is not. And time after time, the reason it is not, when all the mealy-mouthed generalities have been exhausted, is that some goalkeeper played out of his skin.

Look carefully at any 'giant-killing', and there, often among other admirable heroics, you will find a goalkeeper doing things he could not reasonably have been expected to do. Even when the giant is not quite slain, in those drawn games which so often get forgotten when the likely defeat comes around at the replay, there is a goalkeeper at the centre of it. Playing well in any one game depends on making goals and scoring them. But playing well over a season or a cup-run depends on defending. For their share in that, which is at the heart of football, goalkeepers get indifferent applause if they get noticed at all. Many, many goalkeepers have won the League, the Cup, the Under-15 Shield or the next round of beers for teams who have hardly noticed that they played, let alone that they played superbly. When sub-editors pick goalkeepers to figure in their headlines you can be sure that something quite exceptional has happened, something strong and rare enough to replace goal-scorers and their unjustifiable right to be considered news.

People are funny about goalkeepers. It is so easy to run the simple syllogism: we conceded a goal; the goalkeeper is there to stop that; therefore the goalkeeper was at fault. In black and white it sounds ludicrously unfair. It *is* ludicrously unfair. But any football team beneath perfection needs a scapegoat, and why look further than the obvious man for the job? How can it be that goalkeepers crossed the million-pound transfer threshold ten years after outfield players? It's absurd.

Let's see. Trevor Francis was worth a million in 1979. In 1979 Ray Clemence completed a season in which he played forty-two times in the League and conceded sixteen goals. Sixteen! You could easily concede sixteen goals in a game; it's been done, although not often at professional levels. Every schoolboy has conceded sixteen goals in a single kick-about. Clemence's team, Liverpool, were wonderful, and they deservedly won the League that year. But you can't tell me that a goalkeeper capable of preventing all but sixteen goals in a season was anything less than the rock upon which that team was built. He was a miracle, a force of nature. Statistics rarely help, and they are difficult to apply to goalkeepers anyway, but sixteen goals in forty-two games! That's better than a goal every two-and-a-half games. It means that determined and skilful (and occasionally lucky) forwards were only able to score past him every three and three-quarter hours. Worth a million? The next year, he and they won the League again. Clemence let in thirty goals in forty-one games. The year after that, 1980/81, they didn't do so well in the League, but they won the European Cup. After that Liverpool sold Ray Clemence to Tottenham. He hadn't got any worse. His record, if you care for such things, was second to none. His stature in the team and in the game was as high as it could be. The price: £300,000. Now admittedly, in the strange way of football business, that price was a consciously low one with which to reward his long and incredibly distinguished service to Liverpool. They wanted to make his sale go through easily. Which means that they felt, they *knew*, that neither Tottenham nor anybody else would pay, say, half a million, half of what Trevor Francis had cost several years earlier, for a player of immeasurably greater value. It's an insult, born from the habitual contempt in which goalkeepers are held.

Pat Jennings tells us in his autobiography that he thought it was impossible for clubs to stick to a 'wage structure', and that players were entitled to bargain for what they could get. But he admits that it never quite worked out like that. In his last season at Tottenham Hotspur, he tells us that he was on £15,000, having been on £11,500 the season before that.[1] By his own estimation, these were modest amounts for an established First Division star at the time. When Tottenham let him go, thinking that his younger understudy Barry Daines would be quite good enough to see them through a season in the Second Division, and would cost the club half as much in wages, they did it with as much unpleasantness as possible, because they did not like the possibility of his going to their neighbours and closest rivals Arsenal. When he went to White Hart Lane to bid his team-mates of thirteen years goodbye, the directors cut him dead in the car park. They simply refused to acknowledge he was there. And they cancelled, at discourteously short notice, his invitation to go on a closed-season friendly tour of Sweden, which he might have enjoyed.

Now one can argue about whether Jennings was the greatest ever goalkeeper, or only one of the greatest. Whatever else he was, he had been a fantastic goalkeeper for Tottenham, good enough that he had probably in fact kept a middling team in the First Division for some years before they finally went down. These people just owed him. They owed him gratitude and respect, and Jennings was bitterly hurt by this treatment. It's all part of the same parcel. The whole football world undervalues goalkeepers, in money as well as in the more abstract kinds of worth. In fact, Jennings nearly went to Ipswich Town, then just about to enter on a fine period of football. They were twice runners-up in the League in the early 1980s, and no doubt Jennings could have made the difference between that and winning had he gone there. He nearly went to Manchester United, where Tommy Docherty had a short-list of two goalkeepers to sort out a relegation season; Jennings and Peter Shilton, and either could have made all the difference there, too. Manchester United had a habit of being sanctimonious about the interests of the club and the 'ethics' of wages, but at the time their players were on £300 a week, apparently (and incredibly, to anybody who has watched their recent plutocratic behaviour) the lowest wages in the division.[2] As it happened, Docherty was sacked before he could hire either. Shilton wanted £400, and went to Nottingham Forest, and Jennings did go to Arsenal, where he was paid about £200.

Still today, when the cost of players (in England particularly, but elsewhere, too) has reached the stratosphere, the goalkeeper remains the best bargain to be had. If you want to strengthen your team, you should look very hard at the goalkeepers you already have, and make getting a great one an obvious and urgent priority. But they just don't see it. Football club directors, managers, and coaches just don't seem to realize what a goalkeeper is worth. The market for goalkeepers bears no real relation to their value. I remember when Bryan Gunn of Norwich was injured a few years ago, Alan Hansen quite bluntly said on television that they had a chance of staying in the Premier League if they spent the money to get an experienced goalkeeper to replace him. It wouldn't have been a lot, but they didn't, and they dropped. Brian Clough used to say that Peter Shilton was worth ten to twelve points a season to Nottingham Forest, which is a nice compliment, even if it is an underestimation. On Shilton's earlier move from Leicester to Stoke for a then record fee for a goalkeeper of £335,000, Hugh McIlvanney wrote in *The Observer* in October 1983 that it was 'ludicrously low in relation to the sums handed over for some outfield players who couldn't trap a curling stone'.

Agents don't seem to offer goalkeepers at high prices; if they do they find no takers. As far as I can see through the inevitable fog of guesswork and misinformation, no English goalkeeper has been on the highest wages in his time at the club. How is this possible, when so many have so obviously been the most important player? Even international competitions, the Harrods of football, where everything is available at a price, rarely produce goalkeeping transfers equivalent to the outfield ones they routinely generate. Time and again goalkeepers have shone in international competitions, perhaps from smaller countries or countries to which the scouting-and-whispering system doesn't reach. Very few have been snapped up. Very many ought to have been. Think of the wonderfully athletic Thomas N'kono of Cameroon, and the save he made in Italy in 1990 against Gheorghe Hagi of Romania. Hagi was substituted soon after, seemingly morally broken, and Cameroon went on to win with goals by the amazing evergreen Roger Milla.

N'Kono was officially the number two goalkeeper, after the hardly less amazing Joseph-Antoine Bell (who had been dropped for insisting that the Cameroon Football Federation treat its players properly), but he played through the tournament like a man possessed, even if he did cost them, by upending Paul Gascoigne, the penalty which eventually put them out of the competition. British observers barely noticed him, more excited by the dreadlocks of Makanaky and the exact age of Milla. It's standard: whatever there is to notice in a tournament, the goalkeeper comes last, unless he makes a mistake for saloon-bar merriment.

This whole question of the value of goalkeepers is really double-edged. There is the question of their value to their clubs, expressed in transfer fees and wages, consistently lower than they should be, and connected to that, but distinct from it, is the question of the public appreciation of their worth in a game or a team. Good judges are under no illusion. The Brazilian team which won the World Cup Final against Sweden in 1958, the team that first established the swaggering, samba'ing mythology of Brazilian football, played with astonishing attacking flair to win 5–2. It was Garrincha's game, in spite of Pele's two goals and the threat of others. After the game, Vincente Feola, the Brazilian coach, restrained the journalists eager to get him to talk about this breathtaking display of complete attacking football: 'What you forget is the save our goalkeeper Gilmar made when the score was 1–1. It was just as vital as the goals we scored at the other end. Unfortunately few people yet realize that a brilliant save by a goalkeeper is every bit as important as a scoring shot. The keeper is seldom the subject of back-slapping.' Then, and only then, he went on to praise Pele and Vavà and Djalma Santos and Garrincha.

Nick Hornby staked his claim to representing the voice of the fan with his book *Fever Pitch*; it is not unfair to take his attitude to goalkeeping as typical. In a magazine piece under the strapline 'Who Wants To Go in Goal? Not Me, Says Nick Hornby' he wrote these remarks:

> One can never get that excited about seeing goalkeepers live. They're like newsreaders, or weather forecasters: the chances are, you've seen them seven thousand times before. If you nodded off for a few minutes then you missed George Best's entire career, but even Rip van Winkle would have caught up with Peter Shilton somewhere along the line. Remember Ray Clemence, Joe Corrigan, Alex Stepney and Pat Jennings? You ought to. They played football for most of your life . . . You only end up in goal if you are a) small, b) bad at football, c) easily intimidated by your peers, or d) carrying a minor leg injury. So it is somewhat surprising that goalkeepers end up as six-foot-nine-inch megalomaniacs with no discernible limp whatsoever. The only enviable thing about being a keeper is that you get to shout at Steve Bruce a lot, make that gesture of despair and disgust – the one that looks as if you're chucking a handful of mud straight into the turf – and clip Steve McManaman round the ear.[4]

In the same piece, his token expression of gratitude to *his* goalkeeper is immediately soured by three sharp names which spell that goalkeeper's discomfiture:

'Arsenal fans love David Seaman, and will always think of him with awe and respect; but Gazza, Nayim and Ronald Koeman are never far away either.' Three names, three famous goals supposed to blot a career of enormous distinction. But fans should think of this, that the only goalkeepers whom we cannot associate with famous goals conceded are the ones who were not good enough to be there to be shot at.

It may be funny, in the sad sense that goalkeepers acknowledge that one of their roles is to carry the can, but it's also spiteful: being nasty about goalkeepers allows fans to be nicer about the outfield players, the ones they would themselves like to be, and the ones with whom they identify themselves most strongly. Sure, David Seaman failed to save a famous free kick against Tottenham at Wembley. But Tottenham had on their books the most celebrated taker of free kicks in England, Paul Gascoigne. Arsenal knew that – and it was not Seaman who conceded the kick within Gascoigne's range. There's a sourness about this kind of talk about goalkeepers which is very common, and very wrong. The clear implication is that David Seaman did nothing to get his teams (Arsenal in the case of Gascoigne and Nayim, England against Ronald Koeman) into a position where they might have to deal with these great threats on goal. If you can write a kind of shorthand about David Seaman which is simply three names that represent three huge disappointments, then the proclaimed love, awe, and respect are tempered with something that looks very much like contempt. What it amounts to is that the goalkeeper lets the side down.

All fans do this; it is part of the necessary bigotry of fandom: 'We would have got to the final (or won the final, or beaten the old enemy or whatever) if only the goalkeeper . . .' The goalkeeper, in nine circumstances out of ten, got you that far, or at the very least prevented you from not getting that far. To blame him at the last is craven. Goalkeepers do make hideous blunders. But so does every other player, at least as often. Outfield players don't always get away with them, either. But they are not, in general, expected to carry them around their necks for the rest of their careers. The only possible exception comes when they miss penalties. And even then, they're somehow thought to be unlucky rather than hopeless. There is another thing: if goalkeepers are to be saddled with these burdens of shame, let them at least be clear blunders. When Ray Clemence, playing for England in 1976, let a miskicked shot from his club colleague Kenny Dalglish trickle at a slow walking pace between his legs, that was a blunder. He looked truly stricken when it happened. And the ribbing he must have taken for it in training doesn't bear thinking about. Years ago, J.F. Mitchell, who used to keep goal for Preston North End in spectacles, walked off the pitch before the end of a game after mistaking a whistle in the crowd for the full-time whistle. It cost a goal. That was a blunder, sure enough. But Gascoigne's free kick? Perhaps Seaman might have stopped it on another day, but that doesn't make it a blunder.

It has been said many times that goalkeepers are remembered only for their mistakes. Bruce Grobbelaar springs to mind, dropping crosses all over the place. But Grobbelaar was a fabulous goalkeeper, who by playing further forward than any goalkeeper had done before invented and perfected a technicality which suited his team to perfection. He was Liverpool's sweeper as much as their goalkeeper. His record for them is astounding. It is inconceivable – at Liverpool, of all clubs, who have always seemed to value and appreciate goalkeeping more than their rivals – that he could have kept his place if he was as dreadful as it was fashionable to say. Of course goalkeepers are remembered for their mistakes. Fans claim to feel hurt, let down when *their* goalkeeper makes a mistake. But they give themselves away when it happens at the other end of the field. When *the enemy* goalkeeper makes a blunder, fans try everything to convince themselves that he was forced into it by the excellence of one of their men. The cross was too good for him, the pass too cunning. Most galling of all, and often heard, is the grotesque claim that some miserable deflection was a 'touch'. A tiny handful of great strikers have an ability to read confused and hectic play in front of goal so fast that they can legitimately claim some credit for awkward little contacts that finish off the confusion in the defence. Ian Rush did this, and it was princely to watch. But most of the time we credit a touch when no merit is due, when the forward knew nothing at all about the relationship between the ball, himself, the goalkeeper, and the goal. The truth is very simple: to be always in the right place to make the catch, and to catch everything through a game, is appallingly difficult.

People are trying their utmost to make goalkeeping mistakes happen, with energy and hostility and sometimes with skill. As a proportion of their interventions, goalkeepers make startlingly few blunders.

Take the goalkeeper for Leeds United during much of their eminence in the late 1960s and 1970s, Gary Sprake. Kids far too young to have seen him play routinely shout 'Sprake! Sprake!' at the more lamentable goalkeeping efforts of their kick-abouts. His name has become a byword for hopeless and laughable goalkeeping. I was once offered a Sunday game in goal by some people who had never seen me play 'on condition that you're not Gary Sprake'. Sprake is maligned for one moment above all, in a match against Liverpool, when under no pressure at all he threw the ball into his own net. He collected a back-pass from Jack Charlton, who jogged back upfield. Sprake went to throw the ball to Terry Cooper and seemed to change his mind, perhaps because Cooper was too close to a Liverpool player, perhaps because he had seen somebody in a better position to receive the ball. Sprake checked his throw, but not quite enough; he had given it just the momentum it needed to roll off his hand and bobble, really quite slowly, into the goal. No matter how hard I try to take the goalkeeper's side, it was genuinely funny. The Anfield Tannoy played 'Careless Hands', echoed with delighted glee by the Kop. As Bob Wilson described it, Jack Charlton was close to Gordon Hill, the referee, as the noise made them turn round.

'What's happened?' said Hill.

'I think the silly so-and-so's thrown it in his own net,' replied Jack.

'What shall I give?' continued the ref.

'You've got to give a goal,' said Jack.[5]

And on that one glorious howler, Gary Sprake's reputation was established for ever. Or perhaps not quite. For Sprake was definitely prone, like Bruce Grobbelaar more recently, to making mistakes. He let in such a soft one in the FA Cup Final in 1970 (against Peter Houseman of Chelsea) that he was dropped for the replay, and I have heard several different versions of his letting the ball through his legs, which may well be apocryphal. Nevertheless, Sprake's reputation is hard on him. If one can hardly deny that he failed to achieve the consistent reliability of the very finest goalkeepers, it is still true that for Leeds he was for many years the first-choice goalkeeper in one of the most famous defences there has been. He was an international for Wales at the age of nineteen, and went on to earn thirty-seven caps for his country.

It was not – it could not have been – a con; he clearly was a very fine goalkeeper. It is inconceivable that Don Revie would have kept him in his side if he thought he was not good enough. I think the explanation is different. The Leeds team of Sprake's era was hated as very few teams have been. They were a hard side, founded on a hard defence. Billy Bremner, Norman Hunter, Jack Charlton himself, these were tough men perfectly prepared to play negative football if it got results. Even Johnny Giles, the most talented in the team, was a hard player. They could destroy attackers, and with them the romantic hopes of the fans. In fact, Leeds won rather less than they might have done: in Sprake's time they won the Fairs Cup twice, but they kept on coming second in the League, and twice missed the FA Cup in the final. They were a side who by a whisker failed wholly to impose themselves. The team were disliked and feared for their aggression, and the fans had a thoroughly unsavoury reputation for violence. Leeds were a great side, but conveyed an aura of lack of sportsmanship and sleazy toughness which was resented around the country much more than I think they realized at the time. Gary Sprake became the wider public version of what the goalkeeper has always been: he became the one player in the side to carry the abuse. In his case, it came from the whole country, not just from team-mates and the fans behind his goal. To ridicule Sprake was an effective way to ridicule Leeds United. He was a soft target – he was not as good a goalkeeper as such a great team should have had. Perhaps precisely because it was such a good team, in spite of playing in such a widely disliked style, he was the only target. If you wanted to get at Leeds, but couldn't see any obvious flaws, then Gary Sprake was your goat.

Football matches are taken awfully seriously. It's not surprising that people should try to squeeze what laughs they can out of them. The goalkeeper is the obvious focus. He's within earshot, he can't really move away. If, as Grobbelaar could, he can crack a bit of a joke, the fans will laugh with him. If not, they'll laugh long and ruthlessly at him. That's what happened to poor Gary Sprake; he became a national fall guy. Put another way, he came to represent the banana skin on which people were only too happy to see Leeds slip up.

It's all part of the same deal. Goalkeepers have to get accustomed to being terrifyingly and irretrievably alone when it matters. They train alone, or to be accurate, they train with the team and then do more training, specific to their needs, alone. They can work and work on the technicalities they need to master, and they do, but how do you train to be alone at the death? How do you learn to take the blame? Athletes train to improve something called their recovery rate. I remember a documentary on Sebastian Coe, many years ago, when he was shown running up a long hill in Sheffield or somewhere in winter, in the dark, while his father, who was his coach, tooled along in a car. At the top, he jumped in and was driven down, only to run up it again. And again. The idea was that the few moments in the car should be enough for him to be completely fresh when he started running again, and that his time for the fourth or the seventh ascent should be much the same as for the first. That was improving his recovery rate. Watch stage winners in the Tour de France. They race all day at speeds normal cyclists couldn't maintain for quarter of an hour, up ferocious hills in the Pyrenees or the Alps, perhaps two hundred kilometres of appalling physical effort. It is not rare for cyclists to be unable to stand at the end of a stage; the bicycle carries their body weight, so they can carry on producing enough effort to move forward even after they have exhausted the muscles they use to maintain posture. At the end of a stage they get mobbed by journalists and they give interviews, right there, with the bikes still bolted to their feet. And they can speak. Within a minute of stopping they are no longer out of breath.

Goalkeepers naturally have a similar thing for physical effort. It is quite astonishing how often the goalkeeper makes a first save, and is ready to make a second lunge sooner than the striker. If both have fallen, it is a certainty that the goalkeeper will be up and flexibly ready first. But more astonishing is the way they develop a psychological recovery rate. Watch a young goalkeeper, perhaps in a school match. It matters to him; he wants to do well. He lets in a goal, perhaps a bad one. He'll get upset, get edgy, show nerves, lose concentration. It may well last the rest of the game (or it may be abolished by doing something right later on). He sinks into self-reproach, almost certainly assisted by the vocal and ill-informed criticism of those around. His poise is likely to be shattered for a good while. Then look at a pro. A disaster happens. He may allow himself a gesture or a yell. His nerve may go for a moment, but within seconds he has recovered and is ready to start again. The goal has cost . . . a goal, but it has cost none of the discomfiture, the loss of morale, which might lead to another goal. All is not lost, game on! Three-nil down and time running out? It won't be the goalkeeper who loses morale, for that scoreline is no more than an actual manifestation of the psychological situation goalkeepers are deeply familiar with.

Goalkeepers learn to be lone-minded. Athletes in solitary sports are familiar with such a frame of mind when their performance depends on nothing but themselves.

Beat the clock, beat the other guy, go for a personal best every time. Effort in training translated to a fraction more ease, a morsel in reserve, in competition. In team games, much of this is done through the mechanics of the group. Loyalty and cohesion are fostered and encouraged to a military level, the successes of individuals more than making up (if all goes well) for the shortcomings of others. But goalkeepers, who play in teams, only get the marginal benefits of being team players. When they win the Cup their medal looks like everybody else's but while the game was being played they could not rely on assistance in times of crisis. On the contrary, they fully expected their team-mates to depend wholly on them at several critical points in the game.

Goalkeepers do, in fact, get a lot of help from team-mates, but they cannot rely on it. When a defender clears off the line with the goalkeeper beaten the goalkeeper feels it to be a bonus, a lucky break gratefully received and acknowledged, not a normal part of an exchange of mutual help. A defender heads the ball clear from that awkward intermediate area where the goalkeeper doubts whether he could reach it or would be better advised to stay back and wait. The situation is physically similar to the normal cover any defender gives to any other, but psychologically utterly different. The defender may well tear a strip off his goalkeeper for having left the ball to him, something he would rarely consider doing to another defender. The goalkeeper feels doubt about his decision, perhaps a little shame at having seemed to get it wrong, perhaps a little anger at being called to justify his assessment so immediately and so publicly. If he hasn't built a solid frame of mind to make his own criticism on what he does and then recover immediately, he will be destroyed by this kind of thing.

In dressing-rooms before games, goalkeepers behave differently to other players. No matter how gregarious, how glad to see their friends, they prepare more silently than the rest of the team. A very few are calm before a game, but most are seriously nervous. Speaking only for myself, I know that the butterflies begin well before the game starts, before even reaching whichever park has been booked for the day. Perhaps when the time comes to pack kit into a bag, I start running mental tapes of what the game is likely to bring. I run over mistakes to correct from last week, possibilities brought on by the weather and the team for that particular day, a whole series of general worries which together add up to a state of distinct jumpiness. By the time I'm in the changing-room, in the familiar boastful atmosphere of expectation, my stomach is likely to be churning and my mouth very dry. The kick-about before a game makes it worse, and then as soon as the game is begun, the unpleasant, uncomfortable nerves are replaced by something much more constructive.

That nervous edginess is precisely what I live on as a goalkeeper. It seems to be necessary to perform even ordinarily. I know that on the rare occasions when I haven't got into this flap before playing, I haven't played well. It's as though the nervousness were a necessary part of the concentration. To start a match nervelessly, in my case, is the same as starting without caring much, and it isn't possible to play in goal with indifference. The routine things in goal are so unnatural that I find I need a certain motivating energy to overcome them. Whatever happens, I know I'm likely to get minor scrapes and bruises. To wander into a game in a frame of mind where I'd rather avoid them if I can is to start it already less than committed. I'm slower to dive full-length to save myself from jarred elbows, and slower to cut out crosses to avoid the bumping and colliding that goes with them. Inevitably, this means playing less well. It's not that on some days I am more afraid for my health, and therefore protect myself better by playing a little more easily. It's more that to play really well I need to find it obvious that the ball and the goal come first, and that can only happen with a good dose of nerves. To be nervous overcomes the instinct that says, 'What the hell, it's only a game', and makes it self-evident that the effort is worthwhile. The nerves prevent hesitation, which is obviously very useful at times of real physical risk, like diving to block the ball at somebody's feet, but also eliminates uncertainty at other times. Maybe I'm built differently to everybody else, but as a result I don't believe it to be possible to keep goal without something of this uncomfortable excess of nervousness before the game. Call it the adrenalin beginning to flow, or call it concentration beginning to pull together, but it needs to be there.

There is a revealing pointer to how goalkeepers are going to play in the warm-up before the match. Outfield players are nastily inconsiderate of their goalkeepers at that time, enjoying blasting the ball past them, even from silly range or when the goalkeeper is looking the other way. They have their own worries, of course, and they like to feel that they have their 'shooting boots' on. The goalkeeper wants to get the feel of the ball, the ground, the lighting. He really wants to be eased into his match mentality quite gently. But a goalkeeper who is really nervous, one who is right on his game, will try far harder than is necessary to stop these impossible pre-game shots. I have seen some brilliant saves in pre-match warming-up, particularly when, as a kid, I used to stand immediately behind the goal. How hard it must be for goalkeepers to play in big games which demand two national anthems and a handshake with a posse of 'dignitaries', and maybe a meaningless pleasantry or two with one of them before the welcome dismissal to the penalty area and the kick-in.

The nerves don't go away during the game. They merely become usefully channelled into all the things that goalkeepers do. Anticipation is much sharper when nervous, as are reflexes. Courage is immeasurably increased and muscles work appreciably better. Frank Swift, who was later to become an iconic goalkeeper, captain of England and hugely experienced, fainted at the end of the 1934 Cup Final. As he explains it, the photographers gathered behind his (Manchester City's) goal, perhaps in the hope of a Portsmouth equalizer. Seeing how nervous Swift was, and he himself describes his concentration vanishing in the last moments of the game ('I wonder if the cup takes much cleaning . . .'), they counted down the minutes, and then the seconds to the end of the match. When the whistle went, Swift stooped down to pick up his cap and gloves, walked a few paces out of goal, and fainted. Manchester City trainer Alec Bell, loyal to proper footballing tradition, brought him round by the use of the magic sponge. Swift had found it increasingly difficult in those last few moments to keep his mind off his imminent meeting with the King:

I limped across to where the other players and officials were waiting for our skipper to lead the parade up to the royal dais. I still felt a bit woozy, which is probably why I didn't turn and run away instead of slowly climbing what seemed to be an endless number of stone steps up to the royal box . . . A long, gawky lad of nineteen-and-a-bit stands alone in front of a bearded gentleman with kind eyes. Two minutes previously the boy had lain unconscious on the sacred turf at Wembley. The buzzing in his brain beats against the crowd noises. Then the kindly face of this much-loved man crystallizes from the dizzy mist.

'How are you feeling now, my boy?' says a deep voice. It is the King speaking.

'Fine, Sir,' says the lad.

'That's good. You played well. Here's your medal, and good luck.'[6]

This is a moment of bluff patriotism. The shell-shocked soldier gets his medal from the general. George V has kind eyes, a kindly face, and murmurs a few kind words. Would modern players describe the Queen (supposing she could be prevailed upon to give the medals at Wembley) as 'much-loved'? The tired old cliché seems so right in this context, of Wembley's turf being 'sacred'. The fallen man, his duty completed, rises up that ritual stair to receive the proper acknowledgement of his lord. It is almost a religious passage. Swift allows few emotions in the rest of his book, beyond the hale and convivial norm of a proper English sporting yeoman. But here he seems almost overwhelmed by loyal fervour.

Swift himself leans towards (but does not exactly state) the view that he fainted from a kind of timid stage-fright at the thought of meeting the King, made worse by the photographers' countdown. But it seems more likely that the most important game he had played in his life so far had already put him in a whirl. He had been on the verge of fainting before the game, in the dressing-room. He says: 'I was getting on all right, in a quiet sort of way, until it came to tying my boots. Then I noticed one of the players (he shall be nameless) was having his boots tied by Jimmy McLuckie, the reserve. I turned green. Quick as a flash Alec Bell hauled me into the washroom, slapped my face and gave me a tot of whisky from a flask. "Get back in there, you big lug, nobody's going to eat you!" Which, strangely enough, made me feel better.' Is this, I wonder, a stiff-upper-lip way of telling us that he threw up from nerves? He wouldn't be the first goalkeeper to do so at Wembley, I dare say. During the game itself, he made (by not putting on his gloves after a few spots of rain fell, and failing to grip a shot wide to his right) the one mistake which cost City the only goal they conceded. He then spent most of the second half living on his nerves, waiting for City to score. They finally got the winner, four minutes from the end, and it doesn't take much to imagine the state Swift had been in for forty-odd minutes. Add the four minutes left, with the photographers ticking away behind him, and fainting seems understandable. Remember that the very year before Swift had been an ordinary fan, watching the FA Cup Final from the terraces behind that very goal. Other players have fainted, of course. Peter Osgood did it once, if I recall. But for a goalkeeper it seems more obvious. It gives some idea of the strain we expect them to ignore. The wonder is that we don't see it more.

It's often said that goalkeepers divide into those who worry, like Frank Swift at the stellar level and myself at the earthbound, and those who are brim-full of confidence. Stephen Kelly put the distinction as neatly as anybody, quoting a 'former international goalkeeper' who unfortunately remained anonymous:

> We were watching a couple of young apprentices practising their solemn art on a rainsodden pitch in Lancashire. The wind howled about the open spaces, curling and twisting the ball like a chinaman delivery while magpies nosed and fooled around in the pools behind the goals. 'Neither of them will make it,' he grunted. 'They've got technique but that's not everything.' I expressed some surprise at his reservations. 'Naw,' he drawled, curling his lips. 'Goalkeepers fall into two categories. They're either self-assured and cocky, or worriers. Just look at Neville Southall. Keeps himself to himself. A worrier if ever there was one. Then there's Bruce Grobbelaar. They don't come any cockier than him. Remember the way he clowned about in the European Cup penalty shoot-out. Takes bottle that. These two lads are neither one thing nor the other.'[7]

More likely they were embarrassed at being scrutinized by the 'former international'.

Kelly's distinction is often made, but it may not be a fundamental one. Southall and Grobbelaar are certainly different as men and there is no doubt that these differences of personality affect their manner of keeping goal. But the moodiness of the one and the ebullience of the other are just two ways of dealing with the same terrible overdose of nerves that each, after years of being accustomed to it, still needs to feel to keep goal at his own astonishingly high level. Southall once famously drove off into the night rather than attend a post-Cup Final party; unusually, it was after a final his side had won. He preferred to be alone or with his family, anywhere rather than in that frenzied atmosphere of realized dreams. It is hard to imagine Bruce Grobbelaar doing the same, although the showman-buffoon persona he developed was largely for public consumption, a sort of suit he put on with his shorts and goalkeeping jersey. Southall seems almost sullen, Grobbelaar hyperactive; Southall is famously scruffy, Grobbelaar something of a dandy – but they're not chalk and cheese. After hundreds and hundreds of professional matches, both still felt nervous enough before games to play really well. To lose that and face games placidly would be to lose a proportion of their excellence, and then to lose their place in the team to some hungrier goalkeeper with butterflies in his belly.

Modern sporting argot has a language which seems to cover this kind of tension. Tennis players get 'really fired up' before big games, or more tersely, they 'get really up'. Some talk of being 'pumped up' – it's interesting how all these phrases come from the world of drugs, as though sportsmen urge themselves to achieve levels of desire and performance outside those which can be achieved under their own steam. To my ear, these phrases, and a whole array of similar ones, reveal something rather different. If you have to underline how 'pumped up' you get for the game which really matters, you are surely confessing how unpumped up, how deflated, you usually are. Another day on the circuit, be it at golf, tennis, or American football, any of those sports where the rewards for the giants are huge if they just turn up and go through the motions, and nothing much is at stake. Deflation is the order of the day. Be pleasant to a sponsor or two, take the trouble to give a little time to the press. Another day, another dinar. Goalkeepers cannot have such days. There is no such thing.

Even at the puny level at which I play, all those goalkeeping factors like the risk of humiliation and the near certainty of being held responsible for the results of others' play combine to make it impossible just to show up and go through the motions. Goalkeepers who hide don't play very long. They don't enjoy it, and nobody wants them around. And what makes you able not to hide, week after week, is nervousness. Just to move fast enough across the six-yard line to improve your chances of reaching a ball takes a kind of nervous energy. You can't move too soon, or you present a gaping hole in the goal you're supposed to cover. So when the time does come, you have to scuttle along in a movement that is itself fuelled by nerves. The same applies to perhaps half of all that a goalkeeper does. He has to be pumped up to be at his normal operating level, like a bicycle tyre.

I noticed many years ago that goalkeepers who give away a corner in the completion of a blazing save almost never let in a goal as a result of that corner. Maybe it happens from time to time, but it is very rare. To make the save they had to marshal an explosion of energy, first in the mind to work out what they should best do, and then in the sinews to do it. They pick themselves up, if it was that kind of save, and have to organize their defence for what would normally be a serious threat on goal. Corners are. The ball comes over, and the goalkeeper is noticeably faster and more aggressive in getting to it than he had been before the save of a moment ago. People fall over, his own defenders included, as he makes absolutely certain he grabs the ball before any damage can be done. Then he stands while players move away from the goal, and the extra burst of nervous energy drains out of him. He delivers the ball, and the sequence is over. The nerves build up in the scary moments before the save, as the rapid options unfold before the goalkeeper, and as he manoeuvres to improve his chances. The save uses some of this energy, but not all. What's left deals with the corner. The faster the save – that is to say the more it depended on furiously active reflexes alone, unassisted by planning – the longer this hangover of excitement goes on.

In sports argot, the save has pumped the goalkeeper up. Only it is the nature of his job that he was already in that airy condition. So goalkeepers quite routinely live on multiples of nerves. The whole process, of alarm, then thought, then action, is repeated many times during a game. Even when it is not completed, it is exhausting. A threat develops. The goalkeeper starts to think how it might develop, formulating instant detailed plans so accurate they tell him where to move each foot through each stride of the growing attack on goal. It may come to nothing, as a defender does his job or the attacker fails to do his. Good. But the adrenalin will have flowed copiously before the goalkeeper knows that there is nothing to worry about, this time. Outfield players are often surprised that a goalkeeper who 'hasn't done anything' all afternoon should be tired after a game. There is nothing surprising about it at all. Only the goalkeeper will know how much his mind was churning as the game went on. Others have to imagine an exam, a ninety-minute exam, not about some distant thing like French irregular verbs or the periodic table, but probing right into the marrow of how the goalkeeper defines himself.

It's possible to be too nervous, of course. The coordination of hand and eye or hand and foot goes wrong, and timing becomes like soap, harder to grasp the tighter you grip for it. Every detail of the ability to keep goal is threatened at all times. At first, if goalkeeping defeats you, you let in goals which is bad enough. But there's more. Nerve and nerves are not the same thing, but an activity which depends so much on nerves becomes impossible when the nerve goes. All sportsmen run the risk of mysterious troughs of loss of form. One treatment, chosen by the golfer Nick Faldo, for example, is to attack fundamental techniques of swing (in golf) or of action (for bowlers or snooker players). More goal-keepers ought to address this solution than do, when technical coaching is at last more common and more insisted upon than it used to be.

But it won't deal with the problem in all its aspects. For if a goalkeeper loses his form, several things get damaged which are beyond his own repair. Foremost among them is the respect of his team-mates. Outfield players who work well together are often described as 'having a good understanding'. It means that they avoid making the same run into space, and getting in each other's way. They anticipate each other's intentions, and move early and quickly to make them possible. If they have played together a great deal, they can often pass to each other without looking, a marvellous thing to see. But outfield players lack this kind of understanding with their goalkeepers, even after years of mutual aid. The best they can have is trust. They trust the goalkeeper not to let them down, but don't really understand the mechanics. Once a goalkeeper's form starts to slip, from lack of fitness, lack of confidence, or lack of technique, that trust will inevitably slip too. If the goalkeeper recovers form later there will remain a shadow of mistrust among the outfield players, which makes goal-keeping harder.

There is nothing more inspiring for a team than to play in the full confidence that their goalkeeper is a fine one and to be trusted. But every single outfield player has at some point played with a dodgy goalkeeper. Each thinks there is something intrinsically wacky and dangerous about goalkeeping, and their own goalkeeper, no matter how many years he has been excellent, carries in their eyes some of that infection. So goalkeepers have to master not only the perpetually unstable balance between their own nerves and nerve, but have constantly to re-seduce their team-mates into having confidence in them. This is how Dick Pym, for many years the Bolton Wanderers goalkeeper, put it in 1927: 'Confidence is also an important item and plays a large part in a goalkeeper's career. No other position on the field has so much responsibility. Let the goalie make one mistake during a match, and notice the amount of adverse criticism aimed at him? Yet how many players make fewer mistakes? Unless a player has a very broad pair of shoulders and at least one deaf ear, I wouldn't advise him to take up goalkeeping.'[8] Or try Harry Gregg's version of the same idea: 'As a youngster I didn't go in much for the theory of the game; maybe even today I play mostly by instinct. But I find nowadays that when I am playing well, I run the show in defence . . . if I'm hesitant and out of form, the defenders in front of me soon sense that I've got the jitters – and they become affected, too. Confidence stems outward from the goalkeeper; so does lack of confidence. And I reckon that's one of the things the keeper has to overcome at the start of every match.'[9]

Outfield, it is emphatically not the same. Players may be good or bad, or playing well or playing ill, and their colleagues will still treat them with a cosy familiarity which has nothing to do with trust. Of course a great winger can make a centre-forward's job immeasurably easier, and equally so for all other positions. But the absence of such treats does not lead to the assumption of disaster whenever a less talented or less in-form player comes into the game. With the goalkeeper, it does. Because each goalkeeper is the heir not only of his own disaster last week or last season, but of all the generations of disasters before him. Outfield players like to think of themselves, and by courtesy of each other, as a slinky twist of the hips and a screaming half-volley waiting to happen. The goalkeeper is an outsider; they think of him as the disappointment and the defeat around the next corner. At every moment, let the goalkeeper prove that wrong. It's an insane legacy to heap on a player if you want him to play well. And all the more miraculous that goalkeepers so often do, particularly as they are deprived of one of the factors which usually makes ball-playing easier.

In most sports, the timing of the shot is shared and agreed between the players. In dead-ball games like golf or snooker, you hit the thing (within reason) when you feel like hitting it. Your timing can still go awry, but when it does you have an internal problem of your own not one imposed on you by the other. In exchange-of-rally games a tempo is set by compromise between the players. One of the defining advantages the better player will have is his ability to change that tempo, which is why the meeting of two committed baseliners in a tennis match is so dull. Neither challenges the other's timing, and the contest becomes one of endurance and percentage risk and the ability to make fewer mistakes. The whole point of taking the ball early, ahead of the highest part of its bounce, is the same in all games. By snipping a fraction off the time your opponent has to play his shot, you both hurry him and (which is slightly different) break the grooved coordination he has established. The better you are at taking the ball earlier (or sometimes later) than expected, the more you control the timing and leave the opponent struggling to do the same to you in his turn.

In none of this is timing particularly mysterious. It is one of the many ingredients that make a successful ball-player, one which champions know how to alter to their advantage. It is true that the same word covers several things which are in reality distinct. In its precise sense it has to do with things swung, a club or a racquet, a hand or a foot. It refers to the matching of the movement of the ball with the movement of whatever hits it. More loosely, there can be the timing of the extra effort that an opponent does not expect (as when a middle-distance runner chooses to make his break) or the dosing of efforts throughout a game to suit a player and discomfit his opponent. The extraordinary thing is that none of these applies to goalkeeping.

Goalkeepers quite obviously need exceptional hand-to-eye coordination, and nobody doubts that the best have astonishing reflexes. But they are unique in having so little say in the timing of their movements. A standard goalkeeping gesture, if there can be such a thing, is made not when the goalkeeper wants to make it, nor even within some rhythm established by the preceding exchanges, but on the instant of the demand of the opponent. No goalkeeper has the batsman's luxury of gradually familiarizing himself with the pace of the ball, of 'playing himself in'. There is no pattern of play in front of goal which can give even a rough outline of what the next movement is going to have to be. However methodical a football team's play, however neatly it fits the patterns worked out by boot-room strategists, play in front of goal is always sporadic. It may be predictable in its outlines, but in its detail, never. His colleagues used to pretend to give Jimmy Greaves aspirin after he had scored with his head, so rarely did it happen and so reluctant was he to allow it, but that never guaranteed that the next goal he scored was not going to be a header. The goalkeeper is always at the bidding of whatever the attacker might try next, however unlikely it may be. Anything might happen, any time.

The goalkeeper is the only sportsman to whom that applies. Everybody else has at least some inkling of the rhythm to give him help. The only exception is in the truly epic mismatch in other sports, when one player is so much below the standard of another that he has no real idea of what is going to happen next. Some goalkeepers try to anticipate as much as possible, others rely on their reaction. The majority rely on a combination of the two, but the choice of moment is never their own. Goalkeepers have a nominal advantage over other players in that they may use their hands, but a vast, crippling disadvantage in timing.

Goalkeepers make the save they have to when somebody else wants them to. For their more spectacular moments, this is the exact equivalent of a high diver performing his flawless turns and tucks after being pushed off the board. It is unthinkable, shocking. The speed and rhythm of the next intervention a goalkeeper has to make are never the same as, nor even a variation of, the last one. But no goalkeeper thinks it unusual. For their less desperate moves, it is true, goalkeepers have more say. It is perfectly possible, even necessary, to get into a practised rhythm of taking goal-kicks. The timing of a run out to collect a centre, for example, is critical, but it is the goalkeeper's to get right or to fluff as he will, given that he can cope with the baulking that goes with it. When running to challenge a forward the advantage is all with the forward, but the goalkeeper still has some part of the timing to himself. But for the purest moments of goalkeeping the goalkeeper gets no help at all from one of the things which makes every other ball game easier.

4. Nuts

'They say all goalkeepers are crazy. Maybe they are. I ain't talking. But if they are, I suppose the saying arose because in goal a man lays himself open to all of the kicks (which propel the ball past him) and none of the glories. The goalkeeper's best work is forgotten very quickly. Let him but make one mistake – and there has never been a goalkeeper who did not make a mistake (unless he plays for the heavenly eleven) – and he is not allowed to forget it.'[1] Ted Ditchburn, the lean goalkeeper (he was six feet and three-quarters of an inch tall, but always looked a lot taller) who was almost never out of the Tottenham side from the end of the war almost to the end of the 1950s, voicing the standard goalkeeper's lament.

Almost every goalkeeping memoir tackles at some point, usually on the first page, this assumption that all goalkeepers have a screw loose. Some take a certain rugged pride in living up to the reputation. Both Peru's Ramon Quiroga and Colombia's René Higuita thoroughly deserved the nickname El Loco, the madman. Both would have driven British managers apoplectic, for neither thought anything of playing miles upfield, well into the opposition half. But both were capable of brilliant goalkeeping; spectacular (occasional) misjudgements aside, they were mainly efficient. Scottish supporters should remember Quiroga: he saved Don Masson's feeble penalty in their first game of the 1978 World Cup Finals, so helping to speed them out of the competition.

Later in that same competition, Quiroga was at the centre of a murkier affair. The second-round group matches worked out in such a way that Argentina, desperate as host country to do well, had to beat Peru by four clear goals to qualify for the final. Even the timetabling was not above suspicion: the Brazilians, playing in the same group, had been scheduled to play in the afternoon, the Argentinians in the evening, so they knew exactly what they had to do. Argentina shipped 35,000 tons of free grain to Peru, and the Argentine central bank unfroze Peruvian assets. The Argentine manager, Cesar Luis Menotti, barred his goalkeeper, Fillol, and all his substitutes from his team-talk. Then Quiroga, himself an ex-Argentinian naturalized in Peru, proceeded to let in six in a display of goalkeeping that certainly didn't look of international standard. His reserve goalkeeper, Manzo, later admitted while drunk that his team had been paid to throw the game, but changed his mind the next morning. Nothing was proved, although the stench of corruption around the whole competition has not blown away to this day.[2]

Quiroga, as goalkeepers have to, became the fall guy. His connection with Argentina and the abject way in which he had played made him the principal suspect of allegations that Peru had simply accepted that Argentina needed to win the game and had taken money to see that it happened. Quiroga published an open letter protesting his innocence, which satisfied nobody. Argentina eventually beat Holland in one of the nastier finals so far, thanks to Mario Kempes and great goalkeeping by Fillol, and covered themselves in very little glory indeed in doing so. What to make of this abject story is anyone's guess. But the fate of the Colombian defender Andres Escobar, who was murdered after giving away the own goal that helped put his country out of the finals in 1994, should serve as a reminder that the kind of pressure the Peruvians would have had to resist to perform sportingly in the spirit of the game was perhaps too much to expect them to bear.

Higuita earned his share of the El Loco title mainly for his activities on the field of play. He has always insisted that it is a waste of a player to confine the goalkeeper to his penalty area, and has developed a way of charging forward late in moves that is not in theory as absurd as it looks when it goes wrong. No defence has anybody ready to mark an 'extra' man who appears like this, and Higuita has scored many goals to prove it. As a sweeper, too, he is often effective, although Roger Milla made sure enough that nobody will remember Higuita as a conspicuous success in that department. As a goalkeeper, he is athletic beyond the dreams of most of us, supple and springy and graceful. He thinks too much about the style of his goalkeeping, though, and often drops easy balls as a result, his mind seemingly occupied by the attention that wings towards him at the same time as the ball.

In June 1993, Higuita was gaoled in Colombia for having acted as the intermediary in the delivery of money in a kidnapping between two of the Medellin drug barons, and having taken a reward from one of them for doing so. There is a law in Colombia against profiting from a kidnapping, and although Higuita served seven months in prison, he was never either charged or tried. He was a famous Medellin boy made good himself, and would have found it very hard to refuse the request for assistance from Carlos Molina to help recover his daughter, kidnapped on the orders of his ex-partner in the drugs business, Pablo Escobar. Medellin businessmen are not known for their acceptance of polite but firm refusals. Colombia is different, but all the same, it's hard to say that Higuita didn't earn his nickname more definitely than many goalkeepers.

'In football, they say you have to be daft to be a goalkeeper. And I don't kid myself – I know that many people think I'm the daftest of them all. Well, I *am* daft – about football. I've been praised and insulted, cheered and jeered. There are grounds where I'm not welcome and grounds where I love to play. I've been hailed as a hero, sneered at as a villain, written off as a goalkeeper who can be brilliant one moment and shocking the next . . .'[3] Harry Gregg, going out of his way to claim some of the craziness for himself. Gregg wasn't crazy, far from it. He was a goalkeeper who liked coming far off his line, which he occasionally paid for with a goal. In his first European game, for example, in the first

(Manchester) leg of the match against Red Star Belgrade which would end in the plane crash at Munich, Red Star inside-forward Lazar Tasic saw Gregg well forward and shot early. It went in off the crossbar. Gregg says somewhere that Matt Busby approved when he said that he would do the same thing again, which is surely right. Such decisions have to be left to the goalkeeper – nobody else has any chance whatever of knowing quite what the circumstances are. And goalkeepers tend to admit when they were wrong in such choices. Gregg had a fairly cavalier attitude to getting injured, and something of a fiery temper. But he was not crazy. When he tried too hard to claim that he was, he sounded a little strained:

[Fans and team-mates] began to get suspicious of my sanity. It started the day they discovered a cigarette end in my cap.

I always took a cap on the field in case I needed to shade my eyes from the sun, and when I wasn't wearing the cap, I dropped it on the ground at the back of the net.

After one match, as I popped it on the dressing-room bench, a cigarette end fell out. How it got there I had no idea – but one of the lads spotted it and straight away, with an incredulous look, he asked me if I smoked during a game.

Noting his shocked expression and thinking quickly, I answered: 'Oh, I sometimes have a draw when things are quiet.' That did it.

My words, spoken in jest, were taken seriously. And when I realized the boys really believed I was daft enough to have a quick 'drag' when I thought no one was looking, I decided to keep the joke going.

So before every game, I made a point of putting a cigarette

and a few matches in my cap – and making sure that some of the boys saw me. The result was that some of my team-mates swore that I smoked during games. And the story spread around.

In fairness to the boys, I must say they never held it against me – and they didn't split on me to the boss.[4]

This is a fair example of the kind of barrack-room or boarding-school humour to be found in football teams and football memoirs, but it is hardly crazy. The vast majority of goalkeepers don't get noticed at all; they certainly don't get anything so complimentary as a reputation, for zaniness or anything else. I think the explanation for the crazy tag is this. Goalkeepers do necessary but unpleasant things, like risking being hurt and letting in goals. Their chances of successfully doing what they are there to do are slim, and their chances of blowing any credit they might get for doing it in the succeeding minutes are long. I think that any goalkeeper worth his salt will try whatever he can to nail his attitude onto the game, not as vanity or as showing off, but for the technical reason that he will need, in two or three or five crises, every help in getting opposing players to do something closer to his will than to theirs. In a role of such decided underdoggedness every little helps, and if the goalkeeper, by sheer force of character, can make the penalty area the zone of his despotism, where things are done according to his will, he will tilt the balance a fraction in his favour.

In football-speak, this is called 'imposing one's personality on the game'. It should be impossible. How do you impose yourself on a ball which is at that moment at the feet of somebody else, somebody, furthermore, intent on propelling it past you as viciously as possible? But in practice, it works. Everybody who has watched Peter Schmeichel has seen him howling and shouting at his defenders. The fans think it funny, the defenders taking loud stick from their own goalkeeper. Schmeichel has said at various times that it helps to keep his concentration, keeps him right in the thick of the game. I'm sure it does. But opposing players notice it, too. They can't help but notice that as well as a massive frame, a massive will is opposed to their having their way in front of Peter Schmeichel's goal. And when they get there, they doubt a bit, hesitate a blink, and that's enough for a goalkeeper of Schmeichel's genius to have won the battle.

'I get the feeling that they're conscious of my reputation and determination when hitting shots at me . . . They try and hit the perfect ball all the time and don't give themselves any margin for error. This sounds a little conceited, I know, but I'm sure that against a lot of other goalkeepers, they'd just hit it without thinking quite so much about it.' Not Schmeichel, although it might as well have been, but Peter Shilton, explaining something he called the Peter Shilton Effect in his book, one of the very best there is on goalkeeping, and he was absolutely right.[5] Just imagine yourself trying to score past a Shilton, a Schmeichel, a Zoff, a Yashin, or a Jennings. It doesn't bear thinking about – you'd almost certainly scuff the ground or maybe miss the ball altogether. Forwards should thank the Lord for bobbly pitches – they conceal a lot of failures, although not for goalkeepers. Shilton wonders if it was conceited to have written what he wrote; it isn't, of course. He'd simply spotted another tiny advantage he could crank round in his favour.

Imagine. You, full of all your doubts and insecurities, are one-on-one against Peter Shilton. Do you chip him? Chip Shilton? Too late. Do you shoot? Which corner is even marginally exposed? Too late. Do you dribble round him? Have you really got the balance and ball control it would take? Too late. He's got it. He's *made* you come into his range. It's a conjuring trick, but there is nothing conceited in explaining it, certainly when you've done it as often as Peter Shilton has, and against such a quality of opponent. From the outside, it looks like witchcraft. But if it happens to you, you'll know that for the crucial stride or two you were under the control of a tyrant, who simply wouldn't let you have your way when it seemed there was nothing he could do to stop you. Small wonder people use words like craziness to describe it.

Pat Jennings, a more modest man by nature than Shilton, put the same point in a more humble way. He never worried in advance about playing against Best or Charlton, Greaves or Law: 'All you end up with is an inferiority complex. I'm equally sure that none of these four ever gave a thought to the identity of the opposing keeper before a game. When you are mixing in the highest company you win some and you lose some.' You do, indeed. It's just that he did not happen to lose very many. And see carefully what he is saying. If, in goal, the position with the most self-evident inferiority on the field, he could avoid an 'inferiority complex' against forwards of the skill and reputation of these four, then it is obvious that against more normally fallible players, he had achieved superiority. Which, as we know, he had.

Sheer force of personality, honed and sharpened until it becomes a goalkeeping tool. At the weigh-in before big boxing matches, the fighters square up to each other mouthing a little menace. They usually play that kid's game: the first to blink is a sissy. What they claim to be doing is gaining the psychological edge. They're showing each other how tough they are, giving a little foretaste of the bad things each intends to heap on the other later, in the ring. It sometimes seems to work, a little. Gain a tiny edge before the fight, and it's like playing chess with an extra pawn – it can be turned to a bigger advantage later. But how crudely they do it, compared to master goalkeepers. Perhaps one player in thousands genuinely has no doubt that he can score past any goalkeeper. Gerd Muller gave that impression. So did Jimmy Greaves. Brian Clough must have had it, and Gianni Rivera, and Steve Bloomer. But the rest, who miss far more often than not, are full of doubt. If it's a form of craziness to get hold of that doubt and magnify it, then goalkeepers are crazy. But I don't think it is, and I don't think they are. I think it's one of the sublimest things in sport when a goalkeeper, even before starting any of the physical things he does, marshals his self-possession to such a degree that it overflows and takes a little bite out of the man opposed to him.

As is usual with such extraordinary things, there is no clear cut-off point above which we see that some goalkeepers can do it, and below which others cannot. All goalkeepers can do this once in a while, and they'll enjoy it when it happens. But great goalkeepers cultivate it, learn not to be surprised by it, learn eventually to rely on it. Most extraordinarily of all, some even manage to overcome the vast legacy of mistrust of their position and manage to persuade their team-mates to rely on it, too.

There is another element, I think, in this idea that all goalkeepers are nutters. The top goalkeepers at any time can do things of such extravagant courage and athleticism that even the majority, who have grown up regarding goalkeeping no more than a peculiar impediment to their hunger for goals, has to become aware that they are, for a moment, in the presence of greatness. I don't mean serious goalkeepers as opposed to blokes who'll take a turn in goal when they have to. I don't even mean pros as against amateurs. I mean that tiny handful, perhaps no more than three or five in Britain (which is still reputed for its wealth in goalkeeping) at any one time, who are so good that sensible analysis of what they do falls dumb and only slack-jawed amazement will do. They may be in the Premier League, although it is astonishing how many great goalkeepers have carried on playing for years for miserable ordinary clubs. They may be internationals, although selectors don't always get it right any more than the regular run of punters. These people are scary. What they do looks incomprehensible.

Here is Pat Jennings again. He is talking about the implausible save he made to a close header from George Burley in the 1978 FA Cup Final. 'I was asked how I managed to get to the ball, so I didn't like to tell anybody that I thought I should have held it. There are times when silence is golden.'[7] The modesty is there again, but also something else. To anybody who remembers that save, or to anybody who has the video, there is something utterly deflating in the realization that this moment of such swift and graceful athleticism, so many miles beyond our own abilities, *should have been better.* 'Oh, yes, thanks,' Jennings doesn't say, 'it was a pretty good save. You couldn't do it in a lifetime. But for me it wasn't as good as it should have been.' It's as though a truly great goalkeeper cultivates being possessed, like a whirling dervish or an oracle, by a power beyond the comprehension of the floundering clumsy questioner, beyond analysis, beyond reach. And well beyond the despair of the forward who thinks he's scored until he hasn't.

There is no such power, of course. Great goalkeepers are great athletes, and in the pomp of their greatness sometimes greater than their opponents. Jennings himself on the same page carefully and technically explains how some of the wizardry sometimes works. He is discussing three of his very greatest saves, three in the collection. One was from a volley by Tommy Craig, in a League Cup semi-final at White Hart Lane against Newcastle. A similar one was from a volley by Mike Bailey of Wolves, and Jennings turned each over the bar. The third was against Steve Heighway, who described it like this: 'Pat's save left me wondering how he had got to the ball. I had burst through with half-a-dozen Spurs players behind me, and I had to shoot quickly. I really caught the shot just right, and it was going over Pat's shoulder as he came out. I could hear the crowd behind the goal, stretching right up into the Kop, shouting "Goal!" – but there was the ball in Pat's hands. It was amazing. One of the finest saves I've ever seen in my life.' Jennings explains: 'Those three saves, which earned accolades like "best of the season", had something in common which had nothing to do with me. Heighway, Craig and Bailey all suffered because each, in turn, struck the ball perfectly and I was able to counter by going the right way and doing the right thing. If any had been mishit and screwed off the foot of the striker, I might well have been beaten.'[8]

It sounds loopy to talk about great and powerful strikers of the ball *suffering* for striking the ball perfectly, but it makes sense. It's a perfectly reasonable thing to point out. It is often harder to save a mishit shot, which has unpredictable spin and speed and direction. With Jennings's reflexes, flexibility, and ability to read the trajectory of the ball, those saves were made possible as he explains, by the shots being hit true. If I, or you, had faced a truly hit shot from Steve Heighway it would have whistled past like a freight train. But Jennings is not talking about us. He had the necessary athleticism to make the saves as long as the ball was hit true. Not wizardry, or possession, or an out-of-body experience, although they looked like all of those things seen from the outside. Just a great athlete getting it right. And I must say that I like the footnote very much. If it had been otherwise, Jennings says he 'might' have been beaten. The three saves were fairly miraculous – best of the season, he says. Had they been that much harder to get right, that much more unlikely, that fraction closer to the impossible, he might, he just might, have been beaten. Nothing modest about that. He doesn't tell us that he would have been beaten, that that was it, he had reached the limit of what he could do. But he might conceivably have been beaten. Amazing what confidence can do.

There are, naturally enough, very few goalkeepers at any time who can make saves of this kind. Unbelievable saves, saves which make you turn to your neighbour in the stand (or, to her perennially renewed irritation, to the woman in your life if you're watching on television) shouting, 'Did you *see* that?' Every spectator knows enough about the speed of the ball and the distance the goalkeeper has to cover to realize the lunatic improbability of these rarest saves. But it is precisely those saves which set the standard for top goalkeeping. They come around every so often, averaging a few times a season even though once in a while a goalkeeper makes three or four in one day. They look crazy, but not in the sense that the goalkeepers who make them have to be irrational to make them, but in the more complimentary sense that we have no sensible words with which to describe them.

Descriptions of saves, especially descriptions of saves witnessed in the flesh, tend very quickly to the raw heaps of adjectives that indicate that we aren't really sure what we have seen. Amazement dominates, that such a thing should be possible, quickly followed, in cases where loyalty is felt to be at stake, by whichever emotion is appropriate: frustration or relief. The word that occurs again and again is 'blur'; we don't *see* saves as comprehensible movement. That sense of being beyond understanding trickles down through the ranks until it applies to all goalkeepers. They become 'crazy' because we don't have the language or perhaps the curiosity to understand the details of what they do. It is easier to fall back on the assumption that from time to time goalkeepers will play out of their skins, when all we can do is register that something beyond us has taken place, than to try to work out precisely why and how some phenomenon of athleticism worked as it did.

The mechanics of propelling a ball, for reasons which I don't understand, seem more readily to come to verbal heel than the mechanics of stopping it. We read newspaper reports quite cheerfully reliant on our understanding of the importance of keeping one's head down while striking a ball if it is intended to fly low. We are not surprised to understand that kicking with different parts of the foot results in differences of flight. Quite technical details are fully public: half-volley, square-ball, angled pass. These terms are not meant to confuse, nor are they read as confusing. But for stopping a ball, almost nothing. Nine times out of ten the goalkeeper 'got his hands to it' and that's about as far as it goes. Goalkeeping has not been, for many years, what we are interested in. So how it works can be left to mystery; the 'crazy' tag is the result. Since goalkeepers produce finished results which seem, because of our own incomprehension, to have come from nowhere, we grant them a certain witch doctors' status. Pat Jennings *did* reach that shot from Steve Heighway. Heighway couldn't explain it. To him, it looked 'crazy'. To Jennings, it was explicable as a part of what he had spent years learning to do.

John Moynihan, writing as a spectator, described Gordon Banks's save in Guadalajara in terms which make no attempt to conceal that he had no idea how it was done:

Jairzinho's strength took him past Cooper to the byline and he swept the polka-dot ball, with the ferocity of a trench mortar, over to the far post, way beyond where Labone, Moore and Banks were stationed. And towards the blurred object now hurtled Pele, leaping over Mullery and heading the ball down towards a layer of black netting and all for one were shouting goal and rising to acclaim the 'King'. What happened next remains indistinct in the memory, a blurred and outrageous flash of movement, a combination of sprawling arms and legs. Banks was suddenly over to the right of goal lying sideways with his left leg thrust straight out, his right leg bent at right angles and his groping right hand scooping the ball up and over the crossbar . . . One wondered, amid all the commotion, whether Banks had broken his arm and suffered grievous damage; he lay on his back with his shoulders on the grass, his colleagues standing around too nonplussed to yell their praise. The Brazilians took a very quick corner. It was over before it had begun . . . To this day I cannot recall how Banks managed to get across goal and touch the ball as it rose off the turf towards the roof of the net.

Everything is there as a spectator sees it. The threatening build-up, the fully understood menace of Jairzinho and Pele, and then the aftermath, with Banks down and the defence nonplussed. Moynihan is actually describing the save, but the nearest he can get is the frozen posture of the goalkeeper immediately afterwards. In the middle, nothing but blurred movement. It's terrific writing, and its cadences match the gasping shortness of breath that certainly seized everyone who was there. Moynihan's friend had turned to him as soon as it was over: ' "By Christ, did you see it?" It was a fatuous remark, but he had to say something to relieve his windpipe. He wanted to convince himself that we had seen what he had seen and make sure in his normally placid mind that it was not some figment of the imagination, a confidence trick, a sudden mirage brought on by the unrelenting rays of the sun.'[9] There you have it. Imagination or a trick or a mirage. These might explain what he had seen. That's how goalkeeping has become. It's impossible. But it sometimes happens. Therefore it's crazy.

It is instructive to compare a very different account of the same save. Bob Wilson was an eminent goalkeeper, who turned himself into the finest specialist analyst of all that it takes. He wrote several excellent books on the subject, and became the spokesman of the imaginary Goalkeepers' Trade Union on British television, always ready to take the goalkeeper's side, always ready to explain away errors and demand credit. He has become a teacher of goalkeepers high and low (he coaches schoolkids and pros), a serious and committed expert who knows better than any what he is talking about. He also knows Banks well and has asked him about it. Wilson gives three dense pages to this one save.[10] He quotes 'normal' descriptions similar to John Moynihan's of how it looked, and then makes his own contrasted analysis by detailed sections clearly derived from many hours of rewinding the tapes: The Approach; Covering the Near Post; The Cross; The Header; The Save. And he nails down right at the start the difference of perception: 'Describing it as magical is appropriate but inaccurate. Magic involves sleight of hand and clever tricks of the trade. There was neither sleight of hand nor clever tricks involved in Gordon's save. What was involved was year upon year of dedication in training and season upon season of concentration in games.'

Quite. But the word that springs to everyone's mouth first is precisely that word 'magical'. Bob Wilson puts us right. At one moment, with Jairzinho past Cooper and 'one yard off the goal-line and seventeen yards from the near post', Wilson identifies six immediate possibilities Banks had to have in mind: 'the direct shot; a low, driven cross on which to pounce; a low pull-back to the six-yard line; a deeper angled pull-back to the middle of the goal; a driven low cross to the far post; a chip to the far post'. Six high-risk things about to happen, six terrible threats to be sorted in the instant, guarded against, diminished. And this is not some prat in a Jairzinho T-shirt we're talking about here, as likely to go for selfish but unlikely glory as to trip over his own bootlaces. This is Jairzinho, arguably (but who's arguing?) the best outside-right ever. 'His immediate concern had to be a direct shot. Next came the possibility that Tostão, who was on the near post, would be the target. His worst fear was a chip to the far post. A second later and Gordon's worst fear was realized.'

Wilson goes on, second by second, detailing the

actual movements of ball and goalkeeper as well as the ones which might have happened. When it comes down to it, he makes two fundamental judgements to explain what happened. The first is that Pele made a mistake: 'Pele was seven yards from goal when he powered his header down towards goal. He was so sure he had time to pick his spot that he hung in the air and drew his head back. Had he simply attacked the cross and directed his header at the target, it is extremely unlikely that Gordon would have had time to make up the ground or react to make a save.' This is excellent analysis. Not only did Pele himself describe the header as perfect, which makes it brave of Wilson to point out that it was not, but almost everybody else has done so too. It is standard coaching advice to slam headers downwards and make the bounce add to the difficulty of reading the flight and adjusting to it. In this case, it was wrong. The ball stayed out of the goal just a fraction too long, just long enough for Banks to keep it out. The second point Wilson makes is this: 'What was so staggering about his goalkeeping instinct was that he dived diagonally backwards. Had he dived directly towards the ball, it would almost certainly have hit the floor in front of him and bounced over his arm into the net. By diving backwards towards the goalpost, he bought himself another fraction of a second during which time the ball struck the ground a yard in front of him and bounced sharply upwards.'

This is more doubtful. Certainly, by diving backwards as well as sideways, Banks gave himself more time. But it was that backward movement that forced him to clear the ball up and over the bar, which it only just cleared. A more normal dive parallel to the goal-line would have enabled Banks to shove the ball out past the post. That was closer, and to push the ball there would have used more of the speed of the ball. As he did it, Banks had to take a huge risk in converting the goalward momentum into upward movement. He only just made it, and the ball hung agonizingly before rolling over the bar and away. My point is not to quibble, however, and Wilson's detailed analysis is scrupulous and convincing. The point is that to a goalkeeper, even a save like this, which barely gets mentioned without words like 'miraculous' being tagged to it, is explicable. Though it was difficult as hell, and admirable in proportion, there was nothing crazy about it.

'The five stages of Banksy's super save from Carlos Alberto's pass to the ball clearing the bar took precisely eight seconds, and it contained the following goalkeeping attributes: concentration; anticipation; good footwork; agility; composure; courage; instinct; great reactions; and confidence.' What a list! What a cocktail to bring to one's job! What more do we look for from sport? And he chose not to mention luck, which I would certainly add. You can do all that Banks did, and still concede the goal without a little luck. At that level of difficulty, even though you have done everything right, and even though you deserve the full credit, pure and unalloyed, you have to have the luck as well.

Most of us, when talking about saves in the pub after the game, are closer to Moynihan's than to Wilson's point of view. It is not hard to see why. All other parts of the game (except deflections, which should perhaps be separately credited on the score-sheet, like 'extras' at cricket) have some visible development. Stages connect in a way the spectator understands and can follow. Saves descend on us, seemingly from Olympus. Amateur football watchers tend to watch the ball as they follow play. So do a lot of players. Better players watch the spaces, watch where the ball is about to be, watch players decoying away from the ball or making themselves free where it has not yet arrived. As a result, the majority see every development in the game as a surprise; the minority see choices and patterns ahead. For that minority, the goalkeeper is in the game long before the save, manoeuvring to meet the ball perfectly when it finally reaches him. But most of us, eyes glued to the ball, and brains trailing some yards in its wake, see nothing of the goalkeeper and think of him less until a goalbound ball is stopped. It comes as a tremendous surprise. Where did he come from? How did he get there? Only when you understand that the goalkeeper has seen the possibility of the very shot you saw him stop, as well as several others you had not imagined, long before your eyes were actually upon him, can you begin to strip some of the sorcery from what goalkeepers do. And the more we learn to do that, the more we will see just what astonishing athletes they are, and how much they make out of so little.

That's at the heart of the business of goalkeepers being crazy, that we don't see them until what they have done is over. Outfield-minded spectators – who, after all, in the nature of the game outnumber goalkeeper-minded spectators by ten to one – are well accustomed to thinking through options in the same way as the outfield player they are watching. Hmm. Beaten him down the wing, now, I could pass early, or I could draw a defender more by going on to the corner flag. It's constant. It's how we watch the game, seeing choices open and close as the players reveal them to us. That's why spectators howl abuse at players who've taken the 'wrong' option. They're following the play, they think they know what's up. From the stands it all looks so easy (let alone from the settee). That is also why it is so funny when some particularly unlikely piece of play gets howled at before the fans can see that the player was thinking ahead of them, that his apparently 'wrong' choice was the right one, that he has opened more choices than they had thought possible. I confess to enjoying seeing fans discomfited in this way. If you know so much, says the player who rides their abuse when he knew full well what he was doing, why is it me down here doing it? Little of this applies to goalkeeping. There is, until you have learnt to look away from the ball, nothing to follow until it is done.

There is another aspect to the explanation of why goalkeepers are wrongly assumed crazy, and it is to do with the character of the players, as opposed to what they do. Goalkeepers as eccentrics, cards, oddballs – all that. The knowing half-smile goalkeepers get when people learn their position. We've already seen that people like Rene Higuita and Ramon Quiroga do a certain amount to merit notoriety, off the field as well as on. There are others, of course, plenty of them. The tradition of the eccentric goalkeeper was established almost as early as the game. A fine collection of weirdos have passed into goalkeeping annals. The question is whether the tribe as a whole merits the opprobrium of the collective loose slate, and I think the answer is they do not.

Goalkeepers have always been outsiders in their own teams. Everybody around them hopes for and can reasonably expect to achieve every so often a measure of individual glory. When there is its opposite – call it shame, although it is more like strong embarrassment – outfield players dilute it by sharing. The position for goalkeepers has traditionally been precisely the reverse: personal ignominy or a slice of the collective glory; or a moment's applause wiped out by eighty-nine minutes of contempt; or five fine interventions in a row, erased by one stupid deflection that nobody could really have done anything about. Goalkeepers know this equation. They know it intimately. They see it in the mirror when they shave, and it blinks at them as they turn the light out at night. It is the ghost of goalkeeping, this ever-present sensation that you are only as good as your last performance; the next one, or the one after that, may well be the one that gets you a reputation like Gary Sprake's. Outfield players, if they are any good, build reputations in a steady graph of sweeping peaks. They are judged on their average excellence over long periods. The poor goalkeeper is judged right there and then, daily, for the score which is his responsibility.

The goals against column looks like the goalkeeper's own personal tally, and no goalkeeper is unaware of it.

A good game for a goalkeeper is called a clean sheet. It means a clean score-sheet, of course, but what an absurd measure. Outfield players 'fight for possession' and 'win tactical battles'; they 'attack down the flanks' and when they get close to goal they 'fire' in a 'volley' or simply 'shoot', trying to 'hit the target'. No need to go on. All this stirring military vocabulary stops at the most critical position of all. A rare journalist writes of goalkeepers who have 'held the fort' but the metaphor sounds strained. Normally the poor neglected goalkeeper does the laundry. In fact it's worse than that. The goalkeeper doesn't cause the sheet to be clean, or get it clean. He keeps it clean, like a good child learning not to wet his bed. Well done, sonny, you've kept a clean sheet again. It's not exactly the Victoria Cross, is it?

So nobody becomes a goalkeeper because of a fierce longing for glory. That in itself, in a sport seamed with boastful posturing and self-aggrandisement, is grounds to call their sanity into question. But there's more. Outfield footballers, at everything below the very highest level, to some extent cease to be characters when they come on to the field. They have a role in the team which conditions, for the duration of the game, how they behave. Whatever they are like at home or in the minibus on the way to the game gets left behind on a hook in the changing-room. Within the team, they become an attacking midfielder or an overlapping full-back or a withdrawn centre-forward or whatever. Character has little to do with it. They become a little like actors, with a part to perform, and little room to show us the personality beneath. The way they play depends on how they see their role, not how they bring character to it. Only a tiny proportion at the top of the pyramid can do both. For them, of course, football is a means of expression and we can indeed see something of what they are like under the team strip. If I had to measure it, I would say that any professional footballer has some chance of being able to play as himself as well as play as his position. Of those, perhaps only a fraction reveal anything very compelling. And there is always the need to guard against manufactured 'personality' of the kind marketing men love, but which is not what I am talking about.

It doesn't apply to goalkeeping, at any standard. The goalkeeper is always himself because his role in the team needs no interpretation. Keep the ball out. It's a bald script that leaves almost everything to the player. World-class or Wormwood Scrubs class, the goalkeeper has no choice but to be himself on the field of play. That, too, is deeply suspicious to the fans and the players around him, who are so used to interpreting the other positions in terms of mythical types each strives to recreate. People don't have any illusions when they go in goal. In goal, they're just themselves, up for a hiding. There are a surprising number of ways to hide on a football field, considering that it's just an open area of grass. Outfield players can hide in the part they have to play, like actors hidden from the audience by the role. But in goal, you can't. It's you, even if you are wearing a Lev Yashin-style XXL black replica pullover, endorsed boots, and gloves designed to stop astronauts dropping screwdrivers on an unsuspecting world. Nobody goes in goal thinking

'I'll be Gordon Banks today.' You go in goal as you are, and hope to Christ your left-back has learned to kick with his left foot. Because if he hasn't, it's going to be your fault when he cocks up.

That makes people think goalkeepers are crazy, no doubt. For everybody else, it's a game. Good fun, and the chance to be Georgie Best for a fallacious second or two. The phrase 'a hiding to nothing' might have been invented for goalkeeping. Anybody who voluntarily gets exposed week after week to odds that goalkeepers regard as normal is going to be thought of as mad by his colleagues. From the day he considers himself a goalkeeper rather than just the bloke who's agreed to cover in that position for a day, the goalkeeper accepts a wholly different take on the game. He's agreed that he will be judged as he is, alone when it matters, and often unfairly or unreasonably alone. The only person on a football field so unutterably alone when it matters is the referee, and you really have got to be crazy to do that. Goalkeeping is not crazy. It's just that it has a seriousness built into itself which other footballers only find in rare and desperate moments.

5. Read the Manual, Stupid

Keeping a goal inviolate at football is a highly technical activity and one whose professors hardly agree on the manner in which it is most certainly achieved. It seems so simple. There is the goal, and these chaps want to propel the ball past you and into it without the use of their hands. You may use your hands, although it has been agreed that you will not use them in certain ways. You are not allowed to use your hands as weapons to defend your goal. No rule says you may not construct a large carbon-fibre butterfly-net to make catching the flying ball easier, but it is probably also agreed that you may not. It might be classed as ungentlemanly conduct, and so fall within the ambit of the most improbable law in football. No, we know what the goalkeeper does. He must, by whatever means, frustrate the knavish tricks of his opponents. Childishly simple.

There are 192 square feet in the forward face of the goal. It is enormous in relation to a man; you could hang 192 old-fashioned vinyl LPs on bits of string tied through the spindle-holes in their middles from the crossbar, and a goal would be scored if any one of them were struck by the ball. If I bet you that you could not, in an hour and a half, kick a football past me so as to hit an ordinary front door, you would take my money and set to. A front door is perhaps six and a half feet tall, maybe even seven, and three wide. That is to say a little taller than a man, and a little wider. You would be sure, given as many tries as you could fit into the time, that you could hit it. You might trick me into lowering myself and then aim high. You might rely on speed and blast it mercilessly past me, daring me to get in the way. You might well count on my hand or elbows getting sore after a while, and my door-blocking ability to diminish as time passed until the cumulative effect enabled you to hit it. But you would be certain to take my money and find it easy. A goal is many times bigger, make no mistake. The thing dwarfs even a big man who stands up in front of it. It is indefensible without barbed wire and radar.

The fundamental point about football is that it is incredibly easy to score a goal. These buffoons who miss from five yards, miss from three when the goal is 'open' and the goalkeeper somewhere else, are actually doing something quite difficult. To scoop the ball wide of the post from close range you have to hit the ball beyond where you can see it, right around the corner of your peripheral vision. From close in, the goal blocks everything out, dominates everything. Granted, the ball is normally moving, and granted, people get excited when about to score goals, but still. To miss an open goal in football is to demonstrate incompetence of a startling kind. The goal is vast, the ball travels fast. Even on the great plains of a football field, a goal-mouth looks like a pretty substantial aperture. Anybody who can miss an open goal should certainly not be allowed to drive a car. Something seems very wrong with such a person's perception of space or his coordination. And yet. One of the attractions of football, as I say, is that it remains a low-scoring game in which all sorts of things other than the target being hit are important to the play and agreeable to watch. The goalkeepers do that.

A big man's spread hands barely cover one square foot of space. The ball may come at any angle, from any range, at any speed, to any part of the goal. It behaves in very different ways according to weather, spin, the skill of the man who kicked it. It behaves wildly differently according to what kind of ball it is. There's a thought. For most people, a football is a football. Not for goalkeepers.

The standard (size 5) ball approved for serious football has to be greater than twenty-seven and fewer than twenty-eight inches in circumference, and between fourteen and fifteen ounces in weight. Those limits tell us something, but not by any means enough. Footballs are made of panels, usually of leather, stitched together to form the outer casing that encloses an air-filled bladder. The bladder used to have a valve, to which access was granted via a laced hole in the cover. Lacing is now rare, and the valve is a self-sealing projection from the bladder which can only be reached by a needle attachment to the pump. There are no rules to define the shape, number, or manner of attachment of the panels. The outer coating of the ball, commonly nowadays of one kind of plastic or another to prevent the sponge-like absorption of water from the pitch that used to double the weight of the ball during a game, is nowhere defined. The ball can be inflated harder or softer, and can certainly lose some of its air during the course of a game. It is not all that extraordinarily rare for the ball to be punctured during a game. Balls are now commonly white, patterned with the manufacturer's logo, to make them clearer on television. We forget how much consternation was caused when white balls were first introduced to make them visible for the then newfangled experiment of floodlighting. When snow lies on the ground, an orange ball is commonly used, also for visibility. All these factors quite naturally affect the flight of the ball, and if not its flight, then the goalkeeper's ease in following it.

Quite the most serious one is the degree of inflation. All the rules have to say about it is 'The pressure shall be equal to 0.6–1.1 atmosphere (= 600–1,100 gr/cm^2).'[1] This says really nothing, a variation so big that the ball can quite legally be almost squidgy or almost rock-like. I don't think I or anybody else has ever seen a ball checked with a pressure gauge, anyway. If a player (often a goalkeeper) complains to the referee that the ball is under-inflated or burst, the referee checks it by hand, a quick squeeze. Within wide limits, the ball feels about right – play!

The absolute inflation is of fundamental importance to the bounce and flight of the ball. More than that, the inflation relative to the weather also makes a huge difference. It is no great trick to kick a football in such a way that it swerves. Any competent kicker can with practise learn, for example, to swerve five or six out of ten corner kicks into the goal. It is extremely useful to be able to do so, to curl a pass into the stride of a team-mate, or to bend a free kick around a defensive wall. A rock-hard ball can be made to swerve more than a softer one. A *light* and hard ball can swerve viciously, like a beach-ball. It will often swerve far more than the kicker intends, out of the control of all but the few players who train constantly with such a ball. There is no doubt that footballs occasionally describe shallow S-shapes in the air, as spin, momentum, and the friction of the air across the surface fight out the battle of their various forces. When it happens to a goalkeeper he looks as though he has been beaten by a deflection. It is not at all rare for professional goalkeepers to set off to make a save well to one side of them and only just be able to reach the ball going to their other side. Occasionally you will see a full-blooded dive, the goalkeeper convinced that the ball was on its way that far out of his reach, only for the swerve to take it past his feet, a curl of a minimum of six or seven feet in whatever distance the ball has travelled. The ball can bounce low or high in relation to what players expect. The surface of the pitch has a lot to do with it, and rightly so, since football is played outdoors on surfaces exposed to weather and wear. But surely the ball should be predictable?

Gordon Banks played his first international against Scotland. His first overseas opposition, in 1963, was the Brazilians at Wembley, four days after he had played for Leicester and lost the FA Cup Final at the same venue:

During training for the game [Alf Ramsey] stressed time and again how careful we needed to be against their free kicks. 'They can bend the ball either way,' he warned.

I found out in the worst possible way just what he meant during the first half. They were awarded a free kick just outside the penalty area. I shouted instructions to the wall of defenders in front of me until I was satisfied they were lined up correctly to cover the left side of my goal and I then stationed myself on the right side. Pele danced up to take the kick and struck the ball with fierce power with the outside of his left foot. I saw it rise above the wall on a curve to the left, and as I moved to cover, the ball suddenly swung on a completely different course to my right and went high into the corner of the net with me looking on helplessly. I just couldn't believe it. I would have bet any money that nobody could move the ball that much in the air and also that there was not a goalkeeper in the world who could have done anything to stop it.

Alf fired daggers at me with those piercing blue eyes of his at half-time. 'Don't say I didn't warn you,' he said. 'I gave you exact details of what they do from their free kicks, but you fell for the three-card trick.' I explained that it had moved in the air twice as violently as I had been led to expect, but I could tell from Alf's tight-lipped expression that he thought I should have saved it. All I know is that from his position on the touchline there was no way that he could have seen just how much the ball swerved. I have not seen that much bend on a ball before or since . . . the game had been ruined for me by that free kick. If the ball had not gone into the net, I feel it could have done a circuit of the stadium![2]

Not one of Sir Alf's more diplomatic days; a free kick like that early in an international career could easily have wrecked a goalkeeper's confidence. Next time England were to play Brazil, in the 'little World Cup' (a tournament between England, Portugal, Argentina and England) of 1964, Alf Ramsey replaced Banks with Tony Waiters, who conceded three of five goals to free kicks of that kind. Banks simply notes that 'Alf was not pleased.' Is it unfair to think that he himself might have been just a little?

Wembley is on a bit of a hill, but it is nothing more than a few dozen feet above sea level. At high altitude, notably in Latin America, British goalkeepers have regularly been undone by the flight of the ball in the lighter air, swerving violently, often at the very end of its trajectory. The great brown medicine balls of the past could be made to swerve too, although they never moved as much as the plastic-coated ball of today. They swerved for a different reason, too. An under-inflated, heavy ball does seem to swerve, if hit right. I think it is because such a huge proportion of the weight of the ball is at the very outside that once it starts to spin it spins very fast. Certainly the laces on those old brown balls made a heavy whirring sound as the ball came near to you, very different to the almost silent rushing noise of a modern ball. The difference is like the bubbling noise of an old British motorcycle compared to the electric drill of a modern Japanese one. A modern ball is very shiny, at least when it is new. The spin on it is more like the spin on a snooker ball, fizzing and biting against the cloth until it gets grip. Footballs do that against the nap of the grass, and I think they also, if hit with the right sharp vicious stab, do it against the resistance of the air.

Very few modern players can kick a modern ball absolutely straight time after time. It *always* swerves, and good players have learnt to use the spin, and to play with it, but I think few have full control of it. It helps them; if it's a little unpredictable, so much the better. So when goalkeepers early in the game scream for an early touch of the ball, they are not simply calming early nerves. They are anxious to get some idea, however imprecise, of the degree of inflation the ball has been given, to gauge as best they can how it will behave later. They want to be sure too, of course, that they have the right gloves for maximum grip.

I can think of no other sport where the standard item of equipment is so little regulated. Tennis balls are kept in the fridge and replaced every few games, when the fuzz begins to whirr off them and the heat in the rubber makes them bouncier. The relation between ball and court surface is one to which players have ample opportunity to regulate themselves, and it is normal for adjustments to be made to such things as racquet-string tension and speed of swing to get a favourable balance. In golf, the player chooses the ball that suits him best. People make a huge fuss about the cricket ball, and it is true that it too can do unpredictable things, and that a master bowler can exploit that to the batsman's disadvantage. But batsmen (or their captains) have and use the right to complain if the ball is wrong, out of shape, or deliberately abused to increase some characteristic of flight or bounce. The construction of a cricket ball is tightly regulated, even though some respond oddly to the treatment they receive during play. Fundamental details of a football are open to interpretation. A football can have hexagonal panels or straight ones, wavy stripes of panels or pentagons. The seams can be parallel for long distances around the ball or regularly opposed. They can be sewn almost flush with the surface, or more normally tucked like valleys well below it. These things all obviously affect the flight – and the only person who suffers badly if they are different to what he's used to is the man between the posts.

The goalkeeper never really gets taught about flight and bounce. One reverend and scholarly gent wrote a book which is largely about how the ball is a symbol anyway.[3] To some extent, every shot is different, because forwards are not grooved like tennis players or bowlers. The action does not repeat accurately time after time. The playing surface is natural; it can be wet or dry, or both. It can be plush lawn or all but gravel, and laid on anything from cinders to heavy loam to sand to mixtures known only to groundsmen. A 'bad bounce' is not considered a great handicap in football, it is part of the 'rub of the green', and play goes on. But to a goalkeeper it can be a hideous embarrassment. Tim Flowers once dropped to one knee to collect a routine ball; it struck the divot where he had marked the six-yard box and flew unreachably over his head. Goal. Not so long ago, Ian Walker of Tottenham had the same experience against Steve McManaman of Liverpool: a 'comfortable' dive, simply to make sure his body was behind an innocuous shot with little power, a jerky bounce, much higher than he expected, and the ball jumped over his body. Goal.

Every goalkeeper has had this experience, and what's more the lower the level at which they play the more often it happens. It is unfortunate, but at precisely the level of football where you expect not-very-competent goalkeeping, you also find unspeakable pitches, cratered and hillocked and pitted. It is impossible to trust the bounce of such a pitch, and you don't. But they still 'do you' in horrible ways from time to time. Professional pitches tend to be pretty well drained now. The ball that stops in thick mud is a thing reserved for a few short miserable weeks in darkest mid-winter. But on park pitches, it happens all the time. How do you learn to deal with that? Reflexes, experience, and a good dose of fatalism. A fast ball skidding through on greasy grass, seems to come to the goalkeeper faster than it should. On long grass it can bounce in curvier loops than you expect. (I think because the grass slows down the bottom surface of the ball more than normal, so that it gets a kind of unwitting top-spin for its next hop, almost as if it had tripped up.) On hot days the air inside a ball can heat up so much it becomes like a superball. A ball hit hard into the ground (often not deliberately, a deflection or a shank) can have its spin reversed by the friction, and career off in utterly bizarre directions.

The difference between a ball that feels right and one that seems completely unnatural is inexplicable not only to those who don't play football, but to most players too. A soft ball is hard to catch because it gives at the point of impact, its air goes elsewhere, and you're left holding a scrap of the skin (all in a fraction of a second, but that is what it does). A hard ball bounces from soft hands before they have time to close. It's all unregulated, the goalkeeper just has to get used to it as he goes along.

One of football's rooted certainties is that feet are relatively unsophisticated instruments, which were until recently shod in large boots with all the sensitivity and all the subtlety built out of them. It is even one of the attractions of football that you don't need sophisticated gear to play it. Pele is supposed to have practised with an endless series of grapefruit before he could afford to play with a football. Maradona, who was a child-prodigy ball-juggler in pre-match and half-time entertainment before he was ever a player, could make a football do exactly what he wished. Old English pros wrote in their memoirs of street games with a bundle of rags or newspaper wrapped in string (there was even some skill in making a decent ball with these materials). In theory, any ball will do because twenty of the twenty-two players are hardly affected by the variations. Ball-playing magicians like Maradona are rare. To those few, the exact condition of the ball makes a huge difference. Every time a game is played in the wind, ordinary players overhit and underhit passes like fury. They make errors of 30 or even 50 per cent in the dosing of the forces they apply to the ball, the same when its specially warm or specially cold. It cannot be a precision instrument if errors like these are possible, and to the great majority, it isn't. A neatly judged pass on Hackney Marshes is cause for moderate self-congratulation. So is a well-struck shot that flies as it was meant to fly. As for reading the flight of a ball and trapping it stone-dead with one touch, forget it.

Most players are so surprised when they trap a ball elegantly that they immediately lose it again.

Not goalkeepers. The whole complicated ballistics of the flight and bounce of the ball, of swerve and dip and variation in pace, is their normal business. They can be embarrassed nearly to death if they get it wrong. And yet nobody has bothered to standardize the ball. The plainest pattern of sewn panels on the ball has just over half the stitched length of the more complex ones. It obviously makes an enormous difference. The lift, the minuscule foil-effects (like the effects of aircraft wings or sailboat sails) off each seam, and so the spin and flight of the ball, are all clearly affected. And the poor goalkeeper is expected to get it right from experience, and a pathetic 'early feel' of the ball. Football administrations have for years 'approved' types of ball. They receive good commercial fees for doing so, and tend not to withhold their endorsement if the price is right. But the same 'approved' ball can behave utterly differently on different days. The variations are likely to be within the margins which govern the play of outfield players, but beyond those finer ones to which goalkeepers have to adjust.

Goalkeepers are sensitive to the ball because they have to be. Jack Kelsey tells us that 'it is a known fact that continentals prefer to play with a soft ball, possibly because it suits their style. Here I might say that whenever Arsenal go on a European tour, we always take our own footballs with us and they're invariably blown up in the presence of our trainer, Billy Milne.'[4]

Frank Swift was hardly a whinger, but he once made it perfectly clear that he felt he had been cheated over the ball used. When he kept goal in 1947 in Lisbon

> there was a hold-up to the start, as the Portuguese insisted that their size four football (used by schoolboys in this country) should be used for the match, although it had been agreed previously to play with our full-sized ball. Mr Winterbottom's arguments won the day, and Tommy kicked off with the big ball. Within thirteen seconds we were a goal in front, and that was the last we saw of our big ball! The ball went out of play midway between the centre-line and the Portuguese goal. Billy Wright hurled a long throw up the line to Mannion, who crossed for Lawton to head the perfect goal from about eight yards. Whereas our ball had gone into the net, *their* ball was kicked back to the centre-line.[5]

This could have been very serious. The illustration in Swift's book, of Tom Finney scoring in that game one of the finest goals Swift ever saw, shows a tiny ball, about the size of a water-polo ball. Hard for everybody to get used to, certainly, but it might have been impossible for Swift, in goal. But as he says, 'it didn't really matter, as we scored nine more goals with the little ball'. They did indeed. 10–0 in an away game against a fine team who might well have beaten them. The Portuguese goalkeeper, Azevedo, a great favourite with the crowd at the start, was substituted in a storm of catcalls and whistles. Although clearly not (as he should have been to comply with the rules then in force) hurt in body, it was a profound humiliation. But his replacement, Capela, did no better.

The English forward line that day reads like one of those best-ever selections that are always cluttering up match programmes: Matthews, Mortensen, Lawton, Mannion, Finney. No wonder they could afford to shrug off a less than regulation-sized ball. But Swift knew that things might have been very different. To play the small ball, like using the substitutes, was a form of cheating, and had Swift let in goals because of it, he would have had to make excuses which could only have seemed feeble. He was lucky that he could point it out after a 10–0 win, when he could hardly be accused of lack of sportsmanship. These things can wreck a goalkeeper's reputation, his confidence, and his career.

These tiny details matter to a goalkeeper: the ball itself, the grip of gloves, or chewing-gum rubbed on the hands. (Lots of goalkeepers have spat a chewing-gummy glue onto hands or gloves to improve grip. It sounds repugnant? Less so than feeling a ball squirm out of slippery hands.) There is the gap between the stands that always makes a swirling wind in evening games. The take-off foot that slips in mud; the fall of the ground that makes the left-hand post half a yard further than the right, or lifts the edge of the penalty area just a fraction higher than the goal-line. No wonder that when Adidas recently brought out a new football boot, they advertised it with a photograph of its shooting surface and the words, 'This side has humiliated a lot of goalkeepers.' And no wonder there has always been such a ready market for manuals. Every little bit helps.

Nobody ever learned how to play football from manuals, and yet they have kept on appearing, under the name of the latest star or using the endorsement of whichever latest successful team as their selling point. You won't learn how to pass with the inside of the foot from a coaching manual, nor how to hurdle tackles which would bring down a racehorse. (Was it Stan Bowles, years ago, who answered one of those questions on what particular skills he thought most useful to him in top-class football by drily saying, 'I was always a decent high-jumper'?) You might understand tactical schemes and plans better, simply because a book allows you so much more time to work them out than you get on the field. Coaching manuals are one of the obscure pleasures of the game, best savoured when hopelessly out of date, wrong, and illustrated by chaps in baggy shorts and colonial moustaches.

Many goalkeeping worries are beyond manuals, because goalkeepers deal in the brutal specifics of one team, one player, one moment rather than all. The coaching manuals provide a sense of reassurance, that this frequently painful and shameful business is not as loopy as the mythology would have you believe. Young goalkeepers certainly go to them to pick up tricks of the trade they would otherwise have to learn by letting in a lot of avoidable goals. But they mainly want to be sure that goalkeepers old enough and eminent enough to be asked to put their names on such books have been through the same agonies as themselves, and have found it worth it in the end.

The principal needs of the goalkeeper have hardly changed in a hundred years or more. An early volume devoted to practical football was edited by Montague

Shearman, himself a serious athlete, a good four hundred yards runner of the 1880s. It was a practical book, with advice on diet and training as well as good sections on the history of the game. It was aimed at those unfamiliar with football but eager to try it. Shearman's goalkeeping is wholly identifiable as a close cousin of our own:

Perhaps the most important position upon the whole field is that of the goalkeeper. He must have a cool head, a quick eye and hand, and the longer reach he has with his arms the better. Although, too, he has only to defend the space between the posts, and all his work has to be done between the posts or within a few yards of them, he must be ready to display the greatest possible activity within his limited circle . . . It is sometimes little short of marvellous to see goalkeepers like Arthur, of the Blackburn Rovers, or Macaulay, the Scottish international, stop shot after shot in rapid succession, turning from side to side without ever losing presence of mind or balance of body. The goalkeepers of today have no easy task when the forwards have learnt to pass to one another in the jaws of the goal; and the best that can be said of the modern goalkeepers is that they have proved themselves equal to the task. Doubtless players in this position were as plucky and as resolute in the days when Kirkpatrick kept goal for more than half an hour to the end of a match while one arm was hanging broken from his shoulder; but the modern players have better tactics to contend with and are equally successful in their defence.[6]

But note that in all of Shearman's description, there is no mention of diving at full length. I cannot say it didn't happen, because I am sure goalkeepers overbalanced often enough while stretching for the ball. But diving, as a recognized technique for reaching further than an arm's length from one's body, didn't yet exist. Willy Meisl, himself a high-standard goalkeeper and the author of one of the best theoretical books of football tactics ever written (he was the brother of the great Austrian coach Hugo Meisl), pinpoints the time when he first saw it. He tells us that 'in that year [1899] the first English professionals came over [to Austria], Southampton FC. They beat the Viennese city eleven 6–0 and their goal-keeper, Robinson, showed for the first time how to tackle low shots by flying through the air with the greatest of ease. Until this day [Meisl's book was published in 1955] that type of save is called a "Robinsonade" in Austria and Central Europe. After the match, Robinson gave an exhibition. His goal was bombarded simultaneously with six balls and he blocked most of the shots.'[7]

Robinson was the England goalkeeper around 1900, a stalwart for Southampton, Plymouth Argyle, and, at one period, Derby County, and nobody seemed to think him anything less than utterly reliable. Gyula Grosics, the Hungarian goalkeeper in Puskas's great team, and a goalkeeper impossible to keep out of any greatest-ever list, was in no doubt about Robinson's influence: 'It was Moon of the Corinthians, Robinson, and many other world-famous English goalkeepers who had been pio-neers of this art and they showed the way for all Europe's goalkeepers. The fact that the Hungarians were good pupils has been amply proved by them and can be measured in the achievements of their goalies. Let me just mention the names of Ferenc Zsák and Ferenc

Plattkó from amongst my excellent predecessors who have not only mastered the motion style of English goal-keepers but had developed it to some extent.'[8]

Robinson himself wrote an excellent section (How to Keep Goal) in the great four-volume overview of football in 1905 that is Alfred Gibson and William Pickford's *Association Football and the Men Who Have Made It.*[9] It is great stuff. Robinson crams it all in: Paderewski and Herbert Spencer, C.B. Fry, hypnotism, and the pleasures of pipe-smoking, all in a few pages on goalkeeping. Robinson comes over as sensible, vaguely poetic, and amazingly keen on his goalkeeping. I guess Jack Robinson would have adapted to his own trade the thought that C.L.R. James made famous in another context: what do they of goalkeeping know who only goalkeeping know? He's interested in character more than technique, as if goalkeeping would follow automatically the cultivation of certain virtues. Only later did our understanding of goalkeeping definitively break down into the many specific technical gestures that we recognize in it today. But those gestures existed all along, and they had to be learnt, even then.

Technical skills and attributes of character seem to have appeared side by side from as early as goalkeeping attracted attention. Here is another passage from Gibson and Pickford:

> There was at Eton [in early Victorian times] a most delicious regulation which read as follows: 'Should a player fall on the ball or crawl on his hands and knees with the ball between his legs, the umpire must, if possible, force him to rise, or break the "bully" or

"rouge" [a type of scrum].' What a picture might be drawn of the old-time player, filled with a burning zeal to pierce the enemy's lines and a fine disregard of danger, crawling painfully along with the ball between his legs, the prey to numerous kicks and plunges, and resisting with his utmost strength not only the unlawful attempts of the opponents to upset him, but also the rule-sanctioned prowess of the umpire, whose limitations are so aptly described by the phrase 'if possible'. A Foulke or a Hillman, given the law under such conditions, would have been a formidable engine of attack, while there is no modern referee whose size and power would in the least avail him to force an athletic nineteen-stone player to rise. The crawling method has often been adopted by goalkeepers of latter days, and it is on record how one Doig, a champion of the Sunderland Club, in a great match, so held the ball on the confines of his goal, and resisting successfully all the efforts of the trained band of antagonists to rob him of it for some minutes, finally rolled with it to the side of the goalpost and safely delivered himself of his responsibilities by pushing it over the goal-line.[10]

The vision of William Foulke, who later in his career played at twenty-two stones, as an 'engine of attack' is a whimsical one. But there, among the 'burning zeal' and the 'fine disregard of danger', is a technique of sorts, the 'crawling method', identified for goalkeepers to acquire. It is obsolete now, but the principle remains. The only mystery is how Ned Doig, one of several to earn the title of Prince of Goalkeepers, comes to be known as 'one Doig'. Gibson and Pickford most certainly knew very well who he was; they even illustrate him, in approved style.[11] 'Doig saves a stinging shot' says the caption, revelling in the proper adjective, and there he is, punching the ball away for Scotland against England at Sheffield. So the appellation 'one Doig' is only an aberration. One might find oneself saying 'one Banks', but it sounds a little odd. And Ned Doig was just about as famous, and not by any means embarrassing to mention in the same breath.

People like Doig, great goalkeepers, seemed mysterious to the spectators. Until the advent of the slow-motion replay, it was impossible to see exactly what the goalkeeper did. The word 'miraculous' very soon became overused in the context. A goal was on, seemed already to have been scored. Then it wasn't. But what had taken place was too quick to be followed by eye. Now we have a slightly different problem in that television replays tend to make the save look far easier than it was. Knowing what is about to happen, we follow the flight of the ball, as all television watchers must, because that is what the camera takes as its guide, and the goalkeeper's hand naturally seems to coincide with it. Since the two trajectories, of ball and limb, do in fact meet at the crucial moment, it seems obvious that they should meet. Slow motion takes away a great deal of the unlikeliness of great saves precisely because it shows the save taking place at a finite point in the goal-mouth. The odds against the ball being just there, just then, are not shown, nor the even longer ones against the goalkeeper managing to be there at the same time. All the things the goalkeeper *might* have had to deal with are eliminated; the save is revealed, logically enough, where it happened. But we forget as we look that the goalkeeper had no way of knowing until the last moment where his appointment with the ball was scheduled.

Replays, in other words, by removing all the possibilities which did *not* materialize, make the save seem more certain than it ever was on the instant. Curiously, they do not have the same effect for other passages of play. A fine strike of the ball, replayed, looks more refined than the wallop we might have seen at first, but neither more nor less difficult. Fine balance and ball control outfield look more balletic, more graceful, more difficult when seen the second time, and when seen slowed down. I think this is because outfield players don't deal so much in potentialities. They do what they do in the face of perfectly concrete problems. Weight on this foot, defender turning that way, ball to be hit with just so much strength and spin. The goalkeeper has just such problems to negotiate too, but they are the very last pieces in a sequence the great bulk of which has taken place in their minds. So when replayed, we see only the physical conclusion to what is largely a mental equation. This can be spectacular enough, but we haven't wholly seen just how difficult it was to get right.

A fair proportion of instruction writing for goalkeepers comes in the shadow of this mystery. Good goalkeepers often write in a recognizable there's-really-nothing-to-it tone. If, say the manuals, you narrow the angle in the approved manner, then the miraculous save will be yours to command; like a recipe book. You only have to keep goal for five minutes to discover the trouble: that if you narrow the angle just so, exactly as prescribed, you are very likely to be chipped, or bypassed by a square pass, or beaten by a curler. It is vexing. The manuals have long recognized something of this problem, and dealt with it in differing ways. Doubt is always in ambush. There is, for example, a very interesting frame of mind exposed in a fine piece of instruction by James Ashcroft ('the famous custodian of the Woolwich Arsenal FC. . . . a custodian who keeps goal with his brain') published in 1906 as the first section of the *Football Guide, or How To Play 'Soccer'*.[12]

Ashcroft's advice is more technical than Jack Robinson's or Montague Shearman's. He is in part concerned with how the thing is done. His more straightforward conclusions, about standing at the back post for corners for example, are the plainest resolution of his many years of actually doing it, reduced to a conciseness and certainty that brook no disagreement. Even if one or two of his precepts sound odd to modern ears, they are given as the fruit of experience. They are right because they worked for Ashcroft. Take as an example his overarm punch to clear the ball, striking it with thumb and wrist. It looks for all the world like a smash in volleyball, and the whole point of such a way of striking the ball is to bring it sharply downwards within a very few feet of where it is hit. It would be exceptionally difficult to play such a shot for distance – it would have to be hit behind the head, with every chance of being missed altogether, clearly not a good gamble in the situation Ashcroft intends to use it in. A two-fisted jab, where the knuckle surfaces of the hands meet the ball, travelling up and ahead of the face from bent elbows, is far more likely to get distance in the clearance, and many modern goalkeepers advise it as the only right way. So I suppose that one can pick through Ashcroft's primer and find doubts or methods that have been left behind. But these do not alter Ashcroft's position. By doing it, sometimes wrongly, in training and in matches, he has found this and that to work. But that is only one of the voices in which he presents his advice. The other is a doubtful voice, rather awestruck at the sheer implausibility of his trade. It is as though he had never realized, until asked to write about it, just how appallingly difficult his job had been.

Consider only his description of Leigh Roose, the eccentric Welshman who used never to change his goal-keeping shirt, about to let in a goal at odds of 'all Lombard Street to a penny orange'. As he clears his lines, Ashcroft recognizes that Roose must have felt great: 'It is more than a sensation. It is an ecstasy.' This is Roose in fighting mood, but it lies completely at odds with Ashcroft's demand for judgement and nerve. Roose came out the winner from a goal-mouth tangle in which he was likely to be kicked, and likely to concede a goal. Well and good. The 'shiver of nervousness' is necessary, but so is 'the cool head, which every goalkeeper should possess'. Ashcroft quite correctly understands that contradictory temperaments are necessary for different parts of the goalkeeper's game. He follows each, identifying it and showing how it helps. But to resolve the contradiction is beyond him. These are what you rely on, he says, and if they clash, and you use the wrong one at the wrong moment, well; Ashcroft agrees with every goal-keeper who has ever had a word to say about it, that the goalkeeper 'is absolutely the last line of defence . . . his blunder is nearly always irretrievable'. Concentration, technique, and the expectation of blame if they aren't enough. Here's another version of the same equation:

[Elisha] Scott: there is another of the immortals, whose presence still hovers near the departed glories of Celtic. Scott first played for Ireland in 1920. He played thirty-one times for Ireland, and we were seeing him, I seem to recall, in his last match. Somewhat roughly hewn from granite, Scott held no charm for the aesthete. He was of iron will. In the obstinate tradition of his province he held fast to a single conviction – that the enemy should not breach his defences. They rarely did. Often it was England, or Wales, or Scotland against Scott. Come what may he held them off. And at Liverpool it was the same. A player of the old order, honest in endeavour and ever prepared for immolation in the single cause, Scott abjured fine habits and unfitting ambitions, cheap publicity and popular acclaim, and was all concentration. That, of course, is one way to success. The inflexibility of Scott came to mind in that Irish match of later date in which the unhappy Uprichard negligently dropped the ball at the feet of Lofthouse. All that the luckless goalkeeper could say – belonging to land of saints and scholars – was 'Amici, diem perdidi.'[13]

Like all who describe in precise technical detail what a goalkeeper has to do, Ashcroft found himself describing, in effect, a superman. It is just not ordinary to have the combinations of skills, mental and physical, that he listed. He found himself unable to come to that conclusion, even when his list made it plain. And right there, in an example from 1906, is one of the most enduring puzzles in the history of goalkeeping. You need all those things, starting with 'immunity to influenza', and passing through athletic talents like speed and strength to considerable resources of character like patience, nerve, and judgement. And at the end of it, you have to pretend that you're just one of the boys.

Ashcroft would never have described himself as a superman. Leigh Roose might have done, for he was splendidly self-confident, an amateur goalkeeper who played for Stoke for many years, and also liked to 'guest' for many other clubs when asked. He had something of a reputation for losing the ball upfield, and, as many other goalkeepers since, had to be exceptional to get away with it. He died on the Somme in 1916. The 'great' Foulke would have had no hesitation in calling himself a superman or anything else which paid witness to his girth. He enjoyed playing up to his gargantuan image. There are several accounts of Foulke stark naked after matches chasing referees and reporters in dispute, notably one splendid occasion when he offered to fight J.A.H. Catton, who wrote for both the *Sunday Chronicle* and the *Athletic News* under the pseudonym 'Tityrus', about a disputed offside goal in the 1902 FA Cup Final. Catton was only five feet tall, and Willie Foulke could certainly have drop-kicked him into the next county.[14]

The early manuals, then, were to a large extent explanations of the kind of character needed to keep goal. The technical stuff was there too, but it served as the hard-core in a construction which was largely about character. By the time Ashcroft was writing, pluck was the great British virtue; as early as 1856, Emerson had been able to write, 'The only thing the English value is pluck.'[15] Pluck is not quite the same as courage. It was to become the virtue that hopelessly ill-generalled British tommies showed in the Flanders mud. It was one of Kipling's virtues, still peculiarly assumed to reside in this sceptred isle. I suppose it took great courage to attack a machine-gun nest on foot through barbed wire. But as I understand it, it took pluck to keep thinking the war could be won under the perpetual barrage of heavy artillery. In other words, pluck is a kind of negative courage. Perhaps indomitability comes closest to it. It is by pluck, as in Regency English it had been by *bottom*, that you are still there when by rights you should have lain down and admitted defeat. Pluck implies long odds against. As such, it was the root virtue of goalkeeping when sport was more widely seen as a measure of virtue than it is today.

Long after the manuals have left the goalkeeping virtues to speak for themselves, and concentrated instead on the technical skills that make this extraordinary activity possible, I smell pluck as the aroma lurking in the background. I think, for example, that the very British assumption that 'continental' goalkeepers are no match for our home-grown yeomen of the soil is rooted in the idea that pluck is a virtue denied to foreigners. If the British are richer in pluck, and it is clear that goalkeeping demands just that, then it is obvious that poor foreigners won't be able to hold a candle to our boys. The answer, that nobody in this country either knew very much or cared very much about foreign goalkeepers until Channel 4 began to broadcast the Italian Serie A only becomes obvious with hindsight (I know that the fledgling Sky had broadcast Italian football earlier, but without much impact). Foreign goalkeepers were what our lads beat every time we did well in international competition, at whatever level. So who cared about them? And if, from time to time, they were called Jan Tomaszewski, they had whatever virtues they had (mainly luck, if absurd British comments on the Polish goalkeeper's performance at Wembley in 1973 are to be swallowed) but couldn't have pluck because that was our virtue.

This assumption survives, admittedly in something of a residual form. Behind every hard-won 0–0 draw against a better team, behind every useless team that should have been relegated but scraped another year of survival, there is not found, as I would find, a skilled technician of astonishing athletic ability and of enormous value to his side. There is a plucky goalie. It is meant to be a compliment, but it's a sour one.

Pluck has a long career as the assumed foundation of good goalkeeping. But very occasionally a voice is raised that puts it firmly in its place. Nobody who ever saw him keep goal would ever doubt Pat Jennings's courage. Yet in his second season at Watford, the manager, ex-Bournemouth hard man Bill McGarry, told him, 'You'll never be a goalkeeper, son, until you've had your head kicked in a couple of times.' Jennings's answer was typically mild: 'It was a classic McGarry statement, but it's one bit of advice I've managed to ignore in later years. I happen to think that the good goalkeepers are the ones who don't get their heads kicked in.'[16] How refreshing, and what a neat put-down of McGarry's idiotic comment. Some goalkeepers do get badly hurt, of course, but they don't go looking for it and they don't regard it as a qualification.

Courage is not what makes goalkeepers great. Not even notably brave goalkeepers, like Harry Gregg or Bob Wilson or Bert Trautmann, can live on courage alone. It's like downhill skiing. You can have all the courage in the world, but if you don't have technique and balance and a fierce competitive desire to win and a wealth of experience, you won't be very good at it. I don't even say that there is a minimum level of courage beneath which goalkeeping is impossible; goalkeepers can certainly find themselves in positions where the logic of lots of training and lots of experience, allows them to dominate situations they would avoid like the Black Death if thinking about them cold. The courage follows the goalkeeping habits, not the other way around.

And gradually, over the years, the mystique of pluck has receded to something like its proper place. By the time Peter Shilton published his excellent training manual, in 1992, courage had become only fourth of the six 'vital ingredients' of good goalkeeping he lists, and the one he treats at briefest length: 'In any activity you pursue in life, and in particular in sport, you must have courage.' Common sense, stripped of the shrillness that had accompanied it for a hundred years. He makes a distinction between mental and physical courage, and then says baldly, 'a keeper has to throw his body and head into dangerous areas among flying boots. Outfield players do not face quite the same risks. It's no use going in feet first and getting your head out of the way. By doing that you are more likely to get hurt. If you are courageous and take responsibility then you are less likely to suffer injury.'[17] And that's it. No drama. It isn't quite that he has abolished the need for courage by developing technique to circumvent it. It *is* an ingredient, and Shilton urges his readers to acquire it. But it is one of many, and has no higher rank than any other technical requirement he identifies. Courage, he says, presents certain technical problems, such as the risk of injury. But his book is packed with technical solutions to diminish that risk as much as possible. This seems to me a much more measured position.

This is not to suggest that Shilton alone was responsible for the shift. Courage had long been overrated as the defining goalkeeping quality. That had always been one of the things meant by all the old 'got-to-be-crazy' tags. Years late, goalkeepers began to write instruction manuals pointing to other technical demands. Cumulatively, they make a picture of almost impossible skills needed by goalkeepers which could flatly not be explained by the simple catch-all of courage. Shilton, himself both as brave a goalkeeper as you could find and a master technician, is one who was able to see clearly that courage was being used to conceal the real problems in goalkeeping.

Technique is a very loaded word in sports which are supposed to be natural. Football, apparently so much about running freely, is stuffed with techniques. Outfield players in Britain have the reputation of being found deficient in technique when they play European opposition, and there is something to this. Shamefully few outfield players work in training on their weaker foot. How many forwards can confidently even hit the goal with their 'wrong' foot from the edge of the penalty area? Basic skills are not all that basic. It is hard to kill the ball stone dead and ready for one's bidding at the first touch. But no doubt British players could do this more often with practice. I'm not sure that all European players perform miracles of this kind either, I must say, but there does seem to be a culture in British football that effort and speed and ceaseless running will make up for a lot of faults. In good years, they can do, and outsiders envy us; in bad years, they make us look unsophisticated and unskilled. That's fair enough. But outfield, whether in Europe or here, the height of technical perfection is always an experiment: it was daring, and it worked or not. And outfield, too, the failure of technique is shared between players. A 'great' pass finds 'nobody there' in football language; not, as in plain speech, a botched pass to nobody. Goalkeepers cannot conceal lack of technique under something called 'work-rate'. They work at need and not at will. They have to acquire technique of their own, and they have to observe the outfield techniques that oppose them or expose them. Nor is it merely a question of accumulating tricks. This stuff has to work every time, without fail, at no notice.

John Arlott, much more eminent as a writer on cricket, but a marvellous one also on football, quite correctly observed that footballers can put back-spin on the ball. I have never seen a manual that mentions it, and I doubt that Arlott had. But there is no doubt that very highly skilled players can do it. It is useful for getting passes past defenders at fizzing speed, yet slowing them enough to allow a team-mate to receive them with proper control. I have seen it done to spring an offside trap too, the unexpected slowness of the ball in the space behind the defender being exactly the help needed by the forward delaying his run until the ball had been played. Goalkeepers will have no doubt about this: they *have* to have noticed it, or pay the usual price.

But try this: 'Tommy [Lawton, bought by Arsenal at the very end of his career], of course, was a superb header of a football, and he certainly took it very seriously. Heading, indeed, sometimes seemed for him like a cross between a science and a religion. When we were coming back in the car from a match at Preston, I remember him saying to Tom Whittaker [their manager], with great seriousness, "I don't know . . . I should have put bottom spin on that header, but I put on top spin. So it came off the goalkeeper's fists and went over the bar, instead of into the goal." '[18] Jack Kelsey's observation is almost alarmed; I can hear him nervously filing a detail away that might be useful later. It's true that he concluded by saying 'Tom [Whittaker] was afterwards a bit sceptical,' and he implies that he shared that doubt. But that is hardly the point. Lawton, who may or may not have been able to choose the spin he put on his headers (and after all, if anybody could, he must have been that man), felt that he could do it. It was important information for Kelsey. Back-spin! From headers! It was one more thing to learn about, and to learn to deal with if necessary. That is what goalkeepers do, even in the car on the way home from the game.

The old manuals looked to the kind of men who could do these things. The new ones look to the detail of the things to be done. But in all of them the silent assumption is the big one: keeping the ball out is so far from being a simple matter that a manual cannot be what it is elsewhere. If, says the engine maintenance book, you undo these bolts and fiddle here, and clean this, and if you do it all up again properly, the engine will work. If, says the goalkeeping manual, you find some way of combining some of the improbables you might perhaps prevent a goal. It's different. Even in books it's impossible to pretend that it can always work. Goalkeeping is beyond the theoretical guarantee.

6. Throwing the Textbook out of the Window

Nobody needs me to tell them that the language of football is often absurd. All sportsmen speak a jargon-ridden shorthand, rich in technical terms and often light in meaning. I'm sure they always did. Those blokes who fought in Rome with tridents and a fishing net must have given wonderfully Beckettian or Pinteresque post-match interviews, assuming they survived. Modern sportsmen, weaned on a diet of gibberish from the United States, have added the rich lexicon of psycho-babble to the stew, but little has changed. To talk jargon is to proclaim oneself an insider. Footballers, so protected and sheltered in the semi-military, semi-boarding school world they inhabit, certainly like to reinforce the differences between themselves and the outside world, and their jargon does that nicely. There's nothing wrong with technical language in itself, of course, and if ordinary words will not serve, technical ones must be used. But jargon is a terrible mask of clarity of thought.

'Caution', wrote Sir Arthur Quiller-Couch, of jargon, 'is its father: the instinct to save everything and especially trouble. Its mother: indolence. It looks precise, but is not. It is, in these times, *safe*: a thousand men have said it before and not one to your knowledge has been prosecuted for it. And so, like respectability in Chicago, jargon stalks unchecked in our midst.'[1] It sounds uncannily like modern sports-talk. To some extent, it is not the fault of the players and managers that they are obliged to resort to the laughable, the muddy, and the hundred-times-heard-before. Our media are convinced that the appetite for the standard over-the-moon, sick-as-a-parrot interview is insatiable. I don't think it is; I certainly think that in a limited space, on television or in the papers, we should not lose accurate technical coverage of the game to these blatherings.

Keep a sharp ear and eye out for the standard phrases on goalkeeping. They share an impossible imprecision which reveals how little we are expected to follow it in detail. Some, at one end of the scale, are simply absurd but do no great harm. So, for example, I have already mentioned the standard phrase for a goalkeeper who has not let in a goal: he has 'kept a clean sheet'. It is meant to be what goalkeepers are most proud of, most to be congratulated for. It is not even a record that aficionados take seriously. When Jim Stannard of Gillingham broke the clean-sheet record (he kept twenty-nine of them in the 1995/96 season) he smoked an imaginary cigar after each one, until the fans started to send him a supply which he gave to team-mates. It was a considerable achievement, and one which contributed substantially to turning a nearly bankrupt club into one which might achieve promotion. Poor Stannard, who weighed something variously quoted around sixteen stone, was thanked only by a song accusing him of having eaten all the pies.

Other such phrases, by hiding precisely those combinations of athleticism, intelligence, courage and so on that goalkeeping depends on, do a lot more damage. How can we think a goalkeeper has achieved anything of note in particular if all we can say is that 'He stood up well'? Again, I'm not making it up. To stand up well is not some miserable joke about too much lager the night before. Yet commentators use it all the time. It is, in spite of sounding ridiculous, a technical term. It means to stay standing up longer than expected in those moments when a forward has passed the defence and is at leisure to shoot on goal whenever and wherever he chooses. By doing so, the goalkeeper forces the forward to make up his mind on what he intends to do before the goalkeeper has shown his own hand. It is a matter of fractions of seconds, a hideous gamble which can almost only go wrong. It is a version of 'playing chicken', when the first to budge almost always loses, but to wait too long is also disastrous. It is always done at speed, in a crisis, with all the odds against. To get it right is a matter of great pride; it is close to pure goalkeeping. Everything that *might* happen is invisible; when it's over, all you have is a goalkeeper who 'stood up'. As used, it is a phrase which normally implies that the forward has *missed*. He has done nothing of the kind. He has been *made* to miss, by superior judgement, timing, courage, and knowledge of the game. He has, in fact, been beaten by superior technique. To 'stand up', even well, sounds so grudging that it is hard to understand that many of the times it is used, something really extraordinary has been done. The fans don't dare to rank it as a great moment in the game because when they come to describe it, the proper technical term springs to mind. He stood up. Shrug, and pass on. But it's wrong to shrug. The term conceals so much that it often conceals greatness.

Another one, more general, is the collection of phrases based on 'getting a hand to the ball'. Sure, we know that is what the goalkeeper has to do. But getting a hand to the ball is like getting to the railway station on time. Simply to observe that it has been done is to gloss over the perilous probability that until it was it seemed unlikely to be. It seems so minimal an achievement, like stretching out for a conveniently positioned cup of tea. Even getting a *finger tip* to the ball, which at least contains some of the precarious narrowness of the margins within which goalkeepers operate, hardly sounds the stuff of dreams.

Outfield players are described as doing things of a practical kind. They actively deliver the ball to colleagues with accurate passes. They beat opponents by mazy runs or dispossess them with well-timed tackles. They link up and close down and make themselves available. Even if you don't know what these phrases mean, they have an urgency, a busy quality which is the very essence of rapid and effective action. We describe them as we see them, always in motion, and sometimes in purposive and constructive motion. The goalkeeper, if he's any good, 'gets his body behind the ball'. It can be one of the hardest things to do in any sport, providing an extra line of defence so that the defeated hands, unable to hold on, are backed up by something more, a chest or a stomach or, if necessary, a nose or a groin. Yet the only technical phrase to describe it sounds as uninspiring as it could be. It hardly sounds any kind of achievement, to get one's body behind the ball; more like sheltering from the wind, necessary but inglorious.

There is a pattern to these phrases, where time and again the goalkeeper's part is diminished or neutralized. At worst, his actions are seen as the failure of another's, as when a save is described as a miss. Wingers are often censured for crossing 'too close' to the goalkeeper, as though we had forgotten how effective a pass right into the thick of the goal-mouth can be and how difficult it can be for the goalkeeper to get that close to the ball. The language is always grudging, always slanted away from the importance of the goalkeeper and what he does.

When the English national team were put out of the 1996 European championships after a less abysmal run than we had learnt to expect, the whole nation went into a tabloid-led spasm about defender Gareth Southgate's 'missed' penalty, which set the seal on the whole thing. Yet German goalkeeper Andreas Köpke saved that penalty as much as Southgate missed it, as he had saved one from Gianfranco Zola earlier in the competition. Köpke was thirty-four when that competition was played, a goalkeeper who had conceded sixty-five goals in the recent Bundesliga season in which his Eintracht Frankfurt club had been relegated. He had in fact four times been relegated in a career in which he had acquired something of a reputation as a bad luck charm. But

German coach Berti Vogts kept faith with him and was spectacularly repaid.

It was a fine team, and it would be hard to say that Köpke was its star. Yet Köpke had been the only goalkeeper to concede no goals in the first round of the tournament, the rock upon which the marvellous German defence had been built. Critically, he was something of a penalty specialist, like so many modern goalkeepers who have learnt to defeat the unforgiving odds against them in this most unlikely part of the game. For those who like statistics, Köpke's are impressive: of the forty-one penalties taken against him since he had played for the national side, Köpke had saved fifteen, an incredibly high ratio of 36.58 per cent. Better than one out of three! There are many, many penalty-takers who don't *score* so many, in spite of the ludicrously long odds in their favour.

It was not to be expected that the English near-frenzy about the national team's progress to that penalty shoot-out would be objective about foreign contributions to what was being reported as a national epic, but nevertheless, Köpke saved Southgate's penalty. Soon after the competition Southgate made a television advertisement based entirely on a dubious pun on his missing, and in a spate of largely spurious comment on the ethics of his making a great deal of money on the back of his letting down the national side, no British columnist pointed out the central truth that Köpke had done his part. He was the German national goalkeeper; he saved a penalty; England went out of a competition as a result. That is why he was there, even though nobody would *guarantee* that a goalkeeper would save a penalty, ever. How different to the front-page colour photographs of David Seaman as he made his string of penalty saves earlier in the same competition, complete with massive headlines in the tone of 'SEAMAN SINKS ARMADA'. Our goalkeeper? A hero. Theirs, in the same circumstances? Our boy missed.

Penalty competitions are bad (a lottery, nothing much to do with football) and penalty competitions are good (they are the only moment in the game when the strain on an outfield player for one single gesture matches the normal tension goalkeepers live with all the time, as well as being unarguably heart-rending to watch), but to get to a penalty competition at all means that outfield players have not done their job in the game. A penalty competition, even one gloriously 'won' by a David Seaman in miraculous form, is a mark of failure, and outfield players should give thanks at being given that last chance to redeem themselves rather than carping about how they dislike the 'pressure'. They should never miss the goal altogether. It is true that the penalty Köpke saved from Southgate was a weak one, but more power to him; it was weak in part because Köpke managed to impose his confidence on Southgate's nerve in the moments leading up to it, and that is as it should be.

In Italy, in 1990, when England also lost to Germany in a penalty shoot-out – in which, curiously, the great Peter Shilton made not a single save, although he kept on flinging himself the right way and kept on not quite reaching the ball by inches – two British players failed to score. Stuart Pearce's kick was saved by Köpke's predecessor Bruno Illgner, with his legs. And Chris Waddle, unforgivably, blazed the ball over the bar. Which is like giving away the last run in a Test match with a no-ball, or losing at Wimbledon on a double fault. Pearce showed astonishing courage in volunteering in 1996 to take one of the necessary penalties against Spain, with all those years of having 'missed' one on his shoulders, and his roaring relief when he scored it was one of the images of the competition. But the fact was that in 1990 he had not missed; Illgner had saved. It looks the same on the score-sheet, but it is a very different thing. It is as though there were a chauvinist sense that in the end it is easier to claim that one's team has self-destructed than been beaten. The psychology seems like this: we lost, admittedly, but one of our men made a mistake. At least we weren't beaten by *them*. And time and again, that is precisely the mind-set which diminishes goalkeeping to the unfair advantage of other aspects of the game. How many times have we heard a save described with that abysmal lukewarmth that almost overtly regrets it? The goalkeeper 'was in the right place'. Never, you understand, as a reflection of his understanding of the game, his skill, and his timing. He was just there, not somewhere else. Like the lamp-post that you hit with your car.

It is clear that something is going on here. Goalkeeping is talked about in language so sullen, so stripped of the normal admiring mixture of techno-babble with overworked metaphors of glory that we use to describe other sporting activity, that we have to suspect that more than a coincidence is at work. I have mentioned that fans regard goalkeepers as spoilsports. If you live for goals, the man who stops them, even when he is your own man and the goals he prevents would be against you, is an enemy. The average fan has a better week after a 1–0 defeat, wallowing in the teasing at work, wallowing in the richly exaggerated agonies of position-in-the-table and keeping a jealous eye on local rivals, than he does after a 0–0 draw. Few fans will admit this, but it seems to be true. If you lost 1–0 there was at least a goal, to be replayed endlessly in conversation, even if it came the wrong way. After a scoreless draw, there is only blankness, even though it may well have been a fine defensive game, by outfield players as well as by goalkeepers.

Goalkeepers work in a huge void of public understanding. It's all very well knowing that once in a while a goalkeeper becomes the man of the match, that he occasionally gets a Player of the Year award, or even (bless us) an MBE. Goalkeepers, who tend to have long careers, are much loved for their 'service' to a club and for their phenomenal record of playing through injury. It used to be the goalkeeper who exchanged a few words with the crowd, perhaps during the warm-up, perhaps even when play was at the far end of the pitch (it still is at smaller grounds; big ones have so completely fallen for Muzak as a crowd calmative before matches that it is hard to make oneself heard even from the edge of the pitch to the nearest seats). The goalkeeper was often a 'character'. Not necessarily because he was barking, but because his was the only position on the field where the crowd could see a man as well as a player.

There have certainly been much-loved goalkeepers. One thinks of Sam Bartram, so many years at Charlton, of Pat Jennings, with his immaculate reputation for perfect gentlemanliness, years ago of Harry Hibbs and before him of Albert Iremonger, of Joe Corrigan, and many more. But in point of fact it is much rarer for goalkeepers to be named man of the match than it should be. So often when it is the goalkeeper who has made the difference, keeping a side in a game they 'should' have lost, or salvaging a win that others had come close to throwing away, or even playing brilliantly in defeat, it is another who gets noticed. We are not good at watching goalkeeping, not good at understanding what exactly they do. Only four goalkeepers have won the Footballer of the Year award: Bert Trautmann in 1956; Gordon Banks in 1972; Pat Jennings in 1973; and Neville Southall in 1985. The PFA (Professional Footballers' Association) Player of the Year award is voted by the players themselves, and goalkeepers have won it only twice: Pat Jennings again in 1976, and Peter Shilton in 1978. Did the players really not notice the contributions of all those other great goalkeeping seasons? In 1963 Lev Yashin won the European Footballer of the Year award, the only goalkeeper to do so. This is a glorious list, but a pitiful one too. How can any award have gone to anybody other than Ray Clemence after the 1978/79 season when he conceded just sixteen goals? True, Clemence is one of the goalkeepers to have won an MBE, but even so he is less admiringly remembered than any equivalent outfield player would be. But that season he played almost perfect football – all records get beaten sooner or later, but Clemence's sixteen looks out of reach – yet the evidence is that neither the football writers nor his peers noticed.

Or, more recently, how come no award to Peter Schmeichel? Everybody knows the enormous contribution made by Eric Cantona to Manchester United's recent accumulation of titles, but there is a serious case to be argued that Schmeichel did more. Cantona, famously, came with a late rush one year and scored in lots of 1–0 victories at the end of the season. But Schmeichel never, until a brief period in November 1996 when he conceded fourteen goals in four games, went through a bad patch. He certainly saved a goal a game, perhaps more, and not just at the end of a year. Not only did he make unbelievable saves so often that it became expected of him, not only did he learn to start many attacks with his ferociously swift and accurate throws out of defence, but he oozed superb confidence at a time when his side was stuffed with youngsters. Had he not been so assured their confidence would for certain have suffered. That is on the secret side of goalkeeping, but the fact that a large number of young players who made their early steps in the first team with Schmeichel behind them have since gone on to be established, successful, and brim-full of confidence is surely at least in part down to Schmeichel. A bonus, if you will, to the more visible (but still quite amazing) goalkeeping virtue he offered, of being almost impossible to beat. But the 1995/96 Football Writers' award went to Cantona, and Peter Schmeichel has not received one yet. It's almost overt, that to give credit to goalkeepers is somehow to give credit to the negative side of the game that people would rather deny. Goalkeeping *is* negative if all you look for is goals, but the rarity of awards to goalkeepers makes the point that even the people best qualified to judge don't really see what a goalkeeper actually does.

At Premier League level, at any level of professional football, it is quite implausibly difficult to stop people scoring goals. The routine work of goalkeeping is not easy, the bread-and-butter work of collecting back-passes and catching crosses. To do that without major mistakes for a season at a level where the ball is quite routinely hit faster, harder, and with more accuracy than you'd expect at *your* level is difficult enough. Add the miraculous occasions when the goalkeeper must swoop and soar and bounce up and then do it all again, faster, and the task becomes almost impossible. A well-hit drive from any Premier League player, not even from a famous hotshot, a Peter Lorimer or a Bobby Charlton, would wind almost anybody who caught it without expecting the full force, even supposing he caught it properly. The speed and strength needed to reach such a shot at any distance from oneself beggars belief. Yet even within the game, even from people who see fine goalkeeping at close quarters daily, there is a feeling that goalkeeping divides into the simple, which any fool could get right, and the unreasonable, which goalkeepers manage by luck alone. Neither is true.

Most people who watch football have heard the phrase 'narrowing the angle'. Many have used it in a learned way, normally when criticizing a goalkeeper who didn't. But how many know what it involves? As a piece of geometry, it is fairly straightforward. The goalkeeper facing a shot has to defend the whole of the width of the goal. If he stands on the goal-line, he has to cover eight yards. If the attacker, in the obliging manner of geometrical demonstrations, were to stand still and wait while the goalkeeper advanced towards him until only a yard or two separated them, the goalkeeper would have a much diminished breadth to cover. A triangle is drawn with two of its points at the roots of the two goalposts and its third at the ball at the attacker's feet. The further the goalkeeper advances away from the base of the triangle on the goal-line towards the ball, the closer the two sides of the triangle will come to his hands. And that is really it. It is a misnomer to the extent that the angle at the head of the triangle has not changed, but let that pass. What changes is the distance either side of him the goalkeeper has to protect. If played wider than that distance, the ball misses the goal; within it, in theory, it comes within his grasp.

The trouble, and a vexatious and irksome trouble it has always proved to be, is that the attacker does not stay still. Another is that football is not played on a flat two-dimensional graph; the goalkeeper is exposed above his head as well as to either side. The goalkeeper's own position is fundamental to the equation: as he moves to alter one element in his favour, so another element turns against him. Typically, if the attacker is anywhere other than in the dead centre of the goal, the action of moving towards him exposes the goalkeeper to a simple pass square across the face of the goal. In 'narrowing' the angle that existed a second, half a second, ago, the goalkeeper will actually have created the new, wide, gaping angle that has just appeared elsewhere.

Equally typically, the goalkeeper standing under his bar will be able to reach any ball low enough to pass under it. But as he moves towards the attacker, he increases the margin by which a ball can pass over his head and still have time and distance to drop down beneath the bar. It happens all the time, that a goalkeeper gets chipped on his way to a position at which he would have been almost impossible to pass. It gets worse; this precarious balance of unlikelihoods is reversible at any time. Shot or chip? Move to make the shot less likely, and the chip becomes more tempting. Move to deal with the newly favoured chip, and again the shot looks to favour the forward. Perfectly poised to deal with either, for a moment? The pass looks a certainty. In any sport it can be fatal to be caught between two equally 'correct' alternatives. The tennis player who has reached the net to make a volley and hesitates over the selection of the passing volley smacked firmly down the line and the stop-volley dropped stone dead just over the net, with a little back-spin on it to make it that much harder to reach, will very often pump it lamely into the net when it looked as though he could pick his shot. Choice is not always a disaster, but too much of it is. The brain sends messages to feet and hands which contradict each other. Result? Nothing moves. The body weight, trying to move in two directions at once, squashes the feet flat to the ground. And that's what commentators mean when they talk of goalkeepers 'rooted' to the spot. It's like being 'sent' the wrong way, both ways.

In the middle of a typical goalkeeping manoeuvre like narrowing the angle to prevent a forward having all the yawning surface of the goal to aim at, the goalkeeper may well have half a dozen equally threatening contingencies to cover: long pass, short pass, chip, near-post shot, far-post shot, control-and-advance closer. That's six. The ball may be laid back to another forward coming behind the one with the ball. Each attempt on goal may be aimed at any one of the 192 square feet of the goal, and by any one of three or four different trajectories. Each pass may be fast or slow, straight or curved. Each option becomes less tempting the instant the goalkeeper has thought of it, and another becomes favourite in its stead. Other attackers alter the equation, nanosecond by nanosecond, and so do defenders. The state of the ball, the state of the ground, the state of the game . . . is it any wonder that goalkeepers' computers occasionally seize up, and what you see is an ungainly moment when a great athlete simply doesn't move a muscle?

Yes, yes, all goalkeepers know about narrowing the angle. It's just that it's not done on graph paper; it's a nightmare, a kaleidoscope of bad things about to happen, any one of which can be precipitated by a step too far, a shift of body weight, even a movement of the head. Get this dizzying game of instant three-dimensional chess right and you don't get to relax for a moment in the congratulation of team-mates and the applause of spectators. You have to do it again, when it can all go just as disastrously wrong for equally tiny reasons.

A lot of great goalkeepers make their saves to outright shots standing just about on the six-yard line, perhaps a step or two ahead of it. They are gambling that forwards will go for the most likely percentage and shoot more or less for the middle of the goal. Because six or eight yards in front of goal, it requires a prodigious effort to reach anything curling from wide of the goal to either top corner. But then great goalkeepers have such agility, such speed and reach and control of their own movements in mid-air that they have some chance of making the save even then. But see a Sunday morning coach, howling at his goalkeeper to position himself further forward, and you see a man imagining that it's all done on graph paper. If his goalkeeper chooses to stand a yard or so shy of the six-yard line, from where the corners of the goal are still more or less within his reach, but he gives himself a fraction more time to judge the flight and pace of shots nearer the centre, then he is right, and no amount of yelling from the sidelines will make him wrong. Sunday goalkeepers, pub-team players, are not facing brilliant forwards. The forwards are frightened of making asses of themselves. They won't aim for the corners for fear of missing the goal. They won't hit the ball with all the speed of a properly swung professional boot because last week or the week before they swung and connected with nothing. The air-shot is a great boon to lower-level goalkeepers. As long as forwards remember how foolish they felt last time they caught a crab, goalkeepers know they will shoot within themselves rather than flat out. Most Sunday forwards can only strike with one foot, can't volley, and can't put very sophisticated swerve on the ball. Great. A few options reduced. Even better, most of them imagine the thrill of scoring a fraction too early. Mind not on the job, concentration gone, huge percentage reduction in effectiveness right there, even if they do manage to make contact.

No goalkeeper, at whatever level, ever imagines the save complete before it is done. It would run against all the caution goalkeepers learn from day one. They can look so stupid if they ever allow such a thing that it just doesn't survive in their game. Sure, they occasionally take their eye off the ball, or allow a worry about some other part of the kaleidoscope to interfere with the part they should be dealing with at the time. But anybody who daydreams about the completed save in the fraction of a second before it is done is not a goalkeeper.

It used to be said that Arsenal goalkeepers never went into a Cup Final with a new jersey after what happened to the unfortunate Don Lewis in 1927. A Welsh international himself, playing for Arsenal against Cardiff, with about fifteen minutes left he fielded an innocuous shot from Cardiff centre-forward Ferguson. Under a challenge from Davies and Irving he turned and the ball squirted out from under his elbow. His desperate dive to recover the error only sent the ball spinning into the goal. Lewis's crestfallen explanation, that the shiny ball had simply squeezed out of the grip of his shiny new sleeve, didn't satisfy everyone; Ivan Sharpe, who usually knew what he was talking about, wrote that Lewis had simply taken his eye off the ball, which was a little harsh, considering it was in his arms at the time.

Lewis's misfortune goes down as a blunder. It is an

example of how innocuous mistakes by goalkeepers are paid for in goals, and in Cup Final goals at that. It also goes down as a lesson in how goalkeepers have to be aware of even the tiniest details. The lack of grip of shiny sweaters is hardly the stuff of technical manuals, but it cost him the goal 'that first saw the FA Cup carried out of England'. A lot of modern goalkeepers, incidentally, roll up their sleeves even on cold days. Modern football shirts can be very shiny indeed, and sweaty forearms certainly grip the ball better. Others deliberately smear a little mud on the spot in the middle of their chest where they expect to catch the ball, for the same reason – you only need once to feel a snugly caught ball squirm loose to add smirching your kit to the usual pre-match routine.

This is where the technique of goalkeeping borders on obsession. If trivial details can lead to horrible disasters, then it behoves the goalkeeper to worry about trivial details. I have been among the goalkeepers utterly discomfited on Astroturf because we could not mark the centre of the six-yard line. We scrape away at the sandy covering on the ground, making no more than a feeble shadow of a mark. It isn't clear enough to be immediately visible. Then we feel lost in the goal-mouth, unsure of where the posts are behind us, and not having the time constantly to turn around and check. Then confidence goes, and concentration, and it's only a matter of time before the expected becomes hard fact. Good goalkeepers can't afford not to be obsessional. You scurry about in an unpleasantly tense world of your own for ninety minutes, knowing that big obvious things can go wrong at any time. You may let in a goal in any one of several classical ways. At the back of your mind, absurd and unlikely spectres jostle for attention. Sure, you might clatter into your centre-back by making a late call, and it might be disastrous. Avoid it. But shiny shirts are a problem? And shoelaces? Divots, gusts of wind, a loose dog on the pitch?

You think I'm joking, exaggerating to make a point? Chick Brodie will tell you different. He had been the Brentford goalkeeper for years, rather a good goalkeeper, when in November 1970, in a game against Colchester, he got hit in the knee by a dog on the pitch chasing the ball. His studs stuck in the soft ground, his knee twisted badly, and his career was effectively over. The ball went behind for a corner. The dog scarpered.[2] In every goalkeeper's mind there is a tiny but noisy corner reserved for such hideous improbables. You might be lobbed from the halfway line, or you might be badly hurt and considerably humiliated by a dog. You want to be good at judging which centres to go for, and you work very hard on that in training. But what on earth are you supposed to do about the rest of life's little worries? You stew in them, that's what. You file them away and hope not to have to think about them during a game.

'Standard' technique in goal provides a wealth of rules of thumb, but goalkeeping is not an activity in which identical situations ever recur. Technique needs to be adaptable not only to suit particular goalkeepers, their strengths, and their colleagues, but also to the thousand variations of all the main manoeuvres as they occur in a game. Technique as a 'public' body of knowledge shared among all goalkeepers does not cover the little things. So each goalkeeper finds himself revising established tenets in two ways. He revises long term, to modify the guidelines of goalkeeping until they suit his style, but he also has to modify in the immediate short term, to make sure that tried habits come to his rescue when the improbable, the implausible, or the impossible stare him in the face.

Pat Jennings used to catch crosses one-handed. That's hardly recommended practice, but that aside, most people will remember him as a very classical goalkeeper. He was a master. His imperturbability concealed really flamboyant gymnastic ability. He is the first goalkeeper I remember forcing me to notice how excellent his delivery of the ball to his colleagues always was, both from the prodigiously long kicks he could deliver with such accuracy, and from those hard, flat throws that came right onto the toe of the receiver, too fast for opponents a few yards away yet always arriving at the right speed to be controlled and used. Yet memory works in strange ways. Jennings, I am sure, used to save with his feet a lot more than most. It worked, but that isn't classical either, and hasn't been since the end of the last century when goalkeepers decided that they should use the advantage of their hands in almost all circumstances.

Maybe Jennings's classical style was an illusion. He was a smooth goalkeeper, rarely seeming hurried. Perhaps that made him look more like a player from a textbook than he really was. We think of him as a big, rather placid man, but memory again may be playing tricks; he was in fact quite exceptionally fast. Lots of goalkeepers are the fastest men in their side, a fact which always surprises those who think of goalkeepers as stolid and immobile. I would expect that to be true of Pat Jennings, and I know that he played in the same team as Jimmy Greaves. Indeed, Greaves himself confirmed this once: 'I reckon when he was in the mood, Pat Jennings was the quickest player on the Spurs staff. In fact, Pat used to enjoy playing out in practice. He used to play up front and I would get my chance in goal.'[3] Certainly he could play skilful football outside the box when he had to; he headed the ball a lot, and that's not classical either. I remember him playing a thoughtful one-two with Willie Young in the four-game FA Cup marathon Arsenal and Liverpool fought out in 1980, when classical goalkeeping rules of thumb would have said belt it into the tenth row in the stand.

'I have never found coaching manuals much use. On the contrary, the "advice" they contain is often misleading and some of the pet theories about goalkeeping are wide of the mark.'[4] That's what Jennings had to say about it, and he went on to give examples. People say, almost as a matter of course, that the goalkeeper should never be beaten by a shot from outside the penalty area. Nonsense, says Jennings. It might have been so in the days of heavy leather balls. But the lightweight modern synthetic ball with a polished surface is slippery and swervy. 'That's why even the finest goalkeeper can be beaten all ends up by a long-range drive which has been struck with pace and accuracy. Just because you know where it is going doesn't mean you can prevent it getting there.'[5] Similarly, the received wisdom is that 'everything in the six-yard box is the goalkeeper's'. Nonsense again, says Jennings: 'That's all cock-eyed as well, for it all depends on the height and angle at which the ball is played towards you – and on how many bodies are in the way. The goalkeeper used to be encouraged to station himself on the far post for a corner. If he tries it now, there's a fair chance of being obstructed 50 per cent of the time because he hasn't a clear path to move forward if the ball only travels to the near post.'[6] In other words, the apparent classicism of Jennings's way of doing things seems to break down when looked at closely. Jennings made it work, and he managed to look so unruffled doing it that it sticks in the memory as 'pure'. But he found his own solutions to goalkeeping problems, as every goalkeeper must. Some came from his early experience in Gaelic football, a fast game, dependent on faultless handling. Some came from close attention to the game, to that perpetual learning-by-self-scrutiny that seems a hallmark of good goalkeepers getting better.

A proportion of goals result from deflections by defenders or shots hitting divots and changing direction. But most of all you have to safeguard against an opponent miskicking. A mishit shot is the one most likely to end in the bottom of the net after you have prepared to deal with a power drive. And, believe me, First Division stars miskick like schoolboys, even if they don't always admit it. More than once I have seen the scorer of a vital goal go on television after a game and explain, tongue in cheek, how he 'bent' the ball past me when we both knew he intended his shot to go into the opposite corner.[7]

I can't resist that little phrase, 'tongue in cheek'. Jennings knew that scorers are incapable of that kind of subtlety. They boast about all goals, hit right or hit wrong. Irony, as we know, is a weapon to be used as a rapier and not as a bludgeon, and there, dropped into a little inoffensive phrase of three words, is all Jennings's career-long resentment at being beaten so often by other people's mistakes. Of course he's right. The miskick is so unpredictable, it comes at such unexpected speeds and angles, and often after an appreciable delay, that it is always very hard to counter. Forwards argue that 'they all count', that they're not too proud to accept a miskicked goal. But it rankles with goalkeepers.

Jennings came to an unusual perception that the basic skill in goalkeeping, given the required athleticism, is not so different from the basic skill outfield: 'Being a good goalkeeper may call for different skills, but you need a quick brain and plenty of confidence to shine in any position. It is interesting to note,' he writes, and few others have spotted it, 'that the most talented outfield players never shirk going in goal. Tottenham's Glenn Hoddle has kept goal efficiently on more than one occasion after his keeper was injured. Glenn even survived extra time without conceding a goal when Spurs won 1–0 against Manchester United in an FA Cup tie at Old Trafford.'[8] Martin Peters, he notes, used to do 'a sound job in goal', and Jimmy Greaves 'was always hoping to get the opportunity to try his hand between the posts in a League game. Jimmy often turned out in Sunday charity games as a keeper while at White Hart Lane.'[9] Bobby Moore went in goal after Bobby Ferguson was hurt in a League Cup semi-final replay against Stoke City, and stopped a penalty, only to be beaten by the rebound. These players, according to Jennings, were fine athletes and notably good at reading the game. They had the basics for goalkeeping. His argument is essentially, as befits the man, a modest one. He is saying that there is no great magic to goalkeeping beyond the same appreciation for the unravelling of a move or a game that all players have.

But the same argument looks very different turned the other way around. Pat Jennings was such a fine player that there is no reason to believe he could not have shone outfield if he had specialized there. The names he lists as having the *basic* aptitude for goalkeeping are pretty select – Hoddle, Peters, Greaves, and Moore. We can add many others, as we see, for example, with Alfredo di Stefano: 'I will even go between the goals [in training], and it is no secret that I shall not mind if ever called upon to to show my goalkeeping prowess in an emergency! My friend Bobby Charlton of Manchester United takes similar pleasure in being the goalkeeper in training sessions. Perhaps he imagines himself a Frank Swift as I imagine myself a Zamora! It is harmless fun – nothing so serious as the clown wanting to play Hamlet. And none can know if these private "hobby positions" may not one day be useful.'[10]

Jennings can be read as saying that it was precisely because he had the same kind of super-fine antennae for the game as these great and famous players that he was able to do what he did. That's how I think it should be understood. Pat Jennings was one of the all-time greatest, what Americans would call a Hall of Famer. He certainly had both the athleticism and the ability to read the game of any of the players he mentions, beyond question. In the footballing phrase, he made it look simple, just as all great players do. But it would be a mistake to confuse that with classicism. Pat Jennings made it up as he went along, as goalkeepers must. It produced a record second to none in a career loaded with honours, but that is no proof that he did it out of the coaching manuals. Unfortunately, at least for those less gifted than him, it simply proves that he made a technique that worked. Some was inherited, some borrowed, but much was invented. When it came down to it, Jennings was full of respect for the handful of goalkeeping coaches he felt knew their stuff. He singled out three: Bob Wilson at Arsenal, Alan Hodgkinson (who had been the goalkeeper for Sheffield United and England) for England under Bobby Robson, and Harry Gregg at Manchester United. Otherwise, the famous patience and charm of this more than usually patient and charming man wore thin: 'Outfield players haven't got a clue on how to instruct goalkeepers, and even those loaded with coaching badges will admit it if they're honest.'[11]

Pat Jennings gives a good example of the kind of acute observation goalkeepers need to use, and the filing system for disasters they have to develop. George Best was Jennings's room-mate on away trips for Northern Ireland. In a game against England in Belfast, Best lurked behind Gordon Banks and hooked the ball away from him as he was about to clear it upfield and scored. The goal was disallowed. A couple of weeks later, Tottenham

Hotspur met Manchester United: 'The referee was running away, with his back to me, in order to keep up with play. As I threw the ball up to kick it, George's foot came across me to intercept and control the ball all in one movement. Instinctively I had to check: if I'd followed through I would almost certainly have broken George's leg and probably my own as well. I stopped, waiting for the referee to give me the same sort of decision Banks had got – a free kick. But the referee hadn't seen it . . .'[12] The goal was allowed, and Jennings says that he and Best had a laugh about it after the game. It must have been a pretty sour laugh, but I'm sure Best did it to Jennings precisely because he had been at the other end when he tried it on Gordon Banks. Moreover, it would be no surprise if Best hadn't counted on that hesitation, that check, knowing that Jennings would never kick his friend and team-mate.

And then there is the final aspect: I am not sure, and I don't think Jennings was, quite, that the goal was illegal. As he threw the ball up, he no longer had 'control' over it. If Best made no foul on Jennings as he nicked it, it must have been a fair goal. I have seen it done several times since (Gary Crosby of Nottingham Forest did it to Manchester City goalkeeper Andy Dibble in March of 1990, neatly heading the ball off Dibble's hand as he prepared to punt, having arrived from behind him, and George Parris of Brighton did it more crudely to Bristol Rovers goalkeeper Andy Collett in October 1996, clearly fouling him as he nicked the ball) but it has passed into the shared goalkeepers' chamber of horrors. Many, many goalkeepers have since stood stock-still, hugging the ball, after an attack has broken down before looking carefully over both shoulders, like dutiful pedestrians about to cross a busy road, to make sure that nobody is left skulking behind them who might do it again. It has been done, patent George Best. So now, every goalkeeper at every standard has to worry that it may happen to him next.

Gradually, following Pat Jennings, we get further and further from any idea of classical goalkeeping as explained in coaching manuals. When Northern Ireland qualified for the World Cup in 1982, they were very worried that Spain might get another dodgy penalty. They had got one in each previous game, and as Jennings put it, 'I was certainly thinking that way.' Indeed his description of this game (Northern Ireland 1 Spain 0, in Valencia) is as near as he gets to being really sore about a referee, a Mr Ortiz of Paraguay. (Brian Glanville, in the standard work on the World Cup, uses the word 'lamentable' to describe Mr Ortiz.) In Jennings's account, when Spain came to their

> final fling for an equalizer as the game went into injury time, the ball bounced a yard in front of me with Juanito rushing in for the kill.
>
> I could see that the ball was too high for Juanito to reach, and I sensed that if I made contact with him I might be penalized and the game could slip from our grasp. So I knew exactly what I was doing when I tipped the ball over his head and dived to retrieve it. Later I was told that millions of viewers, watching on television all over Britain, had their hearts in their mouths at

that instant. I can only repeat that, however it looked, I had the situation under control.[13]

Here the coaching manual has finally been thrown out of the window. In addition to all the 'normal' goalkeeping problems involved, such as how to prevent a determined and talented forward from scoring, Jennings is telling us that he had factored these other elements into his calculation: the excitability of the last few moments of a game against the World Cup hosts, with a chance of putting them out of the competition, a referee who had made up his mind not to administer the rules fairly, the recent record of the opposition, and his own ability to improvise. There is no reason to disbelieve him. If he says he knew what he was doing, he did. All I can say is that I am as impressed by this description as by many glorious, leaping saves. This is where the chess-like calculating element in goalkeeping, the perpetual weighing of probabilities and subtle sifting then shifting of odds, meets the purely acrobatic. It is a quite amazing thing to have done. It is a territory occupied much more by the mind than by the muscles. And all that the spectators saw, and his team-mates and coaches too, I am sure, was that Jennings appeared to have fumbled the ball then recovered it. '*If you can keep your head . . .*'

In moments of crisis, then, goalkeepers teach themselves. What counts is how they assess the game as it develops before them. They know what they can do, and have to follow that even when it looks odd or risky to a classically minded spectator or coach looking on. They make themselves specialists in the bits of the game that suit them, and then use every stratagem to force opponents to play to their strengths. So one goalkeeper will have a great reputation as a shot-stopper while his rival across town will be reputed to be a great marshal of defensive forces. The marshal may save fewer direct shots, but he will have arranged his defence to allow him to face fewer, too. Risks in the goal-mouth are evaluated and diminished in fractions of seconds. There is no time to satisfy any theoretical principle onlookers may want to apply. Invention is the order of the day, for goalkeepers work extempore even when other goal-keepers have been in similar situations. You could, with patience and a video cassette recorder, find clear examples of utterly different responses to closely similar situations. But that is how it should be; the coaching manuals do no more than accumulate a series of techniques which have more often than not worked for previous goalkeepers. Once you've absorbed those, the rest is yet to be discovered. That is how goalkeeping has kept up with the game. Every new style, each new skill acquired, looked like a disaster until a goalkeeper proved it to work.

If goalkeeping is such an intricately technical activity, and it certainly is, and if goalkeepers find that the coaching manuals are not much help in times of trouble, the question arises as to how they learn to do it. I am suspicious of the ascription of great goalkeeping to 'natural' talent. We can surely see that some goalkeepers work harder at it, while others rely more on the gifts they know themselves to have, but I don't believe any great goalkeeper has ever really been 'natural'. I would put it another way, and say that all great goalkeepers have a fine natural base. They have the figure, perhaps the reflexes, the determination, the agility. But every one of these can be worked on and improved, and must be if the next cross is going to be made to be within reach, or the next race against a centre-forward won. No top-level goalkeeper has ever been able to rely on his natural gifts, however phenomenal, and leave it at that. They have to learn, and, like learning to fly on the trapeze, every lesson can be the last.

I think the answer is that goalkeeping advances dynastically. Goalkeepers tend to play through long careers. Not all club appearance records are held by goalkeepers, but far, far more of them are than the ten to one proportion we would expect. In addition, once established in a side, goalkeepers tend to be fairly certain of their place; there are fewer rivals for the goalkeeping position. Other players can be moved around, 'fitted' into a team. Goalkeepers are either in or out. There is usually a senior goalkeeper who plays unless injured, which does not apply to the outfield positions where it is far more common for a tactical change or the coming and going of players injured or out of contract to force continual rearrangements of the team. A famous exception was the long period of doubt in the England side over Ray Clemence and Peter Shilton. In that case, for years they were first-choice equal, and both must have found the rivalry agonizing. But then, who among us would have liked with certainty to exclude either? But in general, the opposite has been the case. Percy Young, noting in his customarily light way this exceptional longevity of goal-keepers, put it like this:

> As we study the contemporary, or near-contemporary scene, we become conscious of Abraham Lincoln's 'adherence to the old and tried, against the new and untried'. I forget when Swift started to play for Manchester City. After many years he retired. After that he played again. And then he retired again. No doubt after the passage of more time he will come again; but it will be after much more time, for Trautmann would appear not only to be an eminent successor, but also destined for long residence in Manchester. With much ceremony the other day, Alf Wood was conducted from Roker Park by the Sunderland centre-forward. Wood has been with Coventry for seventeen years. Sagar has played for Everton for ever and had I not been aware of Sidlow's antecedents I should have said the same with respect to him and Liverpool. I opened the newspaper – that is to say I turned the newspaper over – one day. Herod was reported injured and Wilkinson – Wilkinson whose toothache set all our canines, incisors and molars in sympathetic vibration more than a decade ago – was back in Stoke's side. All I could do was to repeat Virgil: *O pius pater Aeneas.*[14]

It has always been so. Sam Bartram was 'for ever' at Charlton, like Neville Southall at Everton. Think of Dino Zoff, captaining a World Cup side at forty. Think of Sepp Maier, who between 1966 and 1979 put together a sequence of more than four hundred consecutive games for his club, Bayern Munich, without missing a single one. Arconada, Zubizareta, Sam Hardy, Pat Jennings – it's almost as if to mention a great goalkeeper is also to mention a great veteran. Antonio Carbajal of Mexico kept goal in the five World Cup tournaments between 1950 and 1966.

These players have an enormous influence. Other goalkeepers come and go at their clubs, as understudies or rivals, who train with them and learn while doing it. When they get into international teams, they train with others who are almost by definition not their club colleagues. And on every ground they play, season after season, there is another goalkeeper at the far end who is impressed by the great man, watches carefully, and picks up the habits that he will later sift to decide if they should become his own. The dynasties are not simple progressions from old master to young pretender; few goalkeepers have stayed at the club where they played to carry on as coach to a younger generation, although some have. Of course the arrival of a young goalkeeper threatens the employment of the older one, and many have felt aggrieved, and left to go to another job in fairly short order. When Peter Shilton, perhaps the most aggressively single-minded goalkeeper there has ever been, arrived at Leicester, the incumbent goalkeeper was Gordon Banks, and Shilton was seventeen years old. It took next to no time for Shilton to stalk Banks and then claim his place. Banks was sold on, not yet thirty years old, still the England goalkeeper, and certainly disgruntled at being so summarily ousted. The normal practice has been a lot more patient. Reserve goalkeepers train with the incumbent, learn from him, and eventually either lose patience waiting for him to retire and make themselves available for transfer, or take over from him. Goalkeeping is a world within football where paths tend to have crossed and re-crossed many times. They learn from each other, by direct tips handed about, by emulation, by competition.

Many have acknowledged these debts. Sam Bartram, like so many who watched football in the period between the wars, acknowledged Harry Hibbs as the master. He read all about him, made special trips to go and watch him:

> What he taught me, I should like to teach others. And principally this has to do with positional play. You can make the other fellow, the oncoming forward, put the ball exactly where you want it if you position yourself correctly. Always seek to narrow his shooting angle. Don't stand stiffly but be ready in every muscle to spring to the ball when it is loose. On the other hand, don't jitter about in the hope of putting him off – a good forward is too intent upon his manoeuvring and the finish to his run to bother about a jack-in-the-box keeper.[15]

Harry Hibbs's positional play does really seem to have been something special. A loyal stalwart for Birmingham City, even though they never at the time won much, Hibbs specialized in deliberately unspectacular goalkeeping. Not especially tall, he made it his business to be in the best place to diminish the effort he would have to make to reach any ball. Forwards used to say that he drew the ball to him, which is as pithy a description of great goalkeeping as you will find. Bert Williams, of Wolves, was another to acknowledge how much he had learnt from watching Hibbs. So did Frank Swift:

Many years ago when I was a struggling youngster still playing for my place in the first team, I learned many things from Hibbs. He told me never to be afraid to ask his advice, and I took it on many occasions. He was a master of angles, and each time we played Birmingham I learned something new from him . . . I gave him six inches in height [Swift was taller, even though it sounds the other way] and have frequently made what seemed amazing saves only because the length of my arms enabled me to reach the ball; yet short as he was, I have seen him make similar saves without any last-minute excitement, purely through his amazing positional sense.[16]

Gil Merrick played all his football for Birmingham too, and I expected him to be full of gratitude to his predecessor. But in fact, although Merrick watched Hibbs many times when he was young, he says he hardly knew him later; his own role model was Ted Sagar, by whose apparent confidence he was very impressed. 'I remember thinking how difficult it must be for a forward seeing him like that to score.'[17] Gyula Grosics, as meticulous as ever, tried to be formally clear about the goalkeeping ancestry he traced:

Hungary's football history shows many examples of international goalkeepers turning into football leaders who influence the trend of development in Hungary's football life. Such was, among others, Ödön Hollits who wrote a book with Dr Mihàly Mamusich on football, based on English experiences which had determined the trend of Hungary's football development for dozens of years. Also, Tibor Gallovich, the one-time outstanding goalkeeper, ultimately became Hungary's team manager. I myself am deeply indebted to him for what he had done to make me a keeper of the national eleven's goal.[18]

Sometimes the succession in goalkeeping is brutal. Jack Kelsey remembered sitting on the bench during the Coronation Cup matches between English and Scottish clubs in 1953 when his predecessor in the Arsenal goal, George Swindin, let in a goal direct from a corner. Manager Tom Whittaker tapped Kelsey on the knee and said, 'Get yourself ready for the [off-season] tour.' As Kelsey put it, 'At that moment I knew that I had at last won my place as regular first-team goalkeeper.'[19] In his case the fact that he was part of a team that was immediately routed 6–1 by Rapid Vienna in Bruges didn't affect the transition. He was in and Swindin was out.

These are the lines of descent in goalkeeping. Solutions to vexing problems are lent and borrowed, sometimes with traceable acknowledgement, more often in silence. It is as old as goalkeeping itself. Jack Robinson kindly showed Cartledge how to punch in one particular way, in 1905, and the same exchange had certainly being going on long before. One of the reasons Ned Doig was so admired was that he seemed able to invent an efficient style of goalkeeping as he played, a great deal more efficient than the onlookers expected at the time. A.J. Liebling wrote of boxing that the 'Sweet Science is joined onto the past like a man's arm to his shoulder.' Exactly my feeling about goalkeeping. Some of the things that Chris Day or Michael Oakes or Shaka Hislop (among the crop of young goalkeepers of the present) do are as surely descended directly from things invented or refined by Ned Doig as a man from his grandfather. In part it is a formal line of descent, up and back from disciple to mentor, an unbroken chain of things learnt and passed on.

But in part it is also something less regular, a sense of how the thing should be done, a tradition of goalkeeping emotions, even a visual memory for how the thing should look that sticks in the mind of the young goalkeepers as they strive to replace their predecessors. It is almost as though goalkeepers absorbed from each other an aesthetic of how it should look when right. Harry Gregg put himself in the line of descent from a great goalkeeper he had never seen: 'As a boy, you identify yourself with some famous sportsman when you are playing a game. If it's cricket, you are a Peter May or a Freddie Trueman, depending on whether you are batting or bowling. If it's football, you're a Di Stefano or a Puskas. At football, I was always Johnny Thompson . . . the goalkeeper I had never seen. But I had heard so many stories of his skill that in my heart he reigned supreme as the greatest ever.'[20]

Geoffrey Green was often called the doyen of football writers. Here he is describing a great save by Bert Williams to a sharp volley from the edge of the penalty box, and heading for the top corner in the Scotland versus England match at Hampden in 1950:

That save of Williams, taken within its particular context, was a remarkable effort. The unexpectedness and pace of Liddell's shot, too, was something to wonder at. The whole mechanism of events, in fact – the shot and the save; the question and answer

– made a perfect and satisfying whole. Imagine that searing shot, volleyed as only Liddell can volley – those who have seen him shoot in this sort of mood will understand – and Williams's instinctive reflex action. It was a breathtaking moment. It was an answer as quick as thought itself, with Williams creating a picture of infinite grace as he leapt sideways and upwards as swift as a cat's leap, his yellow jersey lit by the fading sun, in a jack-knife action. One-handed he touched the searing ball up and over the white bar, finally to come to rest, a yellow splash against the green background. They talk about it still at Hampden . . .[21]

Still today that is how goalkeepers dream when they're learning the business, even if they've never heard of Bert Williams, and it is still the collective memory of what great goalkeeping should look like that the spectators have in their mind's eyes when they watch new pretenders to greatness. The snatch of breath of a save improbably made remains the same. So either the goalkeeper was coached by somebody who was understudy to somebody who trained every day with Bert Williams, or he inherits the visual sense that in moments like those the great emotions of goalkeeping combine in marvellous cocktails of high skill which must produce the 'infinite grace' Green mentioned.

Williams's save was great for all to see. But somehow goalkeepers appreciate each other differently. They appreciate the 'yellow splash' of the save, but they cannot leave it at that. Only they really understand the way high applause for goalkeeping normally comes only as a brief interruption of indifference or even contempt. There is a kind of freemasonry of goalkeeping whereby it is taken for granted that non-goalkeepers will not understand. In Britain it is half-jokingly referred to as the Goalkeepers' Trade Union. It involves goalkeepers being quick to defend each other's reputations, quick to thank each other for courtesies received. It is viewed with a little suspicion by those who play elsewhere, as if goalkeepers by ganging together become a little uppity with real football players who don't use their hands.

Goalkeepers in the normal course of matches never play directly against each other. There are odd occasions when one goalkeeper will shoot a penalty against another, or charge up in the dying seconds of a game to add his number to an attack, but normally the very fact that one goalkeeper is active means that the other is not. He can look on in a knightly way, his gallantry unlike that of his team-mates, unsulliable by hard boots or outrageous fortune. Goalkeepers very rarely beat each other. They very rarely actually share passages of play. They watch each other, from opposite ends of the field. They are forced to have sympathy for the other's worst moments, because they know the same might have happened to them, might yet happen at any moment. At the same time, they want the other man beaten; they may be fellow goalkeepers but they are on opposite sides. To see the other man concede a goal lessens the strain at this end. But when he prevents one, he gets a measure of respect filled out by the full understanding of what he has done.

That respect trickles down through football in a way that is different to the usual adulation. To play a park match as, say, an inside-right is immediately to be cast in the same role as a dozen great heroes. A park goalkeeper is not playing a part. He is forced to be supremely himself while the game is on, more so perhaps than at any other time in his life. He may be wearing all the gear, but he is exposed as himself; he succeeds or fails in a bitter muddy world where fantasy offers neither motivation nor protection. Perhaps the majority of park goalkeepers are in fact outfield players, dragooned into the alien position for a game or for a season, but without having themselves become goalkeepers. But those who are, who have learnt to think like goalkeepers and accept it, are automatically members of the same trade union as the very greatest. Because the traditions of goalkeeping were not developed in great stadiums alone. The average or frankly below-average forward of the standard just-for-laughs game can hit a shot just as hard to save as Steve Bloomer or Ian Wright. He doesn't do so very often, of course, and he may well have no idea where it is going, but a sweetly struck football is just that at every level. It needs the same save on Hackney Marshes as it would at Highbury or at Wembley.

Spectators have always tended to be alarmed by the same handful of things goalkeepers do. Increased mobility has been a regular staple of the debate for as long as goalkeeping has existed. Every generation the comparisons are made, and the goalkeepers have to defend their own chosen manner against the coaching manuals of the last. The tendency has been for goalkeepers to try to dominate ever further from goal. How far is not defined in the manuals. Clearly, a fast-sprinting goalkeeper who anticipates well and with sureness will be happier near the edge of the penalty area than one who relies more on gymnastic excellence under the cross bar.

Then there is the system adopted by their team. It is perhaps too easily assumed that competent goalkeeping is a constant which does not vary however the players in that team defend. This is not so. The goalkeeper is a fully paid-up member of the side, and he just as much as any other player has to work in a style which suits that of the team. It is often in fact the precise blend of the qualities a fine goalkeeper possesses which sets the tenor for the rest of the side to follow. By that reasoning, a coach will look at how far forward his goalkeeper can comfortably play and devise his defensive tactics to match. But the opposite also inevitably has to happen, when a goalkeeper has to modify his play to fit in with that adopted by the players ahead of him. For goal-keepers both protect their defenders and are protected in turn by them. They are not, as it is all too easily supposed, independent artisans, commissioned to do a job which is somehow neutral and unconnected.

Some stay back, others go further forward. Both have frequently been criticized, and goalkeepers have been able to play well using both techniques. Here is Ray Wood, the Manchester United goalkeeper whose jaw was broken by Peter McParland in the 1957 Cup Final, taking a friendly bashing from his team-mate Jackie Blanchflower, a fine critic of the game: 'Woody was a good keeper, but he didn't come off his line. "Puffer" we called him, he always had a fag in his mouth. He was a good lad, who could laugh at himself. Old Tosher [one of Manchester United's coaches, Tom Curry, who died at Munich] used to tell him that if a barrel-load of hay went past him he couldn't catch it. When I see him now I say "Woody, you were the second-worst goalkeeper I ever saw in my life." He always asks "Who's the worst?" '[22] Note how a goalkeeper is expected to be a 'good lad' by taking without demur the kind of insult for which any other sportsman would have you outside, jackets off.

Wood's successor in the United goal, Harry Gregg, thought, like many other goalkeepers who have enjoyed rushing upfield to nip danger in the bud, that he had invented it. His superb performance for Northern Ireland against the Germans in the group matches of the World Cup in Sweden in 1958 (drawn 2–2 in the end) included his beating Uwe Seeler twice in 'heading duels' outside the penalty area:

> I saw no sense in waiting inside my 'pen' while he brought the ball under control, with all the time in the world to slip it past me and into the net. So I beat Seeler to the punch, as it were, and nodded the ball over *his* head. And I didn't even stop to take off my cap! That was something novel for the fans – the goalkeeper venturing upfield and leaving his goal completely unprotected. But this wasn't the first time I'd chanced my arm – or should I say, head? In fact, it's a 'bad' habit I've kept up – right from the day I was solemnly warned against standing on the eighteen-yard line while my team-mates were trying to burst the net at the other end of the field.[23]

Later, Gregg compared the two points of view. Jack Kelsey he quoted as saying, 'Now I do not go a yard beyond the goalkeeper's area. I'm governor of the six-yard box, I like to think, but that's as far as it goes.' He then quoted Willy Meisl on Grosics at greater length, with obvious approval:

> Hungary's goalkeeper, Gyula Grosics, again stressed that the keeper of class is the third back, or if you want it that way, the fourth full-back. His personality must dominate at least his penalty area. He must command his defenders. A goalkeeper who thinks his exclusive task is to stand between the posts and produce fine saves when shot at cannot be considered of international calibre. He must rush out, not only to reduce chances from an oncoming forward to hit his target (the goal) by narrowing the angle, but also to intercept. In short, he must live as much and more with the game at any second as every other player.[24]

The debate has rumbled on. The tendency has been inexorably towards goalkeeping even further forward. It used to be that the eighteen-yard line was impassable, a psychological barrier as much as a pitch-marking. Goalkeepers would not go beyond it because the price of being beaten outside was simply too awful to risk. Today, almost all goalkeepers pass it happily, usually unopposed, to make clearances. Goalkeepers like Jorge Campos of Mexico (who regularly plays at centre-forward and likes to combine that, in the same game, with keeping goal), or René Higuita and Bruce Grobbelaar, who play the ball with their feet yards outside that once sacred line, are no longer regarded as a menace. We are not far from the day when some superb athlete will inspire such confidence in that area of the field that he will be allowed to play as a genuine rush-goalie, defending in the back three, and only going back to what used to be his territory when the danger is such that his own midfielders will have come back to relieve him in defence. When we have such a goalkeeper, he will free one defender to play further forward, and football will have another tactical invention to counter. You can be sure that when he does, there will be an outcry every time he lets in a goal that a more traditional style might have prevented. But a brave manager will keep faith with him, a balance will be drawn up of advantage against risk, and the debate will have passed one step further. The quickest goalkeepers in the Premier League are not so very far from it now.

One of the problems with the development of goal-keeping technique, as every spectator will testify, is that the goal-mouth is not the place to experiment. The spectators, even theoretically well-advised spectators like coaches and reserves, have more than a slight tendency to panic when the goal is threatened. For all their supposed appreciation of footballing refinement, crowds get very simplistic when the ball is within reach of goal. 'Boot it into touch!' they yell, 'Get rid of it!' If goalkeepers felt that their defenders had more sympathy with what they do, they would find it easier to explain that they intended to try a change. When it worked in training, they might try it in matches, and if it worked then, crowds would appreciate it more. But it doesn't happen like that. Defenders have no real idea what goalkeepers do. They want certainty from their goalkeepers. Loud call. Defender gets out of the way. Goalkeeper's ball.

Defenders like formulae that have worked for years. Only the best are able to adapt to new formations of play, and even fewer have the improvising ability to abandon a formation for the duration of a game to eliminate some particular forward's advantage. So the goalkeeper who is keen to try something new redoubles the already awkward odds against him; it has to work, or it will upset his defence and so make his own life even harder. The manuals say nothing of this. They talk of establishing 'understanding' with defenders. But 'understanding' turns savagely quickly into blame/counter-blame when things go wrong. So, for example, if goalkeepers are expected to play more often than they were as sweeper, it is to be expected that they will occasionally be beaten far upfield. Yet how many defenders make a practice of seizing the fractional delay the goalkeeper's intervention affords them to race back and cover him on the line? Very few. That only happens at lower levels, my kind of level, where the defenders never really trust the goalkeeper anyway. They are rushing back because they expect a disaster. In point of fact they are right. If a goalkeeper is beaten more than twenty yards from goal, there will almost invariably be time for someone to get back and cover him. But a goalkeeper rash enough to say so, in training or on the bus, will merely get for an answer the standard outfielder's lament that he does enough running as it is.

When the near-post corner became so fashionable in England in the 1980s, aimed for a forward who intended to do no more than flick it on into the crowded six-yard box with a changed angle to cause maximum confusion, it was often described as 'hard to defend against'. Yet defences had traditionally stationed a man on the near post for corners. What was he doing? The answer is a little paradigm of the relationship between goalkeepers and defenders. The corner was expected to be the goalkeeper's to catch if it reached the six-yard area, no matter how high, how fast, or how crowded the space in between. The defender on the near post simply stood there, usually far too close to the post to have any chance of stopping anything bound that way. He tried to get out of his goalkeeper's way but not to get the ball himself. A near-post corner is normally played well short of the near post, to a man who has run there from a more central position. A marker went with him, and invariably the man stationed on the post inched that way too, so that when the ball did arrive in the middle, he was quite out of position for the new angle it presented. Effectively, a slightly new tactic had proved itself successful by removing one defender wholly from the equation. The man on the post did nothing at all. When the worst happened and a goal was conceded, it was always the goalkeeper who had failed to get the corner. Yet by the simple business of talking through with that defender exactly what he thought he was doing with one arm wrapped around the post, the responsibilities could have been divided more equally and more efficiently. The man on the post is there as cover for the goalkeeper who is expected in those circumstances to leave his line. He (unless the angles are untypically fine) cannot provide that cover if he is within touching distance of the post. Yet the near-post corner still works embarrassingly well.

It is as though defenders refused even to contemplate the little bit of goalkeeping technique that might in special circumstances apply to themselves. When it comes down to it, they'd rather concede an avoidable goal than concern themselves with the most elementary fractions of goalkeeping.

Footballers don't like to think about technique. They certainly haven't, in Britain, liked to practise it, although that may be changing thanks to increasing awareness of foreign styles and increasing contact with foreign players. People in the British game who have been interested in the big techniques of strategy or tactics, or the little techniques of ball control, have traditionally been rare, and rather despised within the game. For every Herbert Chapman, admired for strategic innovation, there have been many like the FA's director of coaching Charles Hughes, publicly reviled for concerning themselves with tactics at all.

The exceptions are goalkeepers, who have no choice. It is possible to catch the ball in lots of ways. But if you don't think about how you catch it, why it works for you, then the day will come when you don't catch it. On which day you will either stop keeping goal, or start thinking about technique. Yet the very language with which we discuss goalkeeping slurs the technical precision it uses. Never mind whether great individual goalkeepers follow the accepted habits of their day; most do not, as I have tried to explain. They invent a derivative that works for them. But the spectators can't tell because they aren't given the words to describe how they think it ought to be done, let alone to describe how it is changing. It's so absurd to assume that goalkeepers have a screw loose, that they are flaky and hilarious, when we can't even describe what they do. Again: goalkeepers are the most important players in any football team. If we make no effort to understand more precisely what we ask them to do, what we admire them for being able to do, and revile them for occasionally not doing, then we are not really very interested in understanding the game. There is a huge interest in football, and a vast exchange of knowledgeable views upon it. Is the goalkeeper really so strange that it should all stop short of him?

7. What Price Heroism?

In 1963, Tottenham Hotspur won the European Cup Winners Cup, beating Atletico Madrid in the final in Rotterdam. As with any such campaign, people remember it for varying reasons. It was an important victory because English clubs were still groping their way in European competitions. Spurs had themselves reached the semi-finals of the European Cup the year before, and the year before that they had achieved the League and Cup Double. The Double seems to have become more achievable recently, but when Spurs won it in 1961 it had not been done in the twentieth century, and although both Wolverhampton Wanderers and Manchester United had missed it by a small margin in the late 1950s, many thought it was impossible to achieve in the modern era. The Spurs side managed it, and managed it in a style people liked, for its elegance as much as for its effectiveness.

In the League in that 1960–61 season, Spurs lost only seven times, playing a blend of sharp attacking football and resolute (not to call it anything worse) defending. The glory days lasted throughout the early

1960s, with Spurs, under the managership of Bill Nicholson and the captaincy of Danny Blanchflower, playing a refinement of the push-and-run football they had developed under Arthur Rowe the decade before. There was an added element of English league muscle; the spine of the team was very tough indeed: centre-half Maurice Norman, Dave Mackay, and centre-forward Bobby Smith. They played astonishing football, seeming to enjoy playing in short bursts which ripped the heart out of opposing teams. They were stylish, cosmopolitan, and winners. No wonder they became fashionable. Suddenly intellectual figures who would previously have ignored football were writing about Tottenham, people like Karl Miller, then the deputy literary editor of the *New Statesman*, or philosopher A.J. Ayer. 'It was in the European arena,' as Nick Pitt put it, 'that the Spurs Double side was to find its finest expression. European ties on Wednesday nights at White Hart Lane under the floodlights, with the crowd singing "Glory, Glory, Hallelujah, the Spurs go Marching On" became legendary. There always seemed a deficit to make up, and Spurs always seemed to make it up in style.'[1]

Now that Tottenham team was a fine side by any standards. I cannot say that it was all down to the goalkeeper. It quite clearly was not. Great leadership and fine play in all positions would be more like a fair assessment. But it is an almost unbroken rule that when a team puts together a record like the one that Spurs team built (League champions 1961, runners-up 1963, third 1960, 1962, fourth 1964; FA Cup winners 1961, 1962; European Cup Winners Cup winners 1963) there will be a fine goalkeeper at the root of it. And it is a wholly unbroken rule that when there is, he will have got neither the same plaudits as his team-mates, nor the plaudits he was due.

One of the members of that team, bought from AC Milan after the Double was won, was Jimmy Greaves. Greaves loved goalkeeping and was on the pitch a mighty opponent to the goalkeepers he met, although in his second career as a television pundit he made too much capital from crude jibes at goalkeepers, notably those from Scotland. The goalkeeper of that fine Spurs team was a Scot, Bill Brown. Here is Greaves, eating at least a little bit of humble pie, making handsome amends to Bill Brown and giving credit where credit was due:

> Scottish goalkeepers, as any of you who watch *Saint and Greavsie* [the television show] will know, have often been the subject of, shall we say, some ribaldry from me. Recently, Jim Leighton has spoiled my bit of fun. Young Jim is the steadiest keeper I've seen in a Scotland jersey for a long time. Scots will remind me of Ronnie Simpson, and, of course, old Ron did give a bit of stability for a few games before a bad shoulder injury forced him to give up at the grand old age of forty. But for my money the best Scottish goalkeeper in the last twenty-five years was my old Spurs team-mate Bill Brown. Bill got the nickname Dracula from the rest of us – the old boy just didn't like crosses – but what a reflex keeper that man was. I've told elsewhere how Danny Blanchflower's pre-match pep-talk won us the European Cup Winners Cup against Atletico Madrid in 1963. But the very fact that we made it to that Rotterdam final was thanks to Bill Brown and a superlative display of goalkeeping against Slovan Bratislava.

We had to play the Czechs in mid-winter and they had a fine team, the nucleus of which actually played for Czechoslovakia in the 1962 World Cup Final against the great Brazil side. It had been such a hard winter in Czechoslovakia that the River Danube had frozen over. When we arrived in Bratislava we couldn't believe the pitch we had to play on. It was covered in ice with a thin covering of water – the thaw had finally set in! But play we had to, and when I say that Bill Brown must have had one hundred and fifty touches of the ball and the rest of us zero – that about sums up Bill's contribution and ours. Suffice to say that I've never seen a display of goalkeeping like it. Almost everything that the Czechs threw at Bill he saved. He had the all-time great Czech players such as Masupost and Popluhar holding their heads in amazement as he touched sure-fire winners over the crossbar and round posts. The shots and headers kept coming but Bill stood firm. In the end though he was beaten twice and we had a two-goal deficit to take back to White Hart Lane in the second leg. That it wasn't 12–0 was down to Bill Brown.[2]

A fairly formulaic tribute to a goalkeeper, I suppose. But how many people today remember Bill Brown except as a sort of privileged passenger in a great team? Sure, it was like that on some days. It's a team sport. But then on days like that one in Bratislava, on ice, and against some of the very best forwards in the world, Bill Brown could force everybody to realize just how very good he was. Great goalkeeping is like that, only time after time the tributes somehow don't get written. I wish Greaves had refrained from the old joke about crosses and Dracula (a standard put-down of goalkeepers, now almost meaningless, like goalkeepers who 'couldn't catch a cold' or 'couldn't catch a bus') and I wish he had been more precise in describing what Brown actually did. But it doesn't matter. That kind of writing, by a team-mate, is so rare about goalkeeping that it just has to be collected. Put in plain words, Greaves says what is all too often lost in the bare accounts of the game: Spurs lost in Bratislava, and could have gone out of the competition. That they lost by a margin they were later able to turn around was entirely down to their goalkeeper. It so often is. When the other players don't take advantage of that, performances like Bill Brown's of exceptional stubbornness and athleticism, of high skill and courage, get buried in the bald fact. Out of the Cup, out of the promotion places, out of this season. Yet somewhere in there is likely to have been goalkeeping which represented everything we hold most fine in ball games.

The three most famous goalkeeping facts known to the British football public are all accidents: Gordon Banks, losing an eye in a car crash; Bert Trautmann, breaking his neck in the 1956 FA Cup Final; and John Thomson of Celtic, dying in a scarlet goalkeeping jersey at the feet of a forward called Sam English in an Old Firm game. All three of those goalkeepers were for different reasons extraordinarily popular. We remember the accidents as a painful coming to earth of three public infatuations.

It is in the nature of the competition, played only every four years, that few goalkeepers have won the World Cup; Banks is one of them. But he was popular before that. There is not much doubt that for some years he was the best goalkeeper in the world. Opposing managers chorused to say so when they saw him play, whether in English league or international fixtures. He played his club football for middling teams, for Leicester and for Stoke. He won little in the domestic game, except the enduring affection and respect of everybody who follows it. He seems to have played better for England than he ever did in the League or the Cup. He seemed more driven by the three lions on his shirt than anybody is today; you could see that it mattered enormously to him not to let his country down, not to let himself down in his country's colours. As a young goalkeeper he was almost Italian in his love of the spectacular, even the slightly-more-spectacular-than-strictly-necessary. An extraordinary gymnast, he later left that part of his game for the moments when nothing else would do, and became instead a safe goalkeeper in the English mould – the Harry Hibbs model. The later-model Banks would have agreed with the Everton goalkeeper Barney Cresswell, who said, 'Great goalkeepers never make good saves.'

Outwardly a modest man, and discreet, almost unassuming in his public appearances, he had reserves of courage and of toughness far deeper than it appeared. A dragon in training, obsessively driving himself through late and lonely practise to levels not far below his successor Peter Shilton, he seems to have refined a mentality rather than any specific goalkeeping style. 'They shall not pass' was Banks's motto, and opponents feared him, felt that they would have to be lucky to beat him. I remember no incident of his publicly 'psyching' opponents in any visible way, yet opponents were consistently 'psyched' by him. He didn't seem a particularly confident man, yet confidence seeped away from those facing him. Bobby Charlton noticed that he was even more goalkeeperly than other goalkeepers:

> He is the only goalkeeper I know who never wants to play in another position, even when we are having a little practice game. Most of them are desperate to play out of goal, to show you what they can do on the wing or knock in a few goals. They often fancy themselves on the ball. But Banksie just wants to stay in there and let you try to beat him. He would have you shooting at him all day. We all lined up on the edge of the area this morning and hammered shots at him and we couldn't put one past him. He was unbeatable. He loves that. If one does get by him, even in a little kick around like that, he gets needled with himself. Starts muttering and trying to work out what went wrong. He thinks you have no right to score against him.[3]

Banks used to recite a little mantra to himself on the field: 'Composure, control, concentration.' Not unusual; many goalkeepers, like many other athletes, have kept little litanies running in their heads. Concentration and composure are obviously necessary, together making that massive presence of mind on which goalkeepers live. But control? Goalkeeping is mainly a reactive business. The whole point is that you don't have any control, the other man does. Yet here was Gordon, taking it and using it to his advantage. He actually expected to be in control of an activity which almost by definition implies other people doing things to you. The effrontery of it is something to admire. That it worked, even more so. Because

Banks *was* in control. All witnesses agree: a goal-mouth with Gordon Banks in the right mood in front of it would cease to gape; it had a very big man filling it. Yet if the 1966 World Cup was Banks's tournament, in which he made absolutely no mistakes and at least one wonderful save (in the semi-final, against Portugal, in the last minutes, with England 2–1 up and struggling to hold on to one of those leads that evaporate so easily, the leads which if held take you into a final), nobody would have bet before it that it would be so. Could Banks outshine the incomparable Lev Yashin of the Soviet Union, or Ladislao Mazurkiewicz of Uruguay, fresh from winning the South American Cup almost single-handed (twice running) for his club, Peñarol, of Montevideo? Perhaps, in the end, he did. He won, whereas they dropped out of the competition earlier. And, as they say, that's what it's all about. In the 1966 competition, Banks simply didn't make mistakes. Neither absurd ones to easy balls, nor just-off-perfection ones to screamers. He was that kind of man. That made him popular.

Bert Trautmann is a much more obvious case. A German paratrooper, a prisoner of war who settled here and stayed, Trautmann became Manchester City's goalkeeper over serious anti-German feeling. He weathered it as very few men could have done. Handsome, charming to fans, a goalkeeper whose enormous courage rather blinded people to his other skills, Trautmann did an enormous amount to rebuild the bridges between Britain and Germany broken by the war. He was the first German after the war to achieve great popularity in this country. People liked him because he became an honorary Mancunian, they liked him because he was for that club a successor to Frank Swift, whom they had expected no one could succeed. Trautmann never qualified to play for England, although he played all his professional football here, and the thought does occur that he might have made the England goalkeeping position his own in the late 1950s and early 1960s.

Everybody who saw him play seems to have been amazed. He was always called the giant, and often a friendly or genial giant. (In fact he was six feet one and a half inches tall, not all that huge. People remembered him as bigger than he was, a slight hint of how they were impressed by him.) A character of great charm, who managed to wring affection from crowds initally ill disposed to him for reasons not of his own making, he is a figure whose importance at the time went considerably beyond football. Trautmann was held in great admiration, of course, for his excellence in goal. But he was also held to be a great man, and I think he was. He was the guest of honour brought back to Manchester by the German Federation for the group matches of the European Championship tournament in 1996, and it was noticeable how Manchester journalists, thirty years after his retirement, still held him in enormous respect. I would have loved to see him play, as much as any other goalkeeper there has been.

John Thomson is perhaps a fraction less well known in England than these other two. The only one of the three whose accident was fatal, it is hard at this range of years (he died in 1931) to be sure how much of his enormous popularity came as a result of his death. In death he became an icon, of sporting grace and skill. Yet it is certain that he was a very popular goalkeeper before he died. He was young, but he really does seem to have been as gifted as his posthumous reputation insists. Jimmy McGrory, the Celtic goalscorer, who knew him well, said: 'He was not just a goalkeeper, he was a great natural athlete. He was not big but he had a magnificently developed body with all the grace and litheness of an Olympic gymnast. He had not big hands but he had neat hands and I have never seen hands that were safer in clutching a ball.' It is well attested that he once, in a game between Celtic and Queen's Park, *caught* a penalty kick from Bob Gillespie, a great player with a famously hard shot, with his hands placed on top and bottom of the ball, against all the rules of good practice, his arms straight out as though he were contemptuous even of the possibility that he might not make a safe catch.

He seemed too frail for the goalkeeping of the day. He habitually caught centres well outside the six-yard box. He was capped for Scotland while very young (he died at twenty-two). He played, for example, in a match between the English and Scottish leagues at Birmingham in 1928, when Scotland, badly outplayed, lost by only two goals to one:

Only John Thomson stood between the English League side and the complete humiliation of the Scots. On one occasion he was on his knees to save a point-blank drive and the ball spun to Hine, the Leicester City inside-forward who stood unmarked twenty yards from the goal line. Here was the perfect situation for him, for his forte was the powerful, thumping shot, hit deliberately. It was the shot that great inside forwards of the day had time to unleash, for the marking then was not so tight or the tackling so fiercely fast.

Ernie Hine hit the shot full on his instep and John Thomson was still on his knees as the ball streaked towards the goal, directed to slip under the crossbar and lodge in the roof of the net. And then with a great gymnast's leap John Thomson rose and in a blur of action his body arched and his arms stretched and his fingers reached the ball and its path was bent and it rose to clear the crossbar. It was for such saves as this that it was written of him that he 'had the spring of a jaguar and the effortless grace of a skimming swallow'.[4]

In 1931, in the same inter-league fixture, at White Hart Lane this time, Scotland lost 7–3, yet Thomson's goalkeeping was still much admired:

The goal that day was a concert platform for him and on it he received modestly the adulation due to a virtuoso. The performance was climaxed by a flourish that did not matter except to show his abundant talent.

The English centre-forward burst through after a running pass but not before the referee had whistled offside. He was furious with frustration and, as John Thomson came out to retrieve the ball for the free kick the centre-forward lashed at it. Straight at the goalkeeper it flew rising over his head but he, without breaking his leisurely walking stride, reached up, held the ball and continued his walk and placed it for the free kick. The nonchalance of the action did not hide the skill of the clutch and the cheering and applause must have been the greatest ever for a non-save.[5]

There are enough other saves to suggest that Thomson really was seen to be something exceptional before his death made it impossible to be objective. He seems to have specialized (if one can call it that; at least he frequently enough managed it that critics particularly noticed) in changing the shape of a dive in mid-air. He did this famously against 'Peerie' Cunningham of Kilmarnock in a League game, and in an international against England at Hampden in March 1931, when he improbably stretched a dive to twice its length to push around the post a shot (from Gordon Hodgson) which had been deflected further from him than he expected.

Admired when alive, his death provoked one of those outpourings of sentiment that football produces every so often, when the huge emotional investment of supporters in their players is cut from its ordinary outlet on match days. There was a lot of sentimental guff in the papers, but at the same time it was perfectly clear that there was also genuine and widespread popular grief. Thomson's death and his funeral became a national event, like the funeral of a war hero. A Mr T. Smith wrote a poem about it.

Hail and farewell! we say of those
Who come, and pass too soon,
The broken arc, the blasted rose,
The life cut short ere noon.

Hail and farewell to you, Dear John,
More regal than a king,
More graceful than the fleet-limbed fawn,

Your year ends at its spring.

The athlete rare who typified
All that is best in life,
Your brilliant deeds! the death you died!
Our lovely lad from Fife.

The unerring eye, the master touch
More buoyant than the ball!
The fearless heart, the powerful clutch,
The genius praised by all.

The squirrel's swift leap, the falcon's flight,
The clear quick-thinking brain:
Alas these were yours for our delight
Never, alas! again.

We did not need your death to tell
You were the sportsman true.
We bow to Fate, Hail and Farewell!
We shall remember you.[6]

Heartfelt and genuine enough, no doubt, but it doesn't compare to the finest poem yet written on a goalkeeper, the lament for Ferenc Platko by the great Spanish anarchist poet Rafael Alberti, with its repeated wailing promise never to forget.[7]

Football has had its share of tragedies, of course, and it knows public mourning all too well. Some have been avoidable, the result of indifference to the foot-soldiers in the crowds or brutality by them. Stands have collapsed or caught alight. Supporters have rioted or been trapped. But there is something that distinguishes those accidents which befall players, full in the public eye. What they do is deprive the fans with brutal suddenness of a player or players they had expected to take years to fade away. One thinks of the air crashes at Superga and Munich, and the more recent one which destroyed the promising Zambian national team. Supporters think of footballers as their own, and untimely death, like theft, prevents them from enjoying their property for the full time they had expected. No doubt the Busby Babes were as brilliant a football team as they were said to be after the air wreck had destroyed them as an eleven. They had done enough for the later legend to be soundly based. But football isn't like that. All supporters know the fickleness of football in more mundane matters than these big and heart-wrenching accidents. A loss of form, an unlucky divot, a row between a player and a coach, all these and many more ordinary little things have a habit of altering the certainties and spicing them with doubt. The tragedies have a way of freezing this kaleidoscopic whirling of football into uncharacteristically solid, doubt-free axioms.

John Thomson was a marvellous goalkeeper in the making, a marvellous goalkeeper already very largely made. On 5 September 1931, four or five hours after being quite accidentally kicked in the head, he died in the Victoria Infirmary, Glasgow. At that moment, supporters were deprived of the ebb and surge his career would have furnished from then on. It is precisely that tide that we enjoy following, in any sport. Thomson, as it happened, died at the zenith of his career, but is remembered as a great talent hinted at but only partially fulfilled. It might have gone wrong. He could have faded as other athletes fade, for any one of dozens of ordinary human or ordinary sporting reasons, and thought and memory about him would have been more complex, richer.

Fans don't pretend to be devastated by the death of a John Thomson. They really are. The puzzle is that goalkeepers are not normally seen as heroes. For lots of reasons, some of them unfair, our relations with goal-keepers are too fraught with disappointment and doubt for that to be possible. The distraught reverence that followed Thomson's death was ordinary enough as a response to the death of a *sportsman*; it compares, for example, to the worldwide reaction to the death of Ayrton Senna. But there are not many such public expressions of how much fine goalkeeping means to us.

When Bill Brown kept Tottenham in that game in Bratislava he did something on a par with anything in sport. The first British success in the European compe-titions depended on it, so the stakes were high enough. The skill, the artistry, the imagination he had to use were masterly. The circumstances (I mean the hard ice and the cold) were thoroughly adverse, the opposition among the most feared in the world. If you ask me, there should be a statue to Bill Brown for what he did that day. I have no doubt at all that by any reasonable standard what he did was heroic. Brown was a Scottish goalkeeper too, remember. Yet we erect (at least in Scotland) meta-phorical statues in the memory of John Thomson, but not to Brown. It takes the hideous hand of tragedy to give goalkeepers a status in our affection equal to that we grant to other players without tragedy, and even then it is hardly guaranteed.

Gordon Banks made an effort (that was genuinely heroic, if you like) to continue playing after he had lost the sight of one eye. But goalkeeping depends so much on judgement of distance and angle that he was unable to do it. Close an eye, and try to catch a tennis ball lobbed gently at you to see how much he was asking of himself. He nearly made it, too, playing enough in the United States to win the NASL (North American Soccer League) Goalkeeper of the Year award after his first year. (He had hesitated to accept his American offer for fear, as he put it, 'that they were going to turn me into some sort of circus freak. "Roll up, roll up, and see the world's only one-eyed goalkeeper . . ." '[8]) Banks was not treated as a hero. This amazing goalkeeper, Britain's only one ever to win the World Cup, found it hard to get work after his retirement. Neither the FA nor the clubs had the imagination or the honour to give him a job as a coach. He knew everything there was to know about goalkeeping, and almost as much about other aspects of the game. You would have imagined that if honour and respect and decent gratitude were lacking, self-interest (that more powerful motive in football) would have made some team snap him up for a handsome salary. But while nobody held him in obloquy, nobody did much to help either.

Trautmann made a good recovery from his accident. (How is another question. It was some days before it was properly diagnosed as a broken neck, during which he not only finished the final, making a couple more head-jarring saves in the process, but also went to an osteopath afterwards, who slapped his neck around to try to relieve the 'stiffness'.) If anything, it added a little to his mystique. Manchester City fans had revered him as a worthy successor to Frank Swift, and a large part of his playing reputation had to do with his courage. His accident made that courage plainer for others to see. Trautmann, like Banks, was also genuinely heroic off the field: he managed to make the transition from enemy alien to much-loved local. He is an impressive man, yet we remember him, as a man, hardly at all. We remember him as an accident.

Hero-status is a suspect thing in sport as it is everywhere else, and not wholly to be aimed at or sought after. But of all the positions on a football field which deserve it, the goalkeeper is the one most frequently passed by. Small boys, prone by some twist of the developing brain more to hero-worship than anybody else, rarely put their goalkeeper on a pedestal as high as their centre-forward or their winger. And in the past, in the great collective memory of small boyhood that is the history of football, the goalkeepers get left out or diminished with a frequency that amounts to exposure of the peculiarly grudging affection we have had for them. Peter Shilton, when it comes down to it, did more to win the European Cup for Nottingham Forest than Brian Clough. Yet Clough is the five-star folk-hero, and Shilton sulkily respected by a public which remembers him without much warmth.

At a less stratospheric level, the story is endlessly repeated. All those goalkeepers in weakish sides, keeping them in competitions longer than they deserve. All those goalkeepers who warmed a season or a decade and then got forgotten by all except the anoraks among their own followers. How can the goalkeepers become just names in record books when the outfield players become the staple of pub conversation and misty nostalgia for a generation after they have quit? It *is* endless, I am afraid. But take just one or two names at hazard. Mervyn Day is now a competent manager for Carlisle United, still in football, worthily working away. But in 1975, while playing for West Ham, he was the Professional Footballers' Association Young Player of the Year, an unheard-of compliment for a goalkeeper. Day could work miracles then, did it as a matter of course. I didn't see him often, but I guess, what with television and the odd visit to the ground, I saw him enough. All I think I need say is that some people were lucky enough to have seen the Ballet Russe, others had Picasso draw on napkins for them, some heard Casals play the cello, and I saw Mervyn Day. His *career* was not especially distinguished, but that has got nothing to do with it. His goalkeeping could light a flare on a Saturday afternoon which would burn brightly all week, all season, and which still smoulders now.

I have the advantage that Day was playing when I was the right age to be impressed, and that's fine; if you like to put it that way, he was of my own personal golden age of goalkeeping. Remember Nigel Spink, coming on to play what I think was his first-ever first-class game (he may have played a handful before) in the European Cup Final for Aston Villa? He replaced Jimmy Rimmer, who'd broken a finger or a thumb, and he held Bayern Munich away like Horatius holding the bridge. Or Paul Cooper, who for so long made Ipswich Town able to compete with bigger, richer clubs than themselves? None of these is despised, you understand. They all have good, if dated, professional reputations as solid performers. Other people's golden ages will be different; I have of course heard people remember other goalkeepers with a gently affectionate respect. Oh, yes, says one, George Farm, he was a great goalkeeper. And John Jackson, remember him? But if you followed a team the chances are that it wasn't quite good enough. The goalkeeper, in the end, let you down. No matter that in reality he may well have concealed the deficiencies of others; disappointment is one of the fundamental emotions in football, and the goalkeeper is the natural focus for it. It is a mean kind of respect we have, which quenches lukewarm gratitude to goalkeepers in the freezing waters of disappointment.

To put it at its simplest, every football team that has been good enough to win affection, whether for one single game, a 'giant-killing', or a relegation threatened and averted, or for a span of games, a season or a competition or a generation has had a goalkeeper who has done incredible things. Even if we agree to a handful of exceptions, where a weak goalkeeper has been shielded by his colleagues, even carried by them, we still have hundreds and hundreds of marvellous athletes lost to all but the most devoted guardians of the faith. It is in the nature of sport that it should elevate us to heights most of which are swiftly forgotten, and there is no doubt that football nostalgia has been dragged too far on the back of the modern explosion in the marketing of sport. Football is big business but it is also popular culture, and the culture has recently been bullied by the business. But goalkeeping is just too difficult; even the marketing people haven't quite got us to the point where we can equably consider goalkeepers as celebrities like any other.

The modern marketing of celebrities is the marketing of blandness; even where the occasional rock star is encouraged to misbehave, he misbehaves blandly, so as to attract the largest possible number of people (who are called market-share). Goalkeepers aren't like that. They walk, like Blondin, a tightrope between triumph and disaster. They resist being marketed because we can never regard what they do as bland. And we, deprived in their case of the enormous commercial assistance to memory that keeps outfield players enthroned as celebrities long after they have ceased playing, simply forget them. Or we remember unfairly, using the goalkeepers as scapegoats of nostalgia as we used them as scapegoats in their day.

On the day when Gordon Banks made his great save from Pele's header in Guadalajara, England were facing the team that heads many best-ever lists. Most football fans can make a good start at naming that great Brazilian side of 1970. Pele, Jairzinho, Tostão, Rivelino, Carlos Alberto, Gerson (although Gerson didn't play in the England game, he played in the even more famous final against Italy). But who was the goalkeeper? Probably not as talented as his immaculate Brazilian predecessor, Gilmar, and always accused of weaknesses against high centres (if he was so obviously weak in that department, why did Alf Ramsey not play wingers against him, and bombard him until he spilled one?), he was still an astonishing goalkeeper. If you're a fan, you're getting frustrated by now. Yes, yes, but what was his name? Only the goalkeeper of the 'greatest team ever', and his name escapes you for a moment. That's how it is with goalkeepers.

Felix. Of course, Felix the Cat, and if we remember him at all it is only for the peculiar . . . felicity of his name. I'll tell you about Felix. England lost that game 1–0, the goal scored by Jairzinho. They should have won. Jeff Astle, on as a substitute, missed a straightforward chance that should have out-Spraked his memory for ever. It was incompetence pure and simple, far worse than the mistakes Peter Bonetti was excoriated for in the same competition. Alan Ball missed (he scraped the bar) another. Francis Lee headed feebly straight into Felix's arms. And Felix saved twice, brilliantly, at the feet of Bobby Charlton; Charlton, more feared abroad even than he was here, the very epitome of ruthless English finishing, who must have had a major advantage just by having the ball in a scoring position. Twice Felix did his stuff and prevented Charlton from doing his, in a game that Englishmen would certainly remember for ever if it had been otherwise. And because he's the goalkeeper we forget his name.

So it goes on. The goalkeeper of Michel Platini's French side from the mid-1980s? Of the Dutch 'Total Football' team of the 1974 World Cup? Who was the goalkeeper? The goalkeeper of Helenio Herrera's polyglot

Barcelona side of the early 1960s?[9] It isn't a quiz. Yet I'll bet that readers have to flick through to the notes before saying 'Of course!' The point is that goalkeepers frighten us by what they do, and they frighten us by what they don't do. Whenever a goalkeeper is involved in the play the spectators aren't cool. It's too close, too risky, and the result is that we don't have the same affection for them as their team-mates. Even the most long-serving, the most consistent goalkeepers struggle for a place in fan-memory half as eminent as players with half their gifts. We don't really understand just how gifted goalkeepers are, and when we do understand something of what they do, we don't like it one bit, for it makes us very, very nervous. Result? Not quite oblivion, but something close to it.

William Foulke, the great Foulke who had tried so hard to entertain as well as prevent goals, ended on the beach at Blackpool saving shots from all-comers at a penny a go. When Sir Stanley Matthews had a testimonial on 29 April 1963, he played against an All-Star international XI which included Schnellinger, Pluskal, Popluhar, Masupost, Kubala, di Stefano and Puskas. At the end of the game, Stan (as he then was) was carried off the field on Lev Yashin's shoulders. It has always been like that. Glory has an easy ride, but what it sits upon may just be more glorious still.

It may be that this picture of the goalkeeper underappreciated and imperfectly understood is beginning to change. There has always been an appeal in the goalkeeper's distinctness. He is the soloist in an orchestra. He looks different, odd rules apply to him and to no one else. And on the rare occasions when there is a fraction of glory to be had in the trenches of the goal-mouth, his team-mates tend to think him welcome to it.

In 1951, in his customary jocular style, Percy Young had this to say about goalkeepers:

> It is significant that very few teams appear to have bad goal-keepers. The standard is remarkable. The reason is clear. The goalkeeper is an individual and is allowed to retain his individuality, even to the extent of remaining unnumbered [which they were, at one time. At another, players were numbered consecutively through both teams, and one goalkeeper would be Number 1 and the other Number 22]. Small boys, who have, however, large egos, want to become goalkeepers. In that calling they may shine in unshared glory (they are, too, allowed to kick the ball further than anyone else) and order their team-mates. They may also go home from school with dirty hands and impunity. I asked the other day, 'What are you going to be when you grow up?'
>
> 'A goalkeeper or a referee.'
>
> I understand that at present, aged seven, my catechumen performs both functions simultaneously; at least to his own satis-faction.
>
> The fact that small boys take to goalkeeping in large numbers (again it may be recalled that two boys can play football provided that there is a goalkeeper and he, of the two, is the more important) allows the best to specialize early.[10]

He made a serious point. Other players have to come into contact with coaches to discover their best position;

goalkeepers know that they are goalkeepers before that, and have already acquired the rudiments of their own manner before learning how it is thought correctly done. There are exceptions, of course, lots of them. Coaches still have a tendency to assume that large immobile boys will be central defenders and large mobile ones goalkeepers. Alan Shearer was famously rejected by Newcastle United as a boy because they put him in goal for the length of his trial. Players can migrate around the field, and the goalkeeping position, while less easily adapted to than others, has been successfully occupied by many players who started elsewhere, and successfully abandoned by players who have gone on to great things further upfield. Shearer's forward partner Les Ferdinand was a goalkeeper as a boy, for example. Sam Bartram started as an inside-forward, but in general Young's perception is right. Even as small boys, goalkeepers have a recognizable mind-set and a desire not to vanish in the collective entity of the team.

In my own case, I was as a small boy attracted to the goal very specifically for the sense of being different. I think I had few illusions about the costs of goalkeeping, the deep unease of living on that perpetually unstable balance between considerable fear and accomplishments which even as a child I knew to be trifling in fact. But I liked the wallowing in details which were mine alone, separate from those of the teams of which I was a part: the identifiably different shirt, the gloves which nobody else needed (black wool with ping-pong bat pimples sewn for grip on the fingers and palms, when I started), small details like that were a pleasure. And when there came a save beyond my own expectations, beyond those of the team too, the pleasure was individually mine and not subsumed in the collective of the team. I knew surely that the mistakes were mine also, but I suppose I found it worth it. I learnt to enjoy even those miserable trudges home after being blamed for a defeat.

Percy Young's throwaway line about dirty hands is spot on. I well remember the faintly guilty delight of pulling long trousers over bloodied muddy legs on odd occasions when there was no time for a shower before going somewhere else after a game, and the pleasure of the mud caking, unknown to anybody but me until a bath was found. Mud is one of the unsung pleasures of goalkeeping. You may have played abysmally, but if you're really coated in the stuff, from hair to boots, then nobody will ever tell you so. Watch a goalkeeper in the depths of winter when play is away from him for a while. He stands on the eighteen-yard line, and as he swings his boot and the mud flies off it in a satisfyingly liquid parabola he will be truly happy for a second. Out of the misery comes a moment of salvaged joy, although it isn't recommended to go so far as to say so to his face. As the mud clogs in his nostrils, and his legs freeze around the red-hot bruises, he might deny it, perhaps intemperately. But he knows that muddy conditions can excuse a great deal. To play well in mud is sometimes easier than to play well in the dry, and always looks much worse.

Keeping goal was always for those who wanted to be seen, and who didn't mind the occasional disasters as the price. The goalkeeper-showman is as old as the game. Fatty Foulke used to station two tiny ball-boys on either side of the goals when he was at Chelsea. Seen beyond Foulke's enormous bulk, the effect was to make the goal seem a little smaller. Bruce Grobbelaar comes to mind again, with his hand stands and his willingness to wear silly hats, and the exaggerated quaking at the knees while waiting for a penalty. Years ago, Albert Iremonger played for Notts County in much the same way. A great goalkeeper when he had to be, but a showman and a crowd-pleaser when there was time for all that.

Somehow, that aspect of goalkeeping seems to have come forward a great deal recently. Safety first is the obvious rule. It has to be, and a crowd-pleaser who lets in soft goals won't remain a crowd-pleaser very long. But after that essential caution, it has become more apparent of late that goalkeeping suits a particular modern sensibility. Individual sports have been fast catching up with team games in popularity; we seem to have an insatiable desire for individuals to admire, even if that desire is largely stoked by a voracious marketing industry. Marketing men think nothing of promoting one of a team beyond the team as a whole. Think of Michael Jordan. The old idea that everybody in the team shares in its reputation is under serious erosion. (Although how much it ever represented more than a pious hope of the public-school ethic it largely came from is a serious question. Was W.G. Grace or C.B. Fry a team player? Fry, that epitome of the all-round Edwardian sporting gent, even had a press agent. Was the great Corinthian centre-forward G.O. Smith not more than an equal component of a constellation?)

Goalkeeping suits this version of sport as the triumph of the individual. In the era of the sound-bite and the photo-opportunity, you can guarantee that when highlights of football games are repeated over and again, there will be one player in all the most dramatic shots, and audiences need make no effort to identify him, as he wears a different shirt. Make no mistake, he never was in reality a disconsolate figure, waiting forlornly for the ball to whizz unstoppably past him. We thought of him like that only because goals were the crude definition of what football was all about. But now we are urged to think differently. The otherness of goalkeeping is itself an attraction. If all your nine-year-old friends are wearing replica team shirts, how tempting to be sold the (even more) garish one, the one with an enormous number one, for 'individual', stretched down its back.

Incidentally, the laws of football say that goalkeepers shall wear a different coloured jersey. It used to be the norm for goalkeepers to wear the shorts and socks of their team, and a goalkeeping top, preferably a yellow roll-neck made of wool, which stank when wet, as modelled by almost all the goalkeepers of the past. The idea was that referees could identify the owner of a hand which touched the ball in a scrum of players by the colour of the sleeve. But some goalkeepers wanted to be smarter, wanted to be recognized. Lev Yashin appeared all in black, Peter Bonetti appeared all in green from top to toe. Now kit manufacturers as a matter of routine sell goalkeeping *outfits*, different in all but the sponsors' logo from the team strip. Jorge Campos, goalkeeper-cum-centre-forward, designs his own kit, and wins the luridity competition hands down. The underlying point is a serious one, even if not terribly important in the great scheme of things. If goalkeepers are valued members of the team, they should wear the team colours so far as possible. They no longer do; they are that much less visibly of the team, and that much more isolated.

When the World Cup was ludicrously staged in the United States, practically the only country in the world without a serious football league, when the international administrators blithely accepted that the competition would 'kick-start' a boom in football there, the US team chose a showman-goalkeeper, Tony Meola, in preference to Jurgen Sommer and Kasey Keller. Both were probably better goalkeepers, but Keller was miles better. Keller is one of the modern masters. But Meola would have been ideal to hang marketing strategies from, if the American markets had ever been any more than tepidly interested. He was loud, and he was there; his rivals, in search of better football, played abroad. Goalkeeping is ideal for marketing. This identifiable figure, the best athlete in the side, always involved in the crises, seems to be a promotions man's dream. Even I wouldn't say that you have to be an intellectual to keep goal, but there is no denying that goalkeepers have to have a very acute version of what is known in the trade as the 'footballing brain'. It all hangs together. We should expect goal-keepers to be the figure heads of the new relationship between football and commerce. And yet, it hasn't really happened.

Goalkeepers have always had a chance to endorse products for the sports market. Peter Bonetti marketed green cotton gloves, for example (they were abysmal in the wet), and Peter Shilton once sold white goalkeeping jerseys and chest expanders. Now Premiership goalkeepers expect a contract with a glove manufacturer at the very least, and hopeful shoppers can insist on whatever they fancy: the 'Tim Flowers' glove by name, for example. In recent years, there have been bits and pieces to suggest that it might spread a bit beyond this basic level. Both David James of Liverpool and Ian Walker of Tottenham did a bit of modelling before it was really clear that they were first-rate goalkeepers, and I dare say others have done so too. Why not? David Seaman, brilliant long before his penalty saves in the 1996 European Championship, but only nationally famous since, has done bits and pieces of advertising, as well he might, a perquisite of modern fame. But the explosion hasn't happened. Goalkeepers are still reckoned somehow not to be quite the thing in the very black-and-white cardboard world of advertising. I can just hear all those 'creatives' in advertising agencies: they let goals in, you see, and the client wouldn't like that. And it is true that when goalkeeping metaphors are used in advertising, they tend to be very obviously negative. Not so long ago the Inland Revenue threatened to make citizens pay penalties for something or other. Huge posters of a goal appeared, with some pun on the word 'penalty' to justify them. But they had to be drawn cartoon-style, to try to suggest that being dunned for tax was funny.

Goalkeeping has the taint of 'bad image' about it.

The image has nothing at all to do with what goalkeepers actually do, but there you are. In this very myopic view, the goalkeeper is always a 'loser', however brilliant. Sepp Maier of West Germany didn't let in a goal for 475 minutes of football in World Cup competition, from the penalty he conceded to Holland in the first minute of the 1974 final to the fifth game in 1978. Dino Zoff conceded no goal in internationals for 1,142 minutes of play. Chris Woods conceded no goal for 1,196 minutes in the season 1986/87 while playing for Glasgow Rangers. These are miraculous things to have done, the stuff of sporting emotion. But at the end of these huge sequences of near perfection, inevitably, a goal. Loser. It's absurd. Now of course Maier and Zoff and Woods haven't done badly out of football, but I wonder what kinds of superstars they'd be if they'd played to that standard in any other position. I would make a perfectly serious argument that Peter Schmeichel has been the greatest player in English football for years. Do you see him all over the hoardings? Does he have a tenth of the advertising pull of half a dozen of his team-mates? Is he paid as much? If the people who want to advertise things choose figureheads their customers are supposed to aspire to emulate or simply admire, are we to understand that the great British public wants no part of the finest goalkeeper there has been this generation, and maybe ever?

'What's the time?' ran the quip after England beat Scotland 9–3 in 1961, and back came the answer: 'Nearly ten past Haffey.' Poor Frank Haffey, substituting for Bill Brown that day, and ever since the yardstick against which all supposedly incompetent Scottish goalkeepers are measured. Haffey actually posed for a newspaper photograph in front of Big Ben with the hands at nine minutes past the hour, which helped to fan the flames; he was thought not to care, not to realize the magnitude of the disappointment he had aroused. By that broad brush are all goalkeepers tarred.

It isn't that all goalkeepers are unpopular all of the time. The leading handful have been nearly as popular as any sportsman could be, held in great affection by crowds almost as the defining personality of a team. A few lucky goalkeepers even find their errors forgiven, as part of a strange rueful pact that crowds can make between entertainment and winning. Tony Macedo comes to mind in this category, the Fulham goalkeeper of the late 1950s and early 1960s. Macedo seemed ultra-confident, with his yelling, and his charging all around the penalty area, and his willingness to barge his defenders off the ball if he felt he should have it. When it seemed likely once that he would be picked for an international instead of Eddie Hopkinson, he was asked whether he was worried about his international prospects. 'I'm not worried,' he blustered, 'but Hopkinson is.' He was very much a showman in what used to be thought of as the 'continental' style, flashy and acrobatic, yet he betrayed his nerves by chewing his nails furiously. 'If I stopped biting my nails, it would all go. Everything.' He once had his ribs broken by a back-pass from Fulham team-mate Tosh Chamberlain, precisely the kind of hideous misadventure that somehow endears goalkeepers to crowds.

Macedo more or less single-handedly got Fulham to

the 1958 FA Cup semi-finals. There, he played nightmarishly badly and took the blame for Manchester United winning 5–3. All sorts of excuses were examined: he had chosen to wear no gloves, chief among them. But the United team, rebuilt by Jimmy Murphy after the Munich crash, had an enormous tide of sympathetic popularity behind it, and although Macedo denied it, it was probable that the occasion rather overwhelmed him. After the game, Macedo was interviewed by Clement Freud, who asked him with something less than perfect charm, 'Didn't you feel badly?' Macedo answered, 'If it hadn't been for me they wouldn't have got as far as they did, so they've got nothing to kick about.'[11] The Fulham supporters didn't seem to mind unduly. It was as if one poor performance couldn't wipe out the debt they acknowledged they had to a fine goalkeeper, perhaps a finer one than they deserved.

Maybe it is precisely because the goalkeeper looks so fallible that crowds can take to him. It has always been clear that one of the things crowds like is unstinting effort on behalf of their team. The spectators feel that if they were picked, they might not be very good, but they would give their all for the colours. Hard-working loyal players are forgiven much more than fancy-dans. Crowds don't yell for cunning flicks and feints, they yell 'Get stuck in!' The goalkeeper doesn't do all that chugging around the midfield, but he always looks as though he's prepared to get well stuck in. It's partly that the goalkeeper ends up lying down so often: Greater love hath no man than he lay down his life for his friends. That danger, visible in one horizontal figure among all the vertical ones, is loved by the crowd. They feel that they would do no less, that their blind love for the team would look like that if they were asked, self-sacrificial and heedless of risk. Win, lose, or draw, the goalkeeper gets knocked about at least a little every game. He gets covered in mud. He looks like he's doing-or-dying, and that's what the crowds want their men to look like. And if, like a Ted Sagar, or a Sam Bartram, or like so many goalkeepers who seem just to play on long after you'd expect them to pack it all in, he goes on looking like that season after season, then the crowds come to regard him almost as the fan's representative on the field. You can see he's trying his best. And if he gets beaten all ends up every so often, well, he's only human.

It takes a long career to win that kind of affection. Young goalkeepers represent all the nervous fear of the crowd, the fear of losing, above all, but also the fear of humiliation. After they've been through that for years, goalkeepers become part of the emotional scene at the ground, like the stanchion that has blocked the view of one penalty spot from the seat you've had for twenty years. It's a curious and painful imbalance. Goalkeepers can become much-loved by the fans, but they have to take an awful lot of abuse before they get there. We have all seen a new striker become the darling of the crowd with one goal in an early game. They chant his name, dream that he will single-handedly change their fortunes. Very quickly, they forgive him his trespasses. For goalkeepers, it's either a broken neck or a minimum of ten years. And even then, the oblivion is quick to return. Somehow you never get to hear of goalkeepers of the time before your own. Young Arsenal supporters have heard a mountain of sentimental stuff about Alex James, Bernard Joy, Charles Buchan, and Cliff Bastin. Yet how many have even heard the name of George Swindin? Jack Kelsey ran the shop at Arsenal for years after he stopped playing; how many of the punters below a certain age had any idea who he was?

Yet the goalkeeper has always been allowed by the strange codes of respect which run in football to be the hero *for a day*. In 1891, on a day when it snowed hard, Burnley played Blackburn. Burnley were three up at half-time. There had been some handbags-at-three-paces stuff, and several of the Blackburn team refused to emerge for the second half. Early in the second half there were more fisticuffs, and all the remaining Blackburn Rovers players left the field with the exception of Arthur, the goalkeeper: 'As they refused to return, Mr Clegg [the referee, later Sir Charles Clegg, of Sheffield, Chairman of FA Council] directed Burnley to recommence the game, with the lone Blackburn custodian to set them at defiance – one man against eleven! In his predicament, Arthur successfully claimed for offside, but dallied so long in taking the free kick that the referee applied the closure, the score standing at 3–0 to Burnley. Old supporters still refer with pride to the unquenchable courage of Mr Arthur on that bitter and exciting day.'[12]

You might think that is how it should be in a team sport, that every player should have his turn. It doesn't work like that. Outfield, you can either score goals, any goals, bad goals if need be, just so long as you score them, or you can do something well enough so that a not very alert public and a lethargic press corps can spot it. Mark a man so well that he 'disappears' from the game, fling crosses in so that your centre-forward has merely to meet them to score, win all the loose balls in midfield, and you will get something approaching admiration for the day. But play in goal, and you normally have to work as well as any of the others *and win.* In other words, the degree of approbation that you may earn depends not on your efforts in the face of opposition alone, but to some extent on the competence of your men. I like spotting fine goalkeeping even in losing sides – like Bill Brown's game in Bratislava – and I think it far from rare. But most spectators normally only cling to a fine display of goalkeeping in defeat when everything else has been so deplorable that it is the last thing left. Goalkeepers are like any other neglected and unfavoured minority: they always have to be *better* than the other guys to get the same amount of respect.

When they manage it, you get splendid goalkeepers' games. Hugh McIlvanney once wrote that 'Most goalkeepers, if they told the truth, would have to admit that they are at their happiest when they are flying around at Anfield, being heroically defiant against superior odds, making dramatic saves and getting a clap from the Kop. Their side may lose 1–0 but they get a good press – "If it had not been for some miraculous saves, the score would have been six." '[13] McIlvanney was making the point that Peter Shilton, almost alone, was not like that. He was right, of course – most goalkeepers *are* at their happiest in those circumstances. But not because they are milking adulation. It is only in those circumstances that the constant niggling refrain of things that might go wrong ceases for a second. It's only when under huge opposition pressure, therefore, that goalkeepers are free to worry about what is actually happening, here and now, rather than about the percentage chance of the next possibility or the one after that. And goalkeepers, like any other athletes, play better and enjoy it more when the adrenalin rush has been provoked. It is very hard indeed to stay sharp and alert when your own side is doing all the attacking and the ball is far away most of the time. It is easier (although of course it may be a great deal more unpleasant) to stay quick because you are in the game, right in the middle of it, than to force yourself to know you *may* be in it at any time. A side gets overrun. A goalkeeper holds out. It happens every so often. And when it does, pay attention. It is one of the most exciting, most agonizing things to watch in sport. If that doesn't get you going, perhaps you should watch another game.

In those circumstances, the goalkeeper may well be on the losing side. If that's what it takes to see a display of great goalkeeping, who cares? Although I grant you that if your team happens to be giving you that particular pleasure *every* week, then perhaps something is seriously wrong north of the goalkeeper. So, for example, when Jimmy Greaves played his first game for Tottenham, in December 1961, he scored a hat-trick and Blackpool were beaten 5–2. Tony Waiters, in the Blackpool goal, behind defenders of the quality of Jimmy Armfield, apparently played out of his skin. 5–2? So what? Greaves was on fire, Waiters was on fire. It's not everything in football, but it would have been worth seeing. There are hundreds of examples of this, but somehow they don't accumulate to the credit of the goalkeepers. Harry Hibbs of Birmingham, in the 1931 FA Cup Final against West Bromwich Albion 'never did a better afternoon's work than in this valiant, unavailing rearguard action against the Albion's strong attack'.[14] Choose any goalkeeper, and you can find a similar story.

Goalkeeping is at its obvious best in adversity. Ted Ditchburn, of Tottenham:

> I pass on to the occasions when a keeper can really shine. And unfortunately for your own team, these periods come when your side is usually having a bad game so that you are given plenty to do.
>
> No keeper can get really warmed up unless he is worked hard. To make one or two good saves a match is most goalkeepers' usual habit, but to give such a show as will have the crowd roaring and yelling, the poor keeper has to be subjected to a rain of shots and a storm of attacks.
>
> This is a sad state of affairs, I must confess, for it assumes you won't shine unless your side is overrun; and though it is possible to finish on the winning side when you have given a brilliant display, more often than not you are bound to finish on the losing end.
>
> The reason I think most goalkeepers get a special cheer from the crowd after a wonder display is because the home team has won after all. Sometimes I wonder whether those cheers would come if the keeper had deprived the home team of a point or two they otherwise fully earned.
>
> Maybe I'm being cynical . . . For it has been my lot to

encounter nothing but goodwill towards me on most of the grounds on which I have appeared and the crowd, especially the fervent fans behind the goal, have never been slow in their appreciation and their applause.

Other players in other parts of the field, on the move as they invariably are, do not hear the crowd most of the time. But the keeper, alone in his little cage, not only hears the crowd but is sometimes tempted to talk back with them or at them.

It is the goalkeeper who knows what the crowd is thinking and what they are yelling and just how they are feeling. That is, unless he is so overrun that he has absolutely no respite. In which case, he probably plays a blinder . . .[15]

This is the introduction to Ditchburn's own description of his 'greatest game', when he got a standing ovation at St James's Park, Newcastle, losing 1–0 in January 1947. It reads as though it was taken straight off a tape recorder, and the knowledge is of one who has been there. In fact, Ditchburn was unlucky. Towards the end of the war he was posted to the Far East, and by the time he came back Frank Swift was ensconced in the England goalkeeping position. Ditchburn was a great catcher of the ball. He'd catch it in flight, at any height, any angle, and it never seemed to bounce away from him when he hit the ground. He would do this in winning games, and he did it as well on days when they lost. It is inevitably so. When the great Scottish team of 1928 which became known as the Wembley Wizards outclassed England at Wembley (the King and Queen of Afghanistan were present, the score was 5–1, the moral victory far greater), Ted Hufton of West Ham played the perfect game-in-adversity. 'Only the brilliance of Hufton in the English goal prevented an absolute rout . . .', 'Hufton saved England from the biggest hiding ever . . .' He was an acrobatic goalkeeper, a brilliant one, who once saved eleven out of eighteen penalties taken against him in a two-year period. Why shouldn't he shine on a day when his team was outclassed?

The brutal fact is always the same: it only takes one imperfection in an otherwise brilliant afternoon for a goalkeeper either to have or to be blamed for a disaster. So that on the rare days when the disaster is clearly the whole team's, not the goalkeeper's alone, it becomes easier to see him as the hero, even if he loses. It's nearly self-explanatory. To have a really spectacular game, the goalkeeper has to be involved a great deal. And whenever that happens, you can be sure his team are not protecting him as much as they should.

There was a game in March of 1996 between Newcastle and Manchester United. Newcastle had led the League all season, playing the kind of convincingly beautiful football which had gone a long way to persuading us that the English game could be as fluent and as seductive as we always hope it might be. Manchester United had gradually hauled them back, reducing the margin like a good fast horse coming up late on a flagging leader. The race wasn't run, and either side could with justice have won the Championship when they met at St James's Park; first and second, with a gloriously rebuilt young Liverpool side drawing nearer to both in third place. If Newcastle should win, the thinking went, they would be in the home stretch and looking good.

Manchester United could give themselves hope, and Liverpool too, by winning, but nothing would be guaranteed them if they did. Precisely the kind of game from which British audiences have learnt to expect disappointment, the risks of defeat weighing so heavily on managers and players that a kind of safety-first, belt-and-braces, give-nothing-away fog descends on inspiration and chokes it.

Unexpectedly, gloriously, it turned out the other way. Newcastle left out Keith Gillespie whom they had brought from Manchester United in an inspired exchange-plus-money deal for Andy Cole, a St James's Park darling who had gone thoroughly and apparently permanently off the boil as soon as he had moved to Old Trafford (leading bad-mouths, my own among them, to note how easy it can be to look like a high-class striker when Peter Beardsley is doing your work for you). In his place played their new star, the Colombian Faustino Asprilla. The Newcastle attack looked fabulous, Asprilla and Les Ferdinand served by Peter Beardsley. And for the first half, and in particular the first half of the first half, they played football of near perfection. Asprilla juggled with the ball, running at full pelt like a kid in the park. He embarrassed good-class defenders every time he came near them. Ferdinand did the opposite, simply getting rid of defenders, getting yards of space for Beardsley to pass into. Ferdinand didn't have the control, perhaps not even the balance of his new colleague, but he was doing as much damage to the defence. It could have been a rout. It should have been a rout. It looked for much of the game as though it was going to turn into that rout. But Peter Schmeichel was in the Manchester United goal, and having a good day at the office.

He saved everything, at feet, in the air, deflected, scuffed, or hit true. Only once did he even seem beatable, when Philippe Albert hit a free kick over the wall curling viciously away to Schmeichel's left, and clattered the bar. Pundits immediately said the words 'beats Schmeichel', 'giving Schmeichel no chance', but they were wrong. The television coverage replayed it several times, from several angles. Albert had indeed hit a wonderful shot, as sweetly timed and as satisfyingly executed as the single stroke of an axe which splits a log right through. But the ball hit the crossbar in the lower third of its circumference; more than half of it was above the bar. To dip under the bar, it would have had to be quite a lot lower, far more than the inch or two sporting cliché demands. And there, plainly there in good time on the slow-motion replay, within four inches of the bottom of the ball, was Schmeichel's hand, wrist locked, ready to flip it away, tip it over, or push it out. I don't know what he would have done if the ball had been to hand, but I know for certain he genuinely, breathtakingly, had it truly covered. Those are the tolerances under which truly great goalkeeping operates: any lower, and it had to be lower to score, and it was Schmeichel's; higher, and it was a miss.

Schmeichel was flawless that day. He threw short and long, always thoughtfully, and always usefully. He also twice kicked monstrous distances, once too far, into Pavel Srnicek's hands (his opposite goalkeeper, down there at the peaceful end of the pitch) on one single bounce, and once brilliantly into the stride of a forward – I think it was Giggs – who fluffed the good chance that resulted. He received back-passes at all speeds and in all positions from a defence near collapse with a coolness that looked like taking the mickey, just taking another few calories of energy out of the forwards by making them come to challenge him. He made eight or ten blinding stops of such refined athleticism that even in the replays, knowing what you were about to see, you couldn't quite believe that such combinations could exist. He seemed to delay his movement too long each time, forcing the forward to commit himself, refusing to anticipate and so be outwitted, bluffing that some particular space was available when in fact he had chosen it, forcing the shot where he wanted it and could deal with it. At close quarters he scared a forward line of considerable physical presence by his own indomitability. It didn't take much imagination to eliminate the lime-green quilted nylon and see him as a hero of antiquity, holding out until the enemy could rush at him no more.

He made one save at the end within three yards of his goal just by crouching and waiting and waiting longer until somebody (I forget who, and it doesn't matter) tried to push it past him to his right and squeeze a shot in as he fell. Schmeichel made three movements: he compressed himself even lower to get spring, flung his weight backwards and sideways, and then stretched an arm. It seemed to take for ever, the ball scurrying low and this big right arm like a broad green snake uncurling to its full extent. He didn't palm the ball away that time. He caught it, one-handed, and it was dead and motionless before the movement of his body had brought his chest close enough to complete the gesture and cradle it in complete protection. Schmeichel was hot that day, and everybody knew it. The television ran a telephone vote for man of the match which he won by a mile. That only happens to goalkeepers when they have done something so extraordinary that all the prejudices against them are swept aside. In the end, the game was won for Manchester United by an ordinary goal from Eric Cantona, and the championship race closed down that little bit tighter. Yet incredibly, the headlines the next day were about Cantona, who had hardly contributed to the game at all.

Ruud Gullit, the great Dutch player making his impressive punditing debut that night on television, cut short a discussion on one of Schmeichel's more unlikely saves by saying simply, 'It's his job.' He was right. You wouldn't come away from a concert by Pablo Casals amazed at his double-stopping. It's impossible. So what? Here's somebody who can do it. That, in part, is where goalkeeping is different from equally improbable sports that stop at the improbability. A high-diver twists into sculptural shapes while falling into the water, or a gymnast fluidly moves through a sequence of poses of which we would be incapable of holding just one, and there is the point. They can do it, and we can't hope to. Our admiration is fixed within circumstances as nearly ideal to them as possible. When Schmeichel starts combining thought and timing, physical grace and courage and coordination, he does it as part of a football game. He does it when somebody else wants him to, not when he chooses. The surface is not ideal. He may well be angry (Schmeichel often is, it is one of the ways he keeps his concentration sharp) at an avoidable error by a colleague that put him under the obligation, just then, of doing the impossible. Whatever he has done, he has done over the wishes of at least one player trying his damnedest to do the opposite. Immediately after he has done it, however marvellous it may have been, he knows that everything is up for total loss again. The game goes on, and he might in an instant make the mistake which wipes out ten or twelve moments of the highest brilliance. Gullit was right. It *is* his job. It's also impossible. Which is why, when one of the great goalkeeping performances comes around, we have to put aside thoughts of the team or the League or the Cup or whatever else may be at stake and take the trouble to admire it.

Schmeichel, admittedly, is no ordinary goalkeeper. But what he did that day was only a bigger version of what goalkeeping is all about, and the surprise is that goalkeepers, who, we are asked to believe, are 'there to be beaten', do something approaching that so often. Schmeichel used enormous physical resources, of course. But he also did something intellectual that day. The only way I can explain is to compare it to a great musician, improvising. The *direction* in which the performance had to go was clear. But the detail, of how each moment could be controlled, brought to its end, and then led smoothly into the next passage was always in doubt. What we, as spectators, watched was the increasing resolution of elements that seemed impossible to combine, until gradually Peter Schmeichel led us to understand that the band could get out of the difficult keys and the awkward rhythms. You can't plot a football game, but Schmeichel came as near to it that day as anybody ever could. That he was agile and brave and fast as a cobra's tongue I take almost for granted – that's what it takes, as a minimum, at that level. But he also, and this is where great goalkeeping is such perfect sport, imposed his mind on the proceedings, by grasping the terrifying intricacies with lightning understanding and imposing a logical will on them until time ran out and the oldest goalkeeping cliché of them all, the word 'unbeatable', was the only right word left. That'll do me, I'm happy to keep looking for it until I find its like again.

8. Remind Me – Who was the Goalkeeper?

A goal, you would have thought, is a goal. One point to the scoring side. But it isn't so in two critical cases. In both the onus is absurdly weighted against the defensive side of football which goalkeepers champion. It used to be that in cup competitions, that is to say knock-out competitions, a draw would lead to a match being replayed later, and again if necessary. It wasn't a perfect system: it made fans pay to see the same game over and over, it clogged up the fixture lists, and at its worst resulted in hours of unadventurous football. But at least a goal was a goal.

Now for some years, in some competitions but not all, a new rule has crept in which limits the endless replaying, and whose advantages are therefore obvious. Away goals, in the fans' universal compression, count double. That is to say in the event of a drawn aggregate score over the two legs, goals scored away from home are more valuable than those scored on one's ground. The idea was a good one. It encouraged attacking football away from home, in place of the packed defences and resolute lack of ambition that had been all that was required to get a draw. It had been possible at least to try to win the two-legged match effectively in only one of the games. It is too late to change it, and on balance, it is an innovation which has worked well enough. But we need to be clear about what it in fact did. There is no great advantage to a goalkeeper in playing at home. The crowd noises may be a little more friendly, the surface of the goal-mouth and the furniture of netting and goal-frame more familiar, but nothing that adds up to much. There is correspondingly little disadvantage to playing away. Perhaps the odd doubtful pitch which would take longer than a normal warm-up to get used to, perhaps a different arrangement of floodlighting or drainage which will affect parts of the goalkeeper's play. But certainly nothing which is recognized in the rules. Home and away grounds are circumstantial components of games, not formal ones.

Goalkeepers strain every sinew to prevent goals whatever the circumstances. To make some goals conceded more important than others is to set a different rate for parts of the goalkeeping obstacle course which are intrinsically the same. The away-goals rule works retrospectively, too, within the context of a game. An 'unimportant' goal conceded earlier can become critical in the light of later happenings. This is to place an almost intolerable strain on defenders, and to reward forwards disproportionately for performing their normal function. For some goals to 'count double' effectively implies that others count less, an impossible thing to ask goalkeepers to believe. We know in practice that some goals *are* less important than others: those 'consolation' goals scored late by well-beaten teams are one example. But these are judgements of value made precisely in the light of circumstances. The away-goals rule is not a judgement. It is a rule which for whatever laudable reasons directly contravenes the notion that goals are the way of tallying points in football. It is a contradiction of the very terms by which football games are won and lost. For a goal, any goal, to 'count double' is a direct attack on the goalkeeper.

For many years, British motorists have understood that they may not park on double yellow lines. The lines mean no parking. Then somebody invented 'red routes', with double red lines instead. What more do they mean? As they say in Ireland, no parking at all, at all. They do nothing more than confirm the discomfiture of authority with the previous prohibition. The away-goals rule is exactly parallel to that. If goalkeepers have done everything possible to prevent goals (or if not, if they at least know that their whole *raison d'être* has been called into question by conceding them), then what kind of sense can it mean to say that some 'count double'? Yet in the name of more certain outcomes to games (in the shadow, I feel, of a very American distaste for draws) we have accepted this as inevitable. Many dozens, hundreds of games have been decided by that rule. But nobody has explained why scoring one point in football should be any different to scoring another. Anything would have been preferable: counting corners, as a measure of the degree of attacking football; counting fouls, as a way of rewarding those who play the beautiful game; that old idea of changing to bigger goals at the end is very appealing – the game would be the same, only the chances of scoring a point would increase; even a penalty competition, appended as it were with apologies to the drawn game. There was a suggestion that after the draw, each team should lose a player every few minutes until they were playing five-a-side, when a goal was likely. Rather, as used to happen, a coin toss, which had the merit of clear separation. The football was drawn when a result was desirable? A winner was found by utterly unconnected means. Tough enough on the loser, certainly, but at least there was no suspicion that some kind of para-football had taken the place of the real thing. As it stands, we accept a nonsense of the whole idea of the loss of a goal, which happens, which just happens, to put even more stress on the infallibility of goalkeepers.

And now a newer version of the same thing has arrived in the shape of the 'golden goal', a goal scored in extra time after a drawn game which ends the match there and then. It is a grown-up version of the scoring system kids use, when they have been playing all afternoon in the park and their mums call them in for their tea. 'Next one to score is the winner!' they shout, before frantically finishing the game. Less pernicious than the away-goals rule, because they don't alter the value of the goal as such, the golden goal still smacks of a desire for highlights (in the televisual sense) sufficiently desperate to displace the real thing. Why not go straight to the golden goal, and do away with the tiresome business of a football match before it? At least with a golden goal teams learn that attack is the best form of defence. If you camp in the opposing penalty area, using all the proper footballing resources you can muster, you have every chance of winning. But in point of fact, there is always time for a little more football properly played. Only television schedules don't like that. And the people who run the schedules control football so much that they are prepared to lose parts of its essence to fit their other priorities. I've never played under the golden goal rule. I get nervous enough in the last few minutes of a game as it is. Imagine trying to catch a flighted cross under the golden goal rule, with all the time in the world for your life to flash before your eyes. Another obstacle flung at goalkeepers? So what else is new?

It all adds up. We need to be sure what we are aiming for when we tinker with the game. If we really want football to become just another quick-action contender in the great entertainment industry, we are going the right way about it. Abolish drawn games. Shorten the gaps between goals. Pretend to make 'fans' happy by encouraging huge scores. All of this plastic surgery can be achieved by constant erosion of the rights and duties of the goalkeepers. The trouble is that we have accepted, for many years, precisely that kind of perpetual attack on goalkeeping, without ever agreeing on the ultimate end it might serve. One can hesitate to accept the relentless water-torture drip-drip on goalkeepers' heads without blindly opposing all change in football. There is certainly room for improved laws. To change something like the offside law, to improve it and so remove frustration and doubt, is clearly no bad thing. Nor is it necessarily completely unacceptable to try to tailor the game to the changing needs of its customers. Obviously enough, if football is losing attention because it no longer represents the only entertainment available to the great majority of its punters, there can be nothing wrong in trying to make it more attractive yet, and to take on newer competition. But I very much question whether the mantra 'More goals!' provides the answer.

The tension between attack and defence is one of the marvellous things in football, and it is a fragile and easily upset balance. There have been times when one or the other dominated more than some spectators liked, as for example the long period after the invention of the sweeper system when all Italian league games seemed to end with only one goal. But those imbalances, the natural extremes of a constantly swinging pendulum, redress themselves in time. Coaches apply their minds to the problem, players learn new ways of working, and the pendulum edges back the other way. It is a part of the business of following football to understand such things, and all supporters clearly do enjoy keeping long-term track of these swings as they enjoy the short-term swings within a single match. To try to alter these rich, slow patterns in the growth of the game for such external reasons as the supposed desires of advertisers is a very dangerous thing to do. It's very easy to decree that goal-keepers should stand still for penalties, or that they should not play back-passes with their hands. But a pattern has gradually emerged in which goals are ever more important, and anything which can be tampered with to achieve them is up for change. Inevitably, because goalkeeping has as its main business the prevention of goals, that means making the goalkeeper's life harder.

This would be fine if the accumulation of goals were all there were to the game.

Goalkeeping is very complex but looks childishly simple. Our attitudes to it should be complex but are often reduced to a tiresome litany of clichés. We find it impossible merely to applaud goalkeepers because the terrible urgency of what they do and the terribly visible price they pay for the slightest mistake make us apprehensive even in the moments of their greatest dominance. We blame them, routinely, for faults which are clearly not theirs. At the same time, we are grateful to them for carrying that blame. We ask them to be supermen, while liking them to be fallible. We are ignorant of and impatient with the skills they have to deploy. Outright admiration, even of the very best, doesn't do.

Viz, the (not very) grown-up Newcastle-based comic, used to run a cartoon about Billy the Fish, a goalkeeper with only rudimentary hands and no feet. The joke (when it wasn't simply so absurd or so lewd that it was funny in spite of ourselves) was that a goalkeeper can't be a hero, even when he never lets in a soft one. Before that, years ago, around the 1950s, one of the comics used to run a strip about a goalkeeper called Bouncing Billy Briggs, who only ever let in one goal. He was a hero all right, but a deeply unsatisfactory one. There was no irony in it, but it was laughable. Even the kids who bought it must have felt uncomfortable, as though the sun had started to rise in the west.

Before that (mainly in the 1930s) a very interesting series of cheap novels called the Aldine Football Novels (from a stable which also produced Aldine Boxing

Novels, Aldine Racing Novels and so on) occasionally dabbled with a heroic goalkeeper. They were cheaply printed, rather gaudy, monthly publications aimed, I think, more at working men keen for a good dose of escapism than at children. We are very close to the territory George Orwell explored so thoroughly in his essay of 1939 on *Boys Weeklies*. In 1927 the Aldine series published at fourpence-halfpenny *The Dandy Goalkeeper* by Peter Woodruff. On the cover an improbably aristocratic-looking goalkeeper *sporting a monocle* is seen throwing the ball out of goal, and the tone is set. The owner of this unusual piece of goalkeeping kit is Terry Blake, a wartime aviation hero called in by an acquaintance from the war to fill the goalkeeping position for Plimford Rovers after the regular goalkeeper had been injured by a violent 'charge'. Blake arrives at the games by plane, landing on the pitch. He plays in immaculate white kid gloves. The whole thing is utterly preposterous, but as Orwell noticed, it is preposterous *within* the world-view of its readers. The bully is an opposing centre-forward, who turns out to be making regular trips to Chinatown for 'snow', which he buys from a group of dastardly oriental plotters. Blake (who is also, naturally, 'a trusted member of – well, let me just say this – it is a Government department of which you seldom hear') beats the bully and defeats the plotters. He is such a master of disguise that he infiltrates a secret meeting without any of the Chinamen present rumbling him. He is forever punching the daylights out of people (once one-handed, after being injured in a football game) in a most impeccably Queensberry style; there is one particularly nasty torture scene. Blake is of course the goalkeeper of daydream, flying about making improbable saves all over the shop. He plays one game after being bitten by a poisonous snake sent to him by the Chinamen.

Throughout the novel, people talk like this: ' "Howard! Howard, my buck, I haven't cast eyes on you since you faced that Boche machine-gun with a walking-stick in one hand and a can of bully-beef in the other, and threatened to hurl the gun-crew into eternity if they didn't surrender." Howard Lester's face reddened, and he said hastily, "Cut that out, Terry! The war's been over a long time." ' The whole thing is like the self-aggrandizing dreams of a luridly-minded child. Blake *foils* everything – forwards, drug rings, oriental plots, his own temporary weaknesses. He plays better when he's hurt, best when his team are in most danger. The odd thing is that the descriptions of football itself are quite precisely written in only a slightly embellished version of the journalese of the day: 'It travelled so quickly that many of those present did not even see the shot. But what they did perceive was the mighty spring that Terry Blake made. His outstretched hand, neatly gloved in white kid, met the whirling sphere and turned it in its flight over the crossbar. It sailed far into the crowd to the right of the goal – as fine a save as one could wish to clap eyes on in a month of Sundays.' Take away the kid gloves, and that could come from a newspaper report; the 'whirling sphere' sounds comical today, but like the 'custodian', in charge of the 'citadel', it was a standard term of the day.

In such a book, the goalkeeper is all-heroic, at least in the very cardboard manner of such things. It looks as if we are supposed to admire him without questioning too much the string of implausibilities and exaggerations which together make the plot. Yet I cannot believe that anybody took it all that seriously. It must have been a laugh, and I imagine Aldine conversations on the terraces rather like modern soap-talk, a copious supply of quipping matter, of which not too much was to be made.

But it is part of a recognizable tradition. Blake is always at his best when prospects look bleakest, and that is an enduring part in the mythology of football which goalkeeping does occupy. It's hardly surprising that it should, given that it is hard for a goalkeeper to excel when the play is all at the other end. But the 'rearguard action' provides one of the standard frameworks for match reports, for example, and certainly survives in fiction. Brian Glanville wrote a novel for teenagers about the rise to Cup Final glory of a goalkeeper, which finishes with him making a blinding save and passing out from the pain of an injury received earlier in the game but heroically overcome.[1] It is a peculiar book in some ways. The names of real footballers and managers and so on are dotted through it, and among them moves the fictional cast. It is not a mere procession of triumphs in the manner of *The Dandy Goalkeeper*, and Glanville makes his hero meet at least some set-backs on the way, but its skeleton is plainly from the genus 'goalkeeper triumphant over adversity'.

So there is, in spite of everything, a certain sporting-hero status which goalkeepers can achieve. Outside books, most get something below heroism, a certain affectionate habituation, like well-worn furniture. Since football people undervalue goalkeeping and underplay its importance, they tend to pay it less attention than other parts of the game. You wake up and suddenly the goalkeeper has been five good years with the team and he's become part of your emotional furniture if you're a fan or a colleague. But the real explosions of awe are often reserved for revelations of goalkeeping from abroad. Time and again it has come as a surprise, almost a complete surprise, to the English football world that these foreign chappies can play a bit.

It is hard to recall now just how little we used to know about foreign football. A very few well-informed football people made great efforts to keep in touch with it, but the old English attitude used to be pretty overtly contemptuous. The British didn't play in the World Cup until 1950 (it was first played in 1930), and hesitated just as fiercely to join the European competitions when they were started. The FA actually refused permission for British clubs to play until people like Matt Busby made it plain that nothing would hold them back. The assumption was that British was best, and since we had taught foreigners to play we could hardly be expected to learn anything from them. But the clubs, almost since the start of organized football, had seen touring as the perfect way to advertise their wares in wider markets.

There has always been a commerce of touring teams from these islands abroad, and of visiting teams here. Club tours were sometimes modest affairs, like the end-of season tours that big clubs arrange now, but occasionally they became huge sporting encounters, avidly followed by the press, and seen very much as tests of the national virtues. There are two famous rude awakenings, when the national English side suddenly realized it could not by any means assume itself to be the best in the world. In 1950, in Belo Horizonte, England lost 1–0 to the United States, a football minnow, and to the marvellous Hungarian side, Olympic champions of 1952 and so nearly world champions of 1954, England conceded thirteen goals (6–3 at Wembley, 7–1 in Budapest) in two games in 1953 and 1954.

The American goalkeeper in 1950 was called Borghi. He played well, very well, but it is nowhere written that he had a miraculous game. It seems more likely that the English forward line simply failed to get their act together that day. But in 1953 it was a different story. Comprehensively outclassing England in almost every position, the Hungarians were regarded as having given a footballing masterclass. It started with Gyula Grosics, a wonderful goalkeeper who seems very much to have endeared himself to the British public. His opponent, Gil Merrick, was a good, competent English pro, solid enough. But Grosics simply looked as though he'd descended from the heavens, a goalkeeper so superior that English goalkeepers were still talking about having tried to master things he'd shown in those games well into the 1960s. Grosics was an unbelievable gymnast, for a start. But he was also a very careful tactical thinker. He worked at his goalkeeping like an accountant getting his sums right. He made it his business to learn everything he could about opponents, and then worked out ways of countering them. If he had to rely on his speed of reaction or his courage, he would, and they would very rarely let him down. But English critics had never seen a goalkeeper who played so far forward. His play was an integral part of the Hungarian system. Another or a lesser goalkeeper would have obliged them to invent some other way of doing it. He prevented many attacks from getting close to goal, tidying up behind the defence often yards in front of his penalty area. He played eighty-nine times for Hungary, and in the World Cup Finals three times.

At club level, not officially representing Britain (although often doing so in the minds of all the spectators), these goalkeeping lessons, both given and received, had been commonplace for years. Herbert Chapman, the manager who made the name of the Arsenal, was impressed by the so-called Wonder Team, the Austrian national side of the early 1930s, as everyone was. In particular, the England team had been held to a goalless draw in Vienna in May 1930, mainly by the brilliance of the goalkeeper of the Vienna club WAC, Rudi Hiden. Chapman actually bought Hiden to transfer him to Highbury. He had left on the journey to England when the UK Ministry of Labour laid down a rule that no foreign footballer would receive a work permit without first having resided here for two years.[2] Hiden sadly counts as a lost hero of British goalkeeping, for it is hard to imagine, given what he achieved away from England, that he would not have done something astounding had he played here for a while, in Herbert Chapman's team. He signed for the Racing Club de Paris instead, and eventually took French nationality and played for France before becoming a manager in Italy.

If by that draw in Vienna the Austrians had shaken some of the British complacency in 1930, they nearly shook it a great deal more in 1932 when they lost to England at Stamford Bridge by the odd goal in seven in a famous game. In fact, England were not to lose at home until the Hungarian lesson of 1953, but they had many times been badly scared before that. One thinks of their first ever defeat, in Spain in 1929, when they lost 4–3. In 1930 they drew 3–3 with Germany as well as 0–0 with Austria. In 1931 France beat England 5–2 in Paris. In 1933 the Italians held England to 1–1. Czechoslovakia won 2–1 in Prague in 1934; on the same tour England lost against the Hungarians, 2–1 in Budapest. And so it went on. Good judges, like Ivan Sharpe and Geoffrey Green, looking abroad, found much in the tactics of European teams to admire, much in English play that was old-fashioned and unsupple. Time and again, they warned against any unjustified assumption of British superiority. Ball skills, tactics, even the apparent intelligence of the play left the best English observers embarrassed. And almost every time, there was a new goalkeeper to admire, or one of our own to thank.

In Spain in 1929, it had been the spectacular Ricardo Zamora, hero of the Spanish team in three Olympic competitions in 1920, 1924, and 1928. Zamora was the origin of the myth of the continental goalkeeper. He was flashy but sure. He loved the limelight, but let in only twenty-seven goals in his first thirty-four internationals. His greatest game was in the semi-finals of the 1934

World Cup, when he defied Italy until so crudely fouled in conceding the one goal of a 1–1 draw that he was unable to play in the re-match. When he left Barcelona to join Real Madrid in 1930 he set a record transfer fee of 150,000 pesetas. He definitely shook England in 1929, but allowed English minds to relax when he failed thoroughly on his only visit here, letting in seven in deep mud at Highbury in 1931. An interpreter said to Dixie Dean that night, 'Zamora says tonight in Madrid he is nothing.' 'Tell him,' replied Dean, in the charming manner of English centre-forwards, 'that he's nothing here, either.' But he wasn't nothing. He was a great goalkeeper.

In 1945 the Moscow Dynamos toured in England. Enormous national pride was at stake, on both sides. The Russians, with their aura of efficient lack of sentimentality, amazed the British press and seduced the public; all except George Orwell, who wrote:

> If you wanted to add to the vast fund of ill-will existing in the world at this moment, you could hardly do it better than by a series of football matches between Jews and Arabs, Germans and Czechs, Indians and British, Russians and Poles, and Italians and Yugoslavs, each match to be watched by a mixed audience of 100,000 spectators. I do not, of course, suggest that sport itself is one of the main causes of international rivalry; big-scale sport is itself, I think, merely another effect of the causes that have produced nationalism. Still, you do make things worse by sending forth a team of eleven men, labelled as national champions, to do battle against some rival team, and allowing it to be felt on all sides that whichever team is defeated will 'lose face'.[3]

But to everybody except Orwell, the Dynamos were fascinating. Were they a club side, or were they a national team in disguise? Would they be able to deal with British conditions, British beef and brawn? They were supposed to be mysterious and unapproachable but turned out the opposite. They gave endless interviews comparing conditions in Russia to the ones they found in England; they presented Chelsea with bouquets of flowers; they went out of their way to be charming. In the end they scored nineteen times on the tour and conceded only nine goals, a marvellously successful propaganda exercise, and their goalkeeper Tiger Khomich became as familiar as any English footballer. Muscular in style, squat in physique, Khomich was in his first year of top-class football (he had attracted attention in a Russian Army team which had won the 'Shah's Cup' in Iran two years before), but he certainly became one of the stars of that tour. He saved a penalty in Glasgow, and made a string of highly athletic saves elsewhere. At a banquet at the end of the tour, Ivan Sharpe cheerfully missed a great interview: 'I sat next to "Tiger" Khomich, the man on the flying trapeze who played in goal. But there's nothing to report. That's the worst of these foreigners; they will speak their own language.'[4] When Khomich was injured, his successor both in the Moscow Dynamo and in the national side was Lev Yashin. Khomich became a sports photographer, and spent many years crouching behind the goals as he had once crouched in front of them. One day I'll track down his own pictures of goalkeeping; nobody ever had a stronger chance of snapping the shutter release at the very right moment.

In 1948 it was the other way round. Frank Swift held the Italians at bay in Turin in the game of his life, and Englishmen were able once again to claim their goalkeepers as top. But Swift was something of a 'continental' goalkeeper himself, and admitted it: 'His tendency to showmanship caused me to say to Frank Swift, of Manchester City, on his retirement from the game after the international match with Norway at Oslo in 1949; "Otherwise, Frank, I would have named you the best goalkeeper I've ever seen." Frank, as genial as ever, replied: "I threw in a bit of showmanship to please the crowd. Football's only a game, after all." '[5] Not in Turin it wasn't, on that summer evening in 1948, when Swift endured one of those twenty-minute periods in which it seems inevitable that something has got to give. Mortensen had scored early, from an incredibly tight angle, beating Bacigalupo at his near post. The Italian response was ferocious. Two 'goals' were offside, and Gabetto hit the crossbar with a header, but the rest Swift saved. And when the storm subsided, England themselves went on the attack, and scored three more. It was a famous victory of the day, and it was all down to Frank Swift.

There have been others, many others. The goalkeeper goes abroad with at least this in his favour, that he is not taken for granted as he is at home. He may play indifferently, but the chances are he will not. The Yugoslav ex-ballet dancer, Vladimir Beara, who got a standing ovation at Cardiff in 1954, and who seemed to take deliberate pleasure in moving for the ball as late and as spectacularly as possible, became incredibly well-known in England. We have always welcomed foreign goalkeepers with a strange mix of contempt and admiration. Jan Tomaszewski was a 'clown' according to Brian Clough, yet he stopped thirty-five separate attempts on goal in putting England out of the World Cup in 1974. Our experts used to think foreign goalkeepers were too protected, that a decent shoulder-charge would unman them. Then we decided that they were not as reliable dealing with crosses as our men. We assumed that we could outshine them, and every so often one put us right. Now we buy them, by the hatful, for our Premier League, where they excel.

Football is less insular than it used to be. Players come and go with ease. Yet we still know less about goalkeepers from abroad than about comparable stars outfield. How many English fans watched in the season 1996/97 as the two established stars of the French league, Fabien Barthez of Monaco and Bernard Lama of Paris St Germain, were outshone by the brilliant youngster Mickaël Landreau, playing for an unfancied Nantes team with a brand of elegant sureness that looked very like genius? Did any British coaches pay attention, and bid for him? We notice foreign goalkeepers who have played (and preferably lost) against English teams. So top Italians, say Peruzzi or Paglialuca, or a van der Sar from Holland, become vaguely familiar. But if even a Schmeichel at home can be undersung, and a Yashin, monument and all, can be known only to connoisseurs, then oblivion stalks close behind the majority.

Every country has a goalkeeping tradition of some sort. The captain of Chile in the 1950 World Cup Finals was the goalkeeper, Eves, but since Chile fared even worse that year than England, one could see that he would hardly attract enormous attention. In 1954 the Turkish captain was also the goalkeeper, Turgay. But goalkeepers do vanish: Zeman, in goal for Austria after the war, Debie, a fine Belgian who kept goal in the 1920s, or Gormlie, another Belgian, who played for a number of English teams and coached both Anderlecht and the Belgian national side after the war. Who remembers them? In 1934 when Czechoslovakia reached the World Cup Finals, they had a much-admired goalkeeper-captain, František Planicka, a squat figure in knee bandages, who had his great game against Romania, making two extraordinary saves on the way to a 2–1 victory. He was beaten by a 'freak' goal in the final, the Argentinian-Italian Raimondo Orsi hitting a shot which curled so oddly that he tried twenty times to repeat it for the photographers the next day without success. Planicka went to the World Cup Finals again in 1938, and was in the end capped seventy-four times. He played for Slavia Prague with enormous distinction, and played occasional veterans' matches (he was born in 1904) into the 1970s. In Britain, not one fan in hundreds could name him.

In the late 1930s, Olympique de Marseille had a Brazilian goalkeeper, Vasconcellos, known as El Jaguar, who had a classic reputation as an 'eccentric'. He used when travelling to send himself bouquets of flowers pretending that they were from (female) admirers. Apparently nobody was taken in, since even the relatively discreet press of the day were aware of it. But Vasconcellos earned a certain amount of notoriety for making opponents miss penalties with his 'humorous' play-acting. Keen followers of Bruce Grobbelaar will find that familiar, but Grobbelaar didn't invent it. Even earlier (he was one of the very first celebrity sports stars in France) there was Pierre Charigués, who played all his career for the now defunct Red Star Club. He won twenty-one international caps between 1911 and 1925, and three successive French cups in the early twenties, when he was good enough to be the subject of consistent rumours that he would be bought by Tottenham Hotspur (in spite of frequent heavy defeats of French teams by English ones at the time, including several in which he played). What do we know about him? He had huge hands, great gymnastic ability, and was an early adventurer far into the penalty area. He was known by a variant of the biblical pun 'super hanc petram aedificabo Ecclesiam meam' as the 'Pierre Nationale', the rock on which the French team would be built, and he ran into trouble for professionalism because of his revenue from advertising. There must be film of him playing (and there are certainly surviving magazine illustrations[6]), as there is of so many other 'lost' goalkeepers. To see them, to judge whether the game was really slower then, to know what their successors improved on and what they abandoned, would be very fine. Because at the moment, we persist in believing that goalkeeping is invented anew by each successive champion. It isn't.

After Charigués, in France, there was Alex Thépot, who worked for customs and played in the World Cup in 1930 and 1934 (he was 'chaired' by the crowds at the

Gare de Lyon on his return from Italy in 1934, even without winning anything at all). In France he is remembered for his considerable part in the first French professional victory over England (5–2 at the Colombes Stadium in Paris in May 1931), which liberated the French from a considerable sense of inferiority in the face of English football which they have never felt since. So one can go on listing them. Obscure at home, unknown elsewhere; to catalogue them makes one feel melancholy. Yet they were just as capable of cutting the breath out of a full stadium as our own dynasties of goalkeepers. Still in France, there was the notably short Julien Darui, who played alongside a young Helenio Herrera in the Division Two Charleville team which surprised everybody by reaching the French Cup Final in 1936. He went on to have a distinguished run in goal for both Lille and France, and after the war got the reputation of being the first really attacking goalkeeper, notably in a sequence of three games in the spring of 1946 when France beat Czechoslovakia, Austria, and then England.

The French tradition is like that elsewhere: it runs seamlessly on to the present. Georges Carnus, who played in 1969 in the famous St Etienne team that overcame a 2–0 first-leg deficit to beat the mighty Bayern Munich 3–0 at home, could have been luckier on his international debut. Playing against Brazil (in 1963) he was unfortunate enough to concede all three goals to Pele. The sour transfer negotiations when Olympique de Marseille wanted to buy Carnus from St Etienne became the first time Marseille acquired its murky reputation. They got their man; Carnus was fired from St Etienne and won for his new club the penalty competition which got them to the French Cup Final in 1972. Some English fans will remember Pascal Olmeta, who kept goal for Marseille when Chris Waddle was there, in the same way as French fans follow Peter Schmeichel because the papers report on Cantona. But few in England will recall Joel Bats's reflex save from Zico, of Brazil, which put France into the semi-finals of the World Cup in Mexico in 1986. France–Brazil: not part of the folklore in England. Understandably so, of course, but it is a pity that football excitement works in such a chauvinist way, because Bats's game was one of the all-time goalkeeping cliff-hangers. He made a string of saves, from Junior, Alemão, and Socrates. In the second half he pulled down Branco, the attacking full-back, and saved Zico's penalty. The Brazilians increased the dosage. The French goalkeeper made more saves, and with the goal looking likelier by the minute, until five minutes from the end of normal time, Bats made his save from a header by Zico. It was appalling to watch, even on television, magnificent, a fierce explosion of reactions and determination, a thrilling save. If I had a picture of it I would keep it in my wallet. The game went to penalties, and Bats saved one of those too, almost casually. It's the same game, but we don't really share our football histories.

Goalkeeping is one of those activities where style matters. We notice foreign goalkeepers first because they look so different to our own. Not in the trivial, amusing details, of Khomich's or Yashin's all-black strip, of Sepp Maier's comically baggy shorts and enormous gloves, of this one who wears track-suit bottoms when we don't find it chilly or that one who never takes his own goal-kicks. But they set themselves up differently for free kicks, time their emergence from goal differently, and punch away when we have come to expect an attempt to catch. We expect all British goalkeepers to be safe and cautious and professional, and all foreigners to be like Zamora or Rudi Hiden. And inevitably, from time to time, one of them obliges. Has anybody forgotten the delightful impudence of René Higuita's scorpion kick? It was all our prejudices about foreign goalkeeping rolled into one enormous somersault. It was, admittedly, done in a friendly, and there was some debate about whether Higuita knew that the offside whistle had blown before he did it. Within a game, it didn't matter at all. But within football it was glorious. It was as though Higuita knew that British observers frown on demonstrative goalkeeping, and simply wanted us to put *that* in our pipes and smoke it. We had to, too. Elisha Scott and Sam Hardy would never have done such a thing. Football is too serious if you play in the English league for any such levity. Grobbelaar might have done it, but then he's a foreigner. I wonder if Zimbabwe, whence he came, counts within the dreaded 'continent', the legendary home of so much flaky goalkeeping? It must do. If Higuita, a Colombian, could be described almost as a standard epithet as a continental goalkeeper, then surely Grobbelaar can. Fog in Channel; Continent cut off.

John Macadam wrote a famous piece about goal-keeping in which he contrasted the 'English' style (actually that of a Scot, Harry Rennie of Greenock

Morton) with the most extravagant 'continental' manner:

A football enthusiast . . . peered through the little window in the corrugated walls. There, in the locker-room, an extraordinary sight met his gaze.

Harry Rennie, in full football strip, was prancing, wide-legged from side to side as goalkeepers do when they are approached by an opposing forward. At a given moment, he would yell 'Shoot!' and dive full-length on the hard, stud-pocked boards. He would lie there outstretched for a bare second, then he would pick himself up, adjust his shorts, and start the business all over again.

This is the part that is difficult to sell to the spoon-fed goal-keepers of today – Rennie did this every day when all the others had finished training and gone. He shadow-saved just as a fighter in training will shadow-box. It gave him speed off the mark, coordination of body and mind, unself-consciousness. But why on the rough, knobbly floor? To harden himself.[7]

When he wasn't training in this spartan manner, Rennie was working out theories, of angles, like all goalkeepers, but also of something he called the Shooting Gesture, which he reckoned revealed a little earlier than the shot itself where the ball was intended to go. Rennie is all science and hard work.

Contrast, as Macadam did, Pietro Olivieri, who came to England with the Italian national side in 1938, 'in the true tradition of Hiden, Zamora and the others, and none of his successors has his colour'. Macadam put them in the context of what their audience expected:

British crowds have a way of concentrating behind the home team's goal because they feel that, since the object of the game is to score goals, it is there that they will see most of the play. A Continental crowd huddles also behind the goal, but for an entirely different reason – to watch the goalkeeper. The Continental goalkeeper is more than a player in a side. He is the supreme artist in the side, the epitome of all athletic prowess. The forwards, the half-backs, the backs can play as they will and they will get appreciation according to their deserts. If the goalkeeper fails for any reason to put up a spectacular show the afternoon is wasted. Any football match on the Continent is a melodrama with two main parts – one for each goalkeeper . . . The British goalkeeper – like Dawson, Swift, Merrick, Williams – awaits an onrushing forward. Excited, the forward foozles his shot and the ball runs slowly towards the goalkeeper. What does he do? He places both feet together as a last line of defence against the trickling ball. He stoops, and with hands cupped together for extra precaution he scoops the ball from the turf and, as quickly as possible, throws or punts it up the field to a position covered by a player of his own side.

Not so Olivieri to whom this copybook business is not only unnecessary but unfair to the crowd. The ball trickles towards the prancing Olivieri. He flings his arms wide in a dramatic acceptance of the challenge he is about to meet. As the moment of consummation nears, he raises himself on his toes and then, when the ball is but a yard from him, he leaps high in the air. At the peak of his rise, the crowd yell with delight and the yell swells to a roar of appreciation as the athlete contorts suddenly and pounces, panther-like to the ground – at the exact moment of the ball's arrival. His hands clutch, his knees and toes sink into the turf. He has it! A bare second he is poised there and then with a sudden electric burst, he is on his feet. He moves left and right in short steps, he bounces the ball before him, he clutches it to him once more and then, the peak of emotion passed, he punts it long and gracefully up the field – anywhere. This accomplished, he sprints back to his goal-line where he takes up a nonchalant, disinterested position, hand on upright, one foot crossed in front of the other with a toe pointed like a ballerina. He adjusts his cap with his free hand in token of applause. His whole posture says: 'Wait! Have patience! There will be more!'

There will be plenty more. There will be leaps that bring his head above the level of the crossbar. There will be pounces on balls that are yards away from him. There will be gesticulations and shouts. There will be Douglas Fairbanks Snr, Errol Flynn, Joe Louis and the Early Christian Martyrs all rolled into one magnificent goalkeeper. The fact that it has nothing whatever to do with football will be the least of anybody's worry.[8]

Traditionally, we're supposed to disapprove of this stuff. It's too demonstrative, too little stiff-upper-lip and it patently involves risk, too. But John Macadam didn't disapprove – he loved it, and so do I. He remembers a game where because of the great superiority of his side Olivieri felt that he had done too little in the first half:

When . . . the players ran off to the dressing-rooms to rest and have their lemons or whatever Continental sides have, Olivieri came to the touchline and summoned two assistant trainers, summoned them imperiously and ordered them to bring an old ball apiece. Then he retreated once more to his goal, and for the ten minutes' duration of the interval had the pair of them fire shots at him. He ran the gamut of goalkeeping through the punch-clear, the clutched-in-flight, the fist-over-the-bar, the full-stretch-dive, the pounce. And when the players returned to resume the game, he raised his cap and bowed to the terrific ovation from behind the goal and dashed off to take up his position in the other goal acclaimed all the way as the artist he was.[9]

In practical terms, if Macadam would forgive me for being so literal, Olivieri was doing a sensible, technical thing. He had not had enough to do in the first half. His concentration and suppleness had ebbed away. An intensive warm-up would allow him to be ready for whatever the second half might bring. Any goalkeeper would want to do the same, and the many sad goals conceded soon after the interval remind us that this unwelcome cooling-down period needs to be guarded against. It hardly matters; the style is the thing, the way of keeping goal. For myself, there cannot be any doubt. I want to applaud both Rennie and Olivieri, and a hundred methods that are not quite of either. I want different ways of keeping goal to be offered to us as connoisseurs, to appreciate them for what they are. Perhaps an Olivieri tries too hard to win that elusive status of hero, perhaps we cannot grant it when so little is at stake? Or perhaps Rennie does too little to entertain? Perhaps so. But you wouldn't criticize a dove for failing to fly like a hawk. Yet both stay up there.

In 1938, Italy won the World Cup. They almost went out in the first round, in Marseille, to a good Norwegian side which had only narrowly lost to them in the previous Olympic final. Norway hit post or bar three times, and had a goal disallowed for offside. At the very end the big Norwegian centre-forward Brunyldsen hit one of those shots of comic-book ferocity, screaming for the top corner. Olivieri saved it and as he rose to his feet Brunyldsen walked slowly forward and shook him by the hand.

It does happen. They can get that esteem. It works in two ways. Either they become much-loved after years of impeccable service, or at least of service so nearly impeccable that their few mistakes are willingly overlooked. In that case, their particular style becomes the only one the fans think right, the one short of which every other goalkeeper falls in some detail. Or they can be the heroes of a single day: Jim Montgomery, who won the FA Cup for Sunderland with that stupendous double-save; Packie Bonner, sending the whole of Ireland mad by diving to his left to save that fifth penalty against Romania; Alex Stepney, turning a European Cup Final decisively Manchester United's way with a triumphant save from Eusebio when the score was 1–1 and the floodgates threatened to burst at any moment. Then the goalkeeper is just a hero, and all the nervy edginess he inspires in us is forgotten.

But you see I argue that the goalkeeper is in fact the man of the match even on occasions less startlingly obvious than these. Only exceptionally does a great forward actually win a football game. That can happen, too, and it's amazing when it does. Somebody catches fire, and the defence are made to look foolish. But attacking play always has that enormous advantage that you only need to get it right once to look pretty good. Defenders' mistakes are often punished, and goalkeepers' almost always. To do nothing wrong looks a great deal less exciting than to do something right. Yet match after match goalkeepers do nothing wrong, sometimes in the extravagant style of a Bruce Grobbelaar or a Peter Bonetti, sometimes in the more reserved one of a Joe Corrigan or a Gordon Banks, and often in a peculiar combination of styles which they have made their own. And remember this too, that if there is no other way of preventing a goal, a great goalkeeper will abandon his style in a fraction of a second, and just do what it takes. You don't normally punch crosses out, and come up against a fierce header of the ball? A dozen successful punches in an afternoon. You normally play fairly far back, and your centre-back gets injured? A gazelle sprints out of the penalty area all day. What we ask goalkeepers to do is heroic. You don't need added melodrama, penalty shoot-outs, or those days when one team is overrun and kept in it only by the desperate plunging and writhing of a goalkeeper possessed (let alone the odd sinister oriental plotter or coke-crazed centre-forward). Ordinary goalkeeping is heroic. To make himself bigger at will, to guard the breach, to provide an embattled rearguard are standard in goalkeeping, not exceptional. It doesn't always work, but it doesn't need whistles and bows to be thought heroic when it does.

There are two types of fact newspapermen love to collect about goalkeepers. One is now so well established that it has become a tiny sub-genre in its own right: if somebody eminent in another field was once upon a time a goalkeeper, that fact in itself is supposed to reveal something about them. It's a strange kind of catalogue,

I'm tempted to say an unholy one. It includes Popes real and imagined: John Paul II and Graham Kelly, the head of the FA, who used to play at Blackpool. Cardinal Basil Hume isn't a Pope, but was a goalkeeper, and David Icke isn't a Pope but is, if I understand rightly, even closer to his own particular divinity.[10] Alistair Cooke, incredibly, was first a gymnast, then a goalkeeper in Blackpool, after his family had moved there from Manchester for his mother's health. 'I cannot', he wrote, 'truthfully say that I was crazy about standing between the goalposts on witheringly dank afternoons.'[11] Perhaps one should say he played in goal; he doesn't sound a full member of the trade union. Nabokov played in goal at Cambridge,[12] Camus at school and university in Algiers (so famously that his by-no-means-joking comment that 'All I know most surely about morality and obligations, I owe to football' has for some years been available on a T-shirt sold by an enterprising company called Philosophy Football). Julio Iglesias was reserve goalkeeper for Barcelona[13]. Peter Taylor, Brian Clough's long-term number two played in goal. Eric Cantona's dad, unlike his son, was a goalkeeper. John Motson's son Frederick was a 'budding' goalkeeper at the time his dad wrote about him.[14] Matthew Engel once wrote that Conan Doyle played in goal for Portsmouth under the pseudonym A.C. Smith, a reference which explains a great deal about Sherlock Holmes.[15] The idea is that the dreaded craziness must reside in them, that nothing they do in later life should surprise you. If a man can be shown to be an ex-goalkeeper, then we're automatically supposed to know all the rest.

Another favoured game is collecting little incidents affecting goalkeepers, both on and off the pitch. Together, they become almost like fables, a Book of Hours of human wackiness. You know the kind of thing:

The big topic of conversation in Brazilian football this week has not been the defection of Emerson from Middlesbrough – he is hardly known in his own country – but the vicious attack by Fluminense fans on an opposing goalkeeper.

Ricardo Pinto, a former Fluminense player, required brain surgery after his beating by fans who ran on the pitch at the end of a game, one of them wielding a large stick. Pinto enraged them in celebrating Atletico Paranense's win over 'Flu' which took Atletico top of the League.

In the pre-game warm-up the fans had chanted abuse at Pinto and during play they pelted him with oranges.

After the attack, Pinto, who did not realize how badly he was hurt, needed eight stitches in a forehead wound. He gave a live radio interview in which he called the fans 'animals' and after being locked in the dressing-room for safety he was driven to hospital by armed policemen while the team bus was stoned.

A Fluminense official blamed Pinto for this episode, saying: 'He provoked the fans. It's entirely his fault . . .'[16]

A Sudanese sports reporter, standing in as linesman in a village match at Hasasheisa, nearly 100 miles from Khartoum, died after being attacked by the disgruntled goalkeeper of a team whose goal he had just disallowed. The daily *Alwan* reports that the goalkeeper raced up to Adel Moustafa and punched him in the head. He died in hospital.[17]

The Derby County goalkeeper Martin Taylor has turned to hypnosis to recover his form and confidence after a broken leg . . .[18]

If a crossbar falls on any other player, it is just one of those things, an accident. If one falls on a goalkeeper, we are supposed to see it as confirmation of what zany world he lives in. Of course goalkeepers do stupid things, lots of them. Not so long ago the brilliantly gifted Australian Mark Bosnich disgraced himself by giving a Nazi salute to the Tottenham fans. Tottenham is thought to be a club with a particularly large Jewish following, and Bosnich used his free hand to sketch a little (black) moustache under his nose, just in case anybody didn't get his drift. It was an offensive and stupid joke, and Bosnich was pilloried for it. Interestingly, in that case, I saw no version of the story which made it out to be a specially goalkeeperly thing to do. The best thing about the whole sorry episode was that he apologized quickly, publicly, and apparently sincerely. Goalkeepers can be indiscreet, unwise, rude, and so on. Several have been involved in corruption scandals, recently and throughout the history of the game. But I don't believe that they are any more of any of those things than anybody else.

On the contrary, I think there is a tendency for these stories to accumulate precisely because we don't understand goalkeeping, and find it easier to assume wackiness and bad behaviour than really to get to grips with their job and their role in our favourite sport. Heroes sometimes, certainly, but buffoons, scapegoats, and fall guys more often. It makes me wonder whether all entertainment needs a built-in jester, and where he is lacking we invent him. Football is awfully serious sometimes, and not just when a real tragedy hits it. It may be that to make it a fully rounded performance we have to find some element to lighten that weight, and that the goalkeeper has fitted the bill. It is a formula, as stereotyped as a Punch and Judy show or a pantomime. The trouble is that for years it has tended to obscure the rest of goalkeeping. And that is something too fine to lie hidden under a cartoon misrepresentation. One of the greatnesses of football is that every shade of human behaviour turns up in it sooner or later. Not for anything would I suggest that it should be otherwise. But is it really necessary for the presumption of heroism always to go to the centre-forward, and the presumption of buffoonery always to the goalkeeper?

9. A Counsel of Perfection

The great pleasures in goalkeeping are as obvious as the stripes on a tiger. There is always that old satisfaction – 'It feels so good when I stop' – and certainly there is a lot of pleasure to be had from tugging off a foul clinging sweater and socks in a quiet chorus of 'Good game, mate' from a group of liked and respected team-mates. But all sportsmen know that pleasure. For goalkeepers the high points are like steeples in a corn-plain: the penalty save, the reflex stop, the top corner properly reached and the ball shoved away. In each case the chance of it being carried off is small.

To make a full-blooded save is to achieve the improbable, when the price of not achieving it is high. There is a simple pleasure in that which no goalkeeper would deny. Who makes such a save, even knowing himself capable of it, surprises himself. The relief, roaring, and churning (although by a kind of goalkeeping etiquette, always inwardly) in the making of such a save is quite something. Somebody gets away from a defender, perhaps four yards in front of you, and volleys the ball, hard, to your left. You don't actually *think* anything. But you're certain he's right-footed because you've watched him carefully, and you can see, by the way he's turned through his balance, that he has to aim *sort of . . . there.* That gets you off. Your body is going in the right general direction. Gather spring from thighs and spine and ankles. Then you get a glimpse, less than a glimpse of the trajectory of the ball. That puts your eyes and your hands in the hunt. It's more precise now. You spring and stretch and your arm shoots out in a gesture that has become habitual. You already know enough that if you do make contact with the ball, you will be able to beat it away. It's too late now to invent anything new.

The gesture you are making might well be a characteristic one: all those photographs of the *desperate* dive, of the goalkeeper *failing* to get to the ball, of the goalkeeper *beaten* by a searing drive, will echo round your head in a moment. But there is contact. Ball smacks on hand, not quite true. No palm on it, and only three fingers have actually touched the thing, one of them bent back at an awkward angle, but you've put some tension in the ligaments of your arm; it's all you can do. But for a while you've no way of knowing whether it was enough. You have had to reach so far that there is no time to get your left forearm to the ground to break your fall; your left hip hits the ground first, then your ribs at their widest point, then the rest of you. Long (it seems long) before your feet come down, trailing uselessly in the air, having done their bit earlier by giving you the grip and the momentum to dive, you know that you made it. You may not yet know where the ball went, you need to be up again quicker than thought, ready to go again, maybe the other way. You haven't got time to lever yourself up with your arms or your knees. You use stomach and back muscles, *bouncing* up more than getting up. Then the sound hits you, of someone, your friend, yelling at the top of his lungs: 'Great save!' And you look and the ball has gone behind for a corner, and there's time to notice that your socks got scraped to your ankles as you fell, that the grit in the goal-mouth has drawn blood, just a scrape, down the outside of your left calf and on the point of your left elbow. I've done it a few times, and the feeling is high.

That's an obvious pleasure. It can be wiped out, in terms of your game, in a second or in an hour and a half, and you daren't dwell on it for fear of it driving other important things out of your mind. But you've done something that was worth getting up for, worth trudging to Hampstead Heath Extension (which sounds closer than it is, miles north in Golders Green) at a stupid hour in the morning, worth all those butterflies-in-the-stomach for hours before the game. But there's another sound that normally hits you a fraction late, which all goalkeepers will recognize. As you take stock, just after you've got back to your feet, a voice will say, 'Unlucky, Ali' (or Bill, or Chas, or whoever). It's outrageous, indefensible. It's some responsible bloke on the other side, the captain or a would-be captain, *keeping up morale*. Because the bloke who shot (you're still not quite sure who it was) might be upset that he didn't score. 'Unlucky, mate.' Like that, deadpan. What the swearing blasphemy do you mean by 'unlucky', you pansy parentless creep? I saved the participle epithet

Anglo-Saxon-adjective ball, didn't I? I did everything right, didn't I? The ball's in the next field and all you've got is a corner, you miserable scatological epithet, how dare you say it was unlucky? He screwed up. It was a sitter and he screwed up. He's a forward, for God's sake, four yards in front of a goal as big as a postal district, and he can't get the ball in it. It's incompetence of a staggering order, idiocy, abysmal and appalling failure, and you think it's *unlucky*? I have to admit that I've had one or two of these tantrums. Out loud, too, I'm afraid, when everybody thinks it's funny, and guess what? The keeper's a nutter. But I figure I might as well stand up for what I believe, and anyway the rushing elation of having reached the ball is going to come out somehow. That's a smaller pleasure in goalkeeping.

On a really wet and slimy day, a forward receives a through-pass which has neatly left both of your central defenders still turning in his slipstream. It's so wet that his footing is just a little uncertain, so he plays the ball a little further than usual in front of him with each stride of the dribbling action. So he may be making contact with the ball every four strides instead of every two (even numbers because the vast majority of players touch the ball always with the same foot). As a goalkeeper you're supposed to come rushing out, narrowing the angle as you do, maybe screaming at your defenders for having allowed it to happen, with a view to diving at his feet. If it's wet enough, and if you time it right, and if you're lucky, you can fling yourself to the ground in such a way that you slide neatly past him, collecting the ball safely on the way without any part of him touching any part of you. It's a lovely feeling, of unlikely grace coming to illuminate the rain and the mud and the awful feeling you've been having all afternoon that you just can't seem to get a true grip on the ball. If done right, you pluck the ball from just in front of his instep just as daintily as plucking a flower for your lapel. The ball is his, with the goal at his mercy (there's another phrase that irks me), and then, without any transition, it's yours and you are yards beyond him. His momentum has taken him *that* way, beyond your feet; yours *this*, away from goal, and the moment when you stole the ball from him has been and gone without there having been a damned thing he could do about it. If you come out really fast, he won't even have had time to alter his stride. He just carries on running, sans ball, sans goal, sans everything. Another small pleasure.

Mind you, I did just that, years ago, at school, at the feet of an enthusiastic winger called Charles Phelps-Penry, about whom I now know nothing. My hands went past him. My head, sliding neatly. Shoulders, ribs, crotch, all past him, and then his absurdly uncoordinated swing of the boot came down and roughly split my knee open to the bone. Less of a pleasure. I must have been something short of six feet tall then. My hands, which grabbed the ball, were fully stretched out ahead of me. So this bloke was so hopeless that he swung to connect six or seven feet behind where he had intended. Maybe a fraction less if I was curled up as I slid. It was an accident, but that's an awful long way to miss a football by. I bled in the taxi on the way to hospital and an anxious teacher who came to see me there *allowed me to smoke* in the waiting-room.

Goalkeepers can throw the ball a long way, some prodigiously far. There is real pleasure to be had from knowing different kinds of throw. You can roll it, underarm. You can bowl, still underarm, but with a lot more snap and speed. You can toss it overarm, on the movement of a lever which is only the forearm, from an immobile elbow. The ball sits cupped on your hand level with your ear, fingers pointing behind you, and you flip your forearm and the ball arcs quite slowly away. It can be slung, roundarm, where your hand wheels round level with your shoulder. Or you can heave it, with all the strength of arm and back and sides you can put into it. But that's not all. I throw right-handed. When throwing to a player on my right, the natural action puts spin on the ball which will make it curl into his stride as he runs forward. I throw ahead of him, aiming at the ground, but appreciably less far ahead than seems right for the ball to fall just so at his feet as he meets it. As the ball bounces, the spin bites, and the ball curls elegantly into a new trajectory, this time the right one. There are never thanks for doing this, but it's important to throw accurately if the receiver doesn't have to stop and tidy up the throw before he goes on. It is the same kind of pleasure as often happens in ball games, of satisfaction at being wholly in control first of the flight, then of the roll of the ball. And you know what? You can do the same thing when throwing the ball to your left. It's much less natural that side, but you can roll your hand over the ball as you release it, so that your last touch folds over it and down its left-hand side, and it will curl just as amiably into the stride of somebody running forward away to your left. Nice.

Some pleasures are negative, really, just damage avoided. For example, when a free kick is given within shooting range of goal, it has been normal for years for players to line up as near to the free kick as they are allowed, to cover at least some of the width of the goal as a barrier to a straight drive. You've seen them, all anxiously clutching their private parts as a feeble temporary defensive codpiece. (Although in fact it is doubtful how much good that does. If you're unlucky enough to find a well-hit football hitting you in the hands when your hands are there, you'll soon discover that the hands travel sharply backwards, and that hurts too.) They're supposed to be ten yards away, and a lot of nonsense is always going on in the wrangling. The players inch forward. The referee moves them back. Everybody's concentration goes, and it's all a great waste of effort. Why referees don't carry a ten-yard string in their pocket, I don't know. It would be so simple. Lay it out, brook no argument, and pick it up after the free kick has been taken. But they don't. Referees move in mysterious ways.

However, the business of placing the wall (of players) is the goalkeeper's responsibility. It has to be, because only he can see the angles that need to be covered. It would be very simple if the ball travelled in straight lines, but as it is, I've always found it difficult to know just how far to reasonably expect the ball to be curled. Every forward can curl the ball a bit, in a steady arc. Some can curl it so that it swerves viciously, late in its flight, with dip enough to make things more fun. The wind can do some of that, too. The ball may be more or less inclined to swerve, more or less flighty. Do you place your wall to reach far beyond the straight line between ball and goal? If yes, you need so many men in the wall that you can't spare any for marking jobs (that is to say tight escorting of opponents, to be in position to prevent their doing anything with the ball should it come to them from the free kick). If no, you can't confidently leave the wall to do its job, and march boldly to the other side of the goal, the one the wall is not covering, without a nagging fear that the ball will appear around the outside of the wall. However many men there are in it, and however it is placed, wider or less wide of the goalpost, the wall always obscures the goalkeeper's vision. It has to be between him and the ball, or it's useless, but that means that it's going to be hard to see through. To stand wide of it is asking for disaster unless the free kick is in such a wide position that the angles work that way. The whole business is dealt with in a hurry; the free kick can be taken just as soon as the referee says so, and if the goalkeeper is slow working his desires out, or the bricks in the wall are slow to get into their bond, the whole team can look very foolish very quickly.

The goalkeeper puts his eye by the post, to get the line of sight right. He screams for obedience from the last man in the wall – 'Go right, go right . . .' – frantically working out how much beyond the post he needs to be. It is very reassuring indeed when the free kick careers into the outside edge of the outside man, and away, successfully defended against. I'm not even sure it's negative, exactly. It just one of those parts of keeping goal which can be done and done right without ever touching the ball. There are lots of these, agonizing chains of choice and bluff. They can go wrong, they often do. When they don't, the other players don't much notice that anything has happened; the crowd (where there is a crowd) certainly don't. Secret goalkeeping, whereby a goal is averted with apparently nothing done. Sure, if you take the trouble to notice, that can be a pleasure too.

Footballers do something called selling a dummy. It means pretending to do something, normally a pass or a shot, in such a way as to convince an opponent that it is about to happen. He moves to deal with it, and in doing so commits his weight and his balance to one side or the other. But that move doesn't arrive. By checking it at the last moment, too late for the opponent to come back to his neutral expectant position, the player is free to go the other way. In American sports talk it's called faking, and it only works if the pretence is convincing enough fully to launch the opponent in the direction you want him to go. Now you would have thought that to do such a thing you have to be in possession of the ball, but it is not so. A defender, running backwards, holding off from tackling an attacker until the moment is just right, maintaining his balance all the time, waiting apparently to react (not to act first), can in fact fake to have found his moment and safely prompt the attacker to go the other way, where the defender had wanted him to go all along. It's cute stuff, a quick game of double and treble bluff, played on speed of reaction and quickness of movement.

There's nothing at all extraordinary in goalkeepers being able to do simple versions of this. The ball safely in his hands, the goalkeeper is looking to punt upfield, but an attacker is standing in front of him, trying to put him off, maybe to stick a larcenous toe into the punting action and nick the ball. Nothing easier than to fake to punt with one foot, make the attacker lurch that way, and clear the ball comfortably on the other side. But most outfield players don't realize that goalkeepers can sell them dummies of far more glorious completeness. In fact, most outfield players don't even realize when it has been done to them.

Some do. In February 1974, Queen's Park Rangers played Leicester in a game that was eventually drawn 0–0. Peter Shilton in the Leicester goal had one of those days which leave forwards holding their heads in what is usually called frustration. It isn't frustration, it is the gesture forwards make to acknowledge a vastly superior goalkeeper, as ritualized as peasants grovelling before kings, or private soldiers saluting officers. Shilton made seven or eight saves by which absolutely sure-fire goals suddenly weren't, amazing saves, saves to stop the heart and have spectators yelling at each other to check they hadn't dreamed. One of the opponents, Terry Mancini, noticed that Shilton was doing something that should be impossible: 'The man is actually "selling dummies" to people about to score. It's unheard of. I had a great chance with a header and I knew I just had to thump it square into the net. But he shaped to cover that side, so I glanced it for the other corner . . . and he was standing there laughing at me as he caught it. He's a magician.'[1] I wasn't there, and I wonder what Shilton actually did. Did he lean two inches that way? Or lift the arm on that side five inches further from his body? Did he move that knee just enough to suggest he was about to move off in that direction? Whatever it was, it was a *tiny* gesture. Just big enough for Mancini to notice, but it had to be small enough for Shilton still to leave himself the time to move the other way.

It's not magical. It's just that great goalkeepers take complete control of the goal-mouth using all the weapons that come to hand. It's psychological warfare, but it's also the most exquisite control of gesture and movement, beautiful timing (because if you get that wrong your bluff can so easily be called), gigantic courage, and thoroughly masterly technique. It's goal-keeping. But do note that the great majority of the spectators would not have noticed what Shilton had done. They would have seen Mancini head tamely straight at the goalkeeper. 'Oh, no! He's missed.' He didn't miss, and was sporting enough to admit it afterwards. As Shilton said: 'It's often said that the main way to make the game more attractive to the general public is to give them more goals, but for me, a 0–0 match in which both goalkeepers are making great saves can be as enjoyable to watch as any high-scoring game.'[2]

Of course I agree, and so should everybody. Good judges apparently do. On 17 February 1991 in the House of Lords, Lord Templeman, with the agreement of Lord

Bridge of Harwich, Lord Brandon of Oakbrook, Lord Ackner, and Lord Goff of Chievely, said: 'Mr Shilton made miraculous saves for Southampton because he was an honourable man and a professional footballer and was contractually bound to do his best for Southampton.'[3] Well, I've been trying to explain that miracles, while nicely complimentary, in a metaphorical sort of way, really have nothing to do with it, but then one doesn't like to contradict their Lordships.

Shilton is Shilton, of course, but if you watch closely enough, you can see variants of this in lots of phases of goalkeeping. For a start, a goalkeeper facing a penalty will almost certainly fake one way; there's not a lot else he can do, once he has taken careful note of the striker's approach to the ball and the swing of his leg and the line of his eye, and the way he placed his last penalty and made sure of his own speed and agility and determination. It's possible to dummy people into shooting a fraction earlier than they'd like. Matt Gillies, Gordon Banks's manager at Leicester City, said somewhere that Banks used quite slowly and deliberately to lick his fingers in one-on-ones with attackers, to put them off. Imagine. Beat Banks, and be a hero. But he's staring at you, licking his fingers before having you for breakfast! You'd scuff your shot right then, anything to get it over with.

Banks knew all about faking. In 1968, England lost their sixty-seven-year unbeaten record against West Germany in Hamburg. Franz Beckenbauer had made a long run down the middle, and had come up to Brian Labone: 'I left Beckenbauer a space on my left to aim at and he accepted my invitation. He had fallen into my trap and I knew I had the ball covered as I moved to my left. But then Brian stuck out a leg to block the ball and it struck his knee and flew off into the right corner of the net. I don't think Brian has ever forgotten the misery of that goal.'[4] And Banks says he once saved a penalty from Carlos Alberto by 'outbluffing' him. With the courage, it is possible to dummy forwards into chipping (that is trying to lob the ball more gently over the goalkeeper's head) in circumstances when a full-blooded shot might be harder to deal with. Lesser goalkeepers can do this; they sometimes have to. I, definitely a lesser goalkeeper, know that I have often dummied people into choosing the near post rather than the far by making it look as if I had just left the gap slightly too wide to cover. It's miserable to get it wrong, when the ball pings right through the precise space I was trying to seduce him into aiming for, but there you go. There's always a convenient platitude somewhere around. Nothing ventured . . . but knowing how miserable it will be then, it's an elegant little pleasure when it works.

Professional goalkeepers will have experienced pleasures that cloggers will never have known. I imagine it is very pleasant to make forty or fifty thousand people swallow the word 'Goal!', but that counts as one of those obvious pleasures. Perhaps a heartening word from the crowd, just heard through the pandemonium all around, is a secret pleasure. Or that marvellously public handshake after a 0–0 draw, when the two goalkeepers honour each other in the fellowship of being the only two people in the stadium who are genuinely pleased and proud to have got the result nobody else wanted.

All these pleasures are stolen right in the face of disaster, which makes them all the sweeter. We know that goalkeeping can go terribly wrong at any moment. I once saw a bear, in Idaho, fishing from a gravel-bank in a fast-flowing stream. It sat there, one front paw lightly raised a few inches from the ground. Every so often, in fact quite surprisingly often, it would explode. The paw would slash into the water, with all that poundage of muscle accelerating its swing, and invariably it would come up with a salmon impaled on the claws. Goalkeepers have reflexes like that, astonishing for their sheer speed, but astonishing also for the control they manage to maintain even in their moments of most frenetic activity. Goalkeepers really can change direction in mid-air. Yet they know from bitter experience that even with their skills, they can be beaten by a hundred things, only one of which is likely to be the skill of the opponent. So to get it right once, to find that improbable cocktail of physical skills and attributes of character all functioning together in the perpetually repeated act of defiance that goalkeeping so often is, is itself a pleasure. Make a good save, at any level of football, from coats-for-goalposts upwards, and you will have done something which was extremely unlikely. It will, what's more, in all probability, not have been fully understood by those present, because only a fraction of it is visible. But then icebergs are even more awesomely beautiful when you know just what sits hidden beneath them. And your save will leave no trace in the score, normally no trace even in the collective memory of the game. The small pleasures are there to be found, goalkeepers know them full well.

All good goalkeepers spend a little time after games analysing play, analysing mistakes, working on theories or ideas of how to improve. Some do this formally, as a part of their training, and more do it in private moments, mulling over this and wondering whether that will work, and trying to remember all the ingredients of something they'd like to repeat. I don't think it possible to keep goal simply by going out there and doing it. It looks so very physical that it is difficult to remember how very ratiocinative a business it is in reality. The physical part, the leaping about, the catching and parrying, is only the end of a process which has started far upfield. To be in a position to make the final gestures in a goalkeeping move, the goalkeeper has to know more about his relation to the rest of the game than any other player. It is impossible to do without careful self-scrutiny. And that, in turn, means that goalkeepers are much more likely to know their own mistakes than other players. Outfield, where perfection is unasked-for and unexpected, imperfections are passed over in silence, or buried in the fluid instability of the game. A ball comes across the goal-mouth in front of a midfielder rushing to meet it at right angles. All he has to do to score is touch it, anyhow. He fears he can't quite reach it, and shoves his feet forwards, falling back as he does so, trying to slide the last few inches. If he misses, the ball goes harmlessly on across the field, and while everybody can see that there was nearly a goal, nobody blames him. He might have been slow to set off, slow in the running, running at a slightly wrong angle. Yet the accepted description is always that he was trying his best, that he didn't make it because he could not have made it. Close, but it didn't come off. There is no such latitude in goalkeeping. Not to make it is *prima facie* evidence of having done something wrong.

But goalkeepers know the difference. Because they have to think slowly and carefully about the game afterwards, they know when they have been left helplessly exposed by an error ahead of them, and they know when the mistake was genuinely their own. To keep goal is to accept responsibility in the fullest possible way. Peter Shilton made quite a thing of his willingness 'to be the first person to hold his hand up in the dressing-room afterwards and say "My mistake . . . sorry." This means so much to me . . . It's so important to me to be totally honest with the players around me.'[5] The vision is an odd one, of having to make a public confession, like a schoolboy, but the fact is there. Since goalkeepers really do understand the game so well in all its details, they have no choice but to understand when the error was theirs. The good ones are happy enough to say so, but all of them have grown used to being blamed when it was obvious to them that the blame was misplaced. Once in a while, a very visible mistake by a defender will be mentioned in despatches as the reason for a goal. But if there's no other candidate, the goalkeeper will always do.

That is simply a fact of life of keeping goal. But the corollary is less plain. Some goals, quite a lot, are described to include some phrase about the goalkeeper having 'no chance'. It is meant as an absolution: the ball came too fast, too far, there can be no blame for him not stopping it. But goalkeepers always have 'no chance', or put it this way, they work within such nightmarishly close tolerances of 'no chance' that to say of one particular goal that it left a goalkeeper with no chance becomes a way of saying simply that one doesn't understand where the goalkeeper could have done something differently to lengthen his chances. Peter Shilton again: 'I hate it when people say "Oh, the goalkeeper had no chance with that goal." Now obviously it's right in some cases, but sometimes I see keepers let in so-called wonder-goals which I've known well they could have stopped if they'd been good enough.'[6] It's a fantastically, almost cruelly high standard to set. But if a football match is a developing series of contingencies, then there is always somewhere in the sequence when something different could have been done which would have changed everything that followed. And if you happen to be Peter Shilton, to shrug that off with a 'no chance' is not to face up to the brutal standard, that nothing less than perfection will do. Anybody as driven as Shilton runs the risks of being seen as arrogant. He seemed greedy for acclaim. He sometimes spoke slightingly of other players, other performers. But it wasn't really that. It must have been almost insufferably frustrating to be the best in the world (I'm not going to argue; say 'among the three best' if you like) at something so public and yet to find that the public had no real understanding of how it worked. Because for a Shilton – and, by extension, for any other goalkeeper – there is no such thing as a goal leaving a goalkeeper 'no chance'. Shilton at his best could face 'no chance' a dozen times a day and beat it every time. So why allow it as an excuse the thirteenth time?

To understand this is to understand where goal-keeping defeats our normal ways of making sense of sports. Other sporting activities are measurable in terms that make at least some kind of sense. Athletes run personal best times. Wide receivers run record yardage. Baseball players and cricketers improve their batting averages. Even when the statistics are absurd – golfers make record amounts of prize money – they still carry some sort of approximate relation to what has actually been done, and translate at least some of the fans' respect for it into concrete terms. The American palaeontologist and historian of science Stephen Jay Gould once wrote an essay on Joe DiMaggio's famous fifty-six-game streak (he got at least one hit in each of fifty-six consecutive baseball games in 1941). In it he tried to show that what DiMaggio had achieved was more than just another sporting statistic:

> My colleague Ed Purcell, Nobel laureate in physics, but for purposes of this subject, just another baseball fan, has done a comprehensive study of all baseball streak and slump records. His firm conclusion is easily and swiftly summarized. Nothing ever happened in baseball above and beyond the frequency predicted by coin-tossing models. The longest runs of wins or losses are as long as they should be, and occur as often as they ought to. Even the

hapless Orioles, at 0 [wins] and 21 [losses] to start the 1988 season, only fell victim to the laws of probability.

But 'treasure your exceptions', as the old motto goes. Purcell's rule has only one major exception, one sequence so many standard deviations above the expected distribution that it should never have occurred at all: Joe DiMaggio's 56-game hitting streak in 1941. The intuition of baseball aficionados has been vindicated. Purcell calculated that to make it likely (probability greater than 50 per cent) that a run of even 50 games will occur in the history of baseball up to now (and 56 is a lot more than 50 in this kind of league), baseball's rosters would have to include either four lifetime .400 batters or 52 lifetime .350 batters over careers of 1,000 games. In actuality, only three men have lifetime batting averages in excess of .350, and no one anywhere near .400 (Ty Cobb at .367, Rogers Hornsby at .358 and Shoeless Shoe Jackson at .356). DiMaggio's streak is the most extraordinary thing that ever happened in American sports. He sits on the shoulders of two bearers – mythology and science. For Joe DiMaggio accomplished what no other ball player has done. He beat the hardest taskmaster of all, a woman who makes Nolan Ryan's fastball look like a cantaloupe in slow motion – Lady Luck.[7]

I don't apologize to English readers, who will have got very glaze-eyed reading that; we know that Americans insist on playing (and calling themselves world champions at) a lot of sports nobody else ever plays. Never mind. Even without having heard of Rogers Hornsby or being impressed by batting averages which seem to hover around one hit out of three, you have to admit that there is one way of talking about sports. The whole point of Stephen Jay Gould's essay is that without great care stats fail to measure something so momentous. 'We distinguish DiMaggio's feat merely by quantity along a continuum of courage; we should, instead, view his 56-game hitting streak as a unique assault upon the otherwise unblemished record of Dame Probability.' You could apply the same thesis elsewhere. Remember Brian Lara, the West Indian batsman, setting an English cricket season alight with that string of centuries, when luck seemed not just beaten but driven from the field? Or the great hurdler Ed Moses, who did things like keeping on winning *even with his shoelace untied*? The thesis fits well enough where there is anything even remotely plausible to measure.

But applied to goalkeeping it's a non-starter. What's to measure? Something didn't happen. Something didn't happen a lot? A lot of something didn't happen? Surprisingly little of something happened? Those figures again: Dino Zoff conceded no goals in internationals for a period of 1,142 minutes between September 1972 and June 1974; Sepp Maier conceded no goals for 475 minutes of the World Cup Finals in 1974; Chris Woods went 1,196 minutes without conceding a goal in the Scottish League season of 1986/87; Jim Stannard of Gillingham kept twenty-six clean sheets in a season (and, as his fans never stopped singing, ate all the pies); and Ray Clemence let in only those sixteen goals in another. Astonishing streaks, all of them, if you like that sort of thing, each including shining moments of glorious athletic genius. But so what? Who's going to beat Ray Clemence's record? The real stats in goalkeeping are that the other fellow should always score, and that each and every time he doesn't Dame Probability has been sent running for something easier to manage, like dice or heart disease.

Modern athletes like to talk about the 'pressure' they're under. It increases in the middle of great streaks, as it increases in cup ties. It is supposed to make it harder to do the simple things, easier to let nerves and the occasion give them the yips. Michael Parkinson, so often a wise and moderate voice in the shrill hyperbole of contemporary sports writing, once got fed up with all the loose talk of pressure: 'Goalkeepers carry the can more than most, or should that be they carry more of the can? In any event they are the only members of a football team who can truly claim to warrant that much over-used word "pressure".'[8] They are. To understand that is to understand the beginning of why goalkeeping is so appallingly difficult. It's not just that you've got to stop a ball from finding its way into that improbably large aperture. It's that you do it under the weight of all those hopes and dreams, every time. It's certainly a fine thing to let in no goals for a long time. Other people are very keen to force goals past you so it's difficult as hell. But merely to be a goalkeeper, a whole goalkeeper, is more onerous than any other player can easily understand. Other sportsmen can measure their climb towards excellence, but goalkeepers have accepted a savage equation whereby they know that the only stats that apply to them are the distance by which they fall short of perfection. For in the end, they always do.

The very stringency of that standard makes goalkeeping more like real life off the pitch, and less like playing games. One of the things I like about football is that it matters enormously while it's going on, but that importance vanishes the minute it's over. Anybody who truly believes Bill Shankly's *bon mot* about football being a lot more important than life and death needs his head examining. Of course it's a competitive sport, it goes without saying that to play it at all is to mind very much about winning. But that's as far as it goes. There is still a lot of value in losing well and with dignity, and there is still a lot to be said for honour and sportsmanship, more I think than is currently fashionable to allow. It is simply impossible to play in the goals without caring passionately about preventing every single attempt on goal. Only perfection will do, even though everybody knows it to be out of reach. And that, precisely that, is the only standard that applies to life outside football. Every single one of us will come, once in a while, to moments when the 'pressure' is up to the standards that are routine in goal. A crisis at work, when suddenly it is not the firm or the department that will cope but you, alone, now, and with something important at stake. Then you become a goalkeeper. Or imagine a dreadful case, of being at home with no telephone and no car when your child has an accident. It doesn't matter what you do as long as it works. There are no guides when circumstances are like that, no 'correct' things to be done. You have to react and your reactions have to be right. That's all. Less than perfection is a disaster, even if it was only a moment or a gesture less. Moments of crisis like that are starkly binary. There is no score on a scale of one to ten; it's either right or wrong. The switch is on or off.

Nearly right is not right. We recognize that rule in crises off the football pitch. If we only understood that goalkeepers live all their playing lives under exactly the same crushing finality we'd be unable to take them so very much for granted.

Anybody can have a single moment of glorious sporting 'rightness'. I suppose that anybody who can consistently reach the short holes in golf is capable of scoring a hole-in-one. In football every single action, from scoring goals all the way to taking nice throws-in, is like that; except goalkeeping. Only in goal do you stand or fall by a very different standard. But that standard happens to be the real one that we apply everywhere else, when it matters enough. Consistent perfection. Now do you begin to understand why I hold even an ordinary goalkeeper in such very high esteem? Leave alone a Tiger Khomich, a Gyula Grosics, or a Peter Shilton.

To reach this kind of standard, even to get near to it, is not the least incredible thing that goalkeepers do. That's why their blunders look so glaring, and why there is such unholy enjoyment to be had from watching them fail. Most of the time, of course, we spectators are not looking at perfection. The goalkeeper, like any other player, can do better or worse on any given day. The difference is that goalkeepers know they are judged only on the unforgiving comparison with the unachievable. They do let in goals they cannot in fairness be held responsible for. But they know – because they are in goal – that there is no consolation there. To let in such a goal is merely to confirm that there is better goalkeeping elsewhere, because somebody, on some day, would have saved it. There is really nowhere to hide. To be any good, quite apart from a physical gymnastic ability that is out of the reach of ordinarily athletic outfield players, involves ruthlessly understanding one's own weaknesses, so that a goalkeeping career becomes a long chain of revelations of one's own imperfections. They can be worked on in training, but only once they have been identified by rigorous self-analysis. Win or lose, the brutally honest dossiers goalkeepers keep on themselves and on the game need updating. On the field, the permanent risk is humiliation, the laughable catastrophe that is never further away than the next dropped cross or poor clearance from goal. And off it, that risk has to be processed, understood, eventually learnt from, and eliminated.

All sportsmen make efforts to improve their performances, of course, and many can make mistakes of terrible finality. But I think only goalkeepers play their sport in such comprehensive disjunction from the past. There is no 'personal best' in goal. What happened last week or the week before has no bearing on what is about to happen. Reputation, confidence, ultimately the ability even to do the simplest routine gestures are exposed and open to be shattered, every single time. We know that goalkeepers are mainly remembered, cruelly, for the goals they let in. No matter the hundreds, the thousands, they prevented. The bad one can always be the next one, is always actually likely to be. And when it comes, there is absolutely no redemption from the past. That's pressure, if you like. A goalkeeper can be the hero for a day, sure enough, but he can be the goat for a lifetime. People *expect* him to make mistakes, his own team first among them. To fight that, to persuade them again and again that it isn't so, that it won't happen this game, this shot, this corner, is a hell of a thing to do. All goalkeepers do it, all of the time. Few of them admit it. When goalkeepers recount, as all footballers have to sooner or later, the 'Match of My Life' they talk about a sequence of events, a save, an injury, a goal conceded. What they'll more rarely admit to is the fragility of the trust between themselves and the team, between themselves and the fans. They won't talk about the neurotic frenzy in which they spend the game, hideous sequences of unpredictabilities lining up like waves on the shore, all to be foreseen in good time.

Curiously, one of the places to find that aspect of goalkeeping best recounted is not in memoir or in reporting, but in a novel. Dan Kavanagh pseudonymously wrote a succession of thrillers about a bisexual private detective called Duffy, a familiar of the London that doesn't get printed on postcards. In one of them, Duffy investigates a football club, a royal straight flush of all that is most corrupt in football. And we learn that Duffy, in his spare time, is the goalkeeper for the Western Sunday Reliables. Duffy is neurotic, all right:

> One of the reasons he liked goalkeeping – and one of the reasons he worried – was that he liked things neat. He liked the neat box of the penalty area; he liked the way that it marked out his territory, his manor . . . He also liked the way that everything in his manor had corners: the penalty area, the goal area, the

woodwork; even the netting was made in squares. He liked these right angles: they reassured him. The only thing on his patch that didn't have corners was the penalty spot. A great big round chalky mess, as if some bloody enormous pigeon up above had decided to unload right in the middle of Duffy's manor: *splat*. Somebody ought to clear that mess up, Duffy thought. He didn't like the penalty spot. For a start, it was much too close.[9]

Duffy spends his games worrying about things that are about to happen. He's not a very good goalkeeper, but nor is he just a bloke who's gone in goal for the day. He has precisely the right understanding that 'Everything he does wrong is vital.' And he knows about being exposed:

Duffy checked his angles, got up on his toes, banged his gloves together and started inching out for when the winger beat the right-back. He would beat the back, of course: he'd done him three times already, no trouble. Once going inside, once outside, once nutmegging him in a show of public contempt. Which would he go for this time?

He went for simple pace – the cruellest method there is. Show the full-back every inch of the ball, give him a couple of yards, then just hare past him as if to say, Give it up, this game, don't bother, you're too fat, you're too slow, you're not smart enough. And that left it up to Duffy. Come out fast, narrow the angle, cut down the winger's options, make him pick one way or the other, don't go down too soon, but when you do go down, really spread yourself. Duffy was muttering the coaching manual to himself for company; there wasn't much other help around. The winger was closing fast. *Now*, thought Duffy, and started to spread himself. Just as he did so, the winger gave a little jink to the right, and took off at speed to the left. He beat Duffy, who couldn't lay a finger on him, legal or illegal . . .[10]

This is right. It is how goalkeepers think. Will I be embarrassed that way, or this? Nothing much good can come out of it either way. Is it possible that the worrying itself is a pleasure in goalkeeping? I don't think so. It is too painful, too often proved right. But to get the feeling of having mastered all that worry, to get to know that it was right to imagine the worst and prepare for it, and then to make the save precisely in that way, that is glorious. All too often, the spectators see the outcome. The forward, with the whole goal to aim for, managed to hit the goalkeeper. Or he didn't. Not a thought about what the goalkeeper had been doing. I say again, if only we could learn to understand that only the crudest bits of goalkeeping are visible, we would understand it better for the incredible activity that it is.

For much of its past, this most spectacular and most visible part of the game of football has been almost a secret pleasure. Aficionados treasure their moments and their men but the great bulk of the football-watching public have barely scratched the surface. Lowly Hereford beat Newcastle 2–1 in a famous FA Cup replay in 1972. The 'public' memory is of Ronnie Radford's goal, driven so fast from thirty-odd yards that it might as well have been hit from three, of which Newcastle's Irish international goalkeeper Ian McFaul said, 'It was the best goal I've had scored against me.' Fair enough. It was a wonderful goal. But imagine what it took to be Fred Potter, in the Hereford goal. To remember him and his performance is quite wrongly thought to be eccentric, as though he played a minor part in the game. He didn't, and goalkeepers don't.

Choose any match, or almost any, and the same can be said, adjusted for names and dates. Goalkeepers seem to vanish from the memory quicker than other players – I think, as I have said, because we cannot watch them with equanimity. We need to redress the balance. We need to acknowledge that everything that happens on a football field is directed from one of them towards another. There are certainly other pleasures in football than watching (and enviously admiring) goalkeepers, lots of them. But those other pleasures come as exceptions, as bonuses. The ordinary staple of any game will be that within it there will have been fine goalkeeping to wonder at, even if it didn't happen to be of the kind that makes the mouth drop open and the eyes start. It is almost self-evident that in any team the goalkeeper will be the one player who could easily make the transition to a higher level of football, where the ball is kicked faster and the time for thinking is less. Since the nature of his job means that he is used constantly to defeating superior odds against him, there is every reason to believe that he will continue to do just that when the odds get even longer. Which is not to say that any park goalkeeper could automatically excel in the Premier League; the elite of goalkeepers in any generation are athletes so far beyond the ordinary that it is absurd to think there might be dozens or hundreds who could match them. Nevertheless, the advantages in play all lie with the forwards, and yet goalkeepers regularly foil them. It isn't ever nothing. And sometimes, just sometimes, it is the most exhilarating, most astonishing thing in sport. To hit a baseball, even a lot of times in succession, is ridiculously easy compared to that.

10. Last Five

How vivid one's memory was in those early impressionable years of one's life, and I can still give the names of practically all the players in the first few years of Pompey's existence. For example, Matthew ('Ginger') Reilly, an Irish international goalkeeper, was a grand player, and the most remarkable goalie I have ever seen. Never, to my mind, has a keeper been known to punch a ball like this ex-Royal Artilleryman; his fist would emerge from a crowd of players and the ball would be returned almost to the halfway line.

In those days a goalkeeper was allowed to advance out of his goal, provided he did not carry the ball over the limited number of steps. I have seen Reilly patting the ball and dodging opponents to well past the halfway line, eventually passing to a forward to enable him to score. I never saw the ball taken away from him. He was unique in the art, and always delighted the home crowd with his antics. Another peculiarity was that he never wore gloves and seldom sported a cap.

He kept goal for Ireland against England on two occasions to my knowledge – I think 1900 and 1902. I have been told, and believe it to be authoritative, that Reilly was responsible for an alteration in the laws of the game. His play was actually a mixture

> of both soccer and rugger, and his wonderful skill of bouncing the ball (to which I have referred above) caused the Football Association to prohibit the handling of the ball outside the penalty area. Truly a mighty goalkeeper was Reilly, and though at that time Jack Robinson of Southampton, the English international, was referred to as the 'prince of goalkeepers', I still have my own definite opinion in this respect.[1]

Thus Alec Whitcher, director of Brighton and Hove Albion, and a more serious writer on football than his chatty style at first makes apparent. Whitcher was one of that band of enthusiastic players whose writings early on tried to address the problem of football being 'only' a working-man's amusement. They wrote from their own pleasure in the game, but they also wrote to counteract the snobbery, the contempt for the spectators, the refusal to treat football seriously that were endemic in the football culture until recently. If football has boomed beyond their wildest dreams (overturning some difficulties and, inevitably, raising others) it is in part due to the feeling they started. Treat football properly and it repays the treatment many times over. Treat it merely as the loutish pastime of persons you are too lazy or too self-interested to see as anything other than loutish themselves and you will have some of the horrors that we have known.

Long before Pete Davies started the 'revolution' in football writing with *All Played Out*, taking advantage of the surge in football passion that accompanied the Italian World Cup in 1990, these writers – who include A.H. Fabian, Ivan Sharpe, Bernard Joy, and later Danny Blanchflower, all far more renowned as players than

Whitcher, who was never more than a keen amateur – held in common a powerful sense that if only they could explain the sophistication under the apparent simplicity of the game, they might persuade readers to think on it in rather more depth. Whitcher became, as I say, the director of a club. Fabian was a famous Corinthian, Bernard Joy a fine player for Arsenal, Sharpe an international amateur, Blanchflower a star at Tottenham. They knew about the passion of football, of course they did, the unreasoning loyalty, the evanescence of glory, the sense of theatre in battle and battle in theatre. But they also understood that footballing virtues do not simply descend from the heavens on a picked and blessed handful. It is nowhere ordained that supporters of Real Madrid shall have perpetual success, nor that playing in a Brazilian national side automatically makes one a stylist of the game, a poet, or a samba dancer. It is not a law of nature that one's own chosen side should be enshrined in glory and the other fellow's mired in confusion.

One of the great advances in the football boom has been precisely that analysis has become a part of the game and a part of the attitudes that surround it. The whole basis of modern football coverage on television, for example, is analysis. To seek to understand more than we saw at first sight, to unravel mysteries, to add comprehension to delirium has become the way, and a good thing too. Not only within the game, either, in the business of shifting tactics, or changing personnel. Football and business, football and sociology, football in almost every connection that it has in our lives, all open to debate and available for understanding. Of course some of it is done ill, and of course some of it throws little light. No matter. Brian Glanville or Simon Inglis on corruption in the game, or Simon Inglis again on stadium design, or the Centre for Football Research on fans' attitudes to football and football's attitudes to its fans, much of what is good around football comes no longer from hagiography or adulation, but from thought. Even such apparently polemical developments as the series of oppositions to boardroom decisions about the financing of clubs, or the rise of the fanzines with their shrill hilarity in the rude collisions of the game, have their roots in a keen appreciation of the value of analysis. Many fanzines are terrible, but others are not, and the serious concerns they have raised have become as much a part of the football agendas as the long-ball game or the third-back of years ago. Serious clubs put the best fanzine editors on their committees, and the Football Supporters Association is more than an ordinary single-issue lobbying group. It is not enough, says our modern attitude to football, merely to leap about in a stripy bobble-hat and muffler. It is not enough merely to assume that they don't make 'em like Skinner Normanton any more. We actually find that we get more from the game if we think about it with precision, in detail and with care.

Analysis need not be, as it was for so long snobbishly assumed, in opposition to the popular, the demotic, and the instinctual. To take an analogy more familiar than football, it seems obvious that we can still enjoy the latest Hollywood action picture in all innocence (that may, given the content of the pictures, not be quite the right word). But for many years there has been a branch of criticism devoted to the cinema which has much more profound analyses to offer than the merely appreciative 'great special effects' or 'pity about the car chase' which may well be all we feel as we emerge blinking from any particular movie. It is right that it should be so, and at long last it seems that the two levels have begun to co-exist in football. We like analysis now, we seek it out and take an extra pleasure from it. It by no means need diminish our pleasures in the game to understand more about it and its ramifications; nor do we need ostentatiously to take learning, scepticism, or theory into the grounds when we go. Football is not beyond criticism precisely because it is not beyond understanding, and the newish manner in which the search for understanding is encouraged to co-exist with the simpler delight in the game is surely an advance. We can have both, and should. Increasingly, we do. We have still the thrilling agonies of the game itself, but we also have the beginnings of a shared delight in turning our minds to it.

But then why, and how, has goalkeeping been so late in getting the same attention? In some respects, it simply hasn't been late. No doubt an Andy Gray or an Alan Hansen can turn the ultra-slow-motion videotapes on passages of goalkeeping as they can on any other type of play, and they do. We know that more clubs now have specialized goalkeeping coaches (although how they ever managed without remains a considerable puzzle), and we see that kit manufacturers devote quite special research to goalkeeping gloves, to padded shorts and shirts, and so on. In a covert, creeping sort of way, goalkeepers seem to have more of a voice than they used to; at least the new glossy magazines devoted to football interview them with a frequency not vastly disproportional to their number within the game. And I believe that small boys, keen in the manner of the times to demonstrate their individuality more than their membership of a caste, are more likely now to hold a goalkeeper as their hero than they ever were. There are discernible signs that goalkeeping is no longer quite the footballing odd man out that it used to be. Gradually, we can say, goalkeepers are creeping up from incomprehension, disdain, and lack of attention to something a little more respectably visible.

But there is so far to go, and the pressures are so great, that it may be too little and too late. Goalkeepers are still not paid the same as their outfield colleagues, though their worth to their sides is likely to be many times greater. Their transfer fees have not caught up; if anything, they are proportionately down on the prodigious (the lunatic?) amounts spent on the top goalscorers. This question of the value of goalkeepers to clubs may have been obscured by the recent influx of foreign goalkeepers into the Premier League (and to a lesser extent into other British leagues). But if the Premier League is now awash with foreign goalkeepers – and it has been for a while, ranging from the Double-winning brilliance of a Peter Schmeichel all the way to the hardly tested and the barely proven – does this mean that there is a shortage of British players of the right standard? Or does it mean that coaches and scouts, not really very alert to the difference between a fine goalkeeper and a great one, have gone bargain-hunting where they could, and felt satisfied with what they have got? Certainly, the old myth of British goalkeeping has had to evaporate a little. Nobody can blithely assume British-is-best any more, when so many clubs have brought their goalkeepers in from abroad. Although it is still true that British league goalkeepers are among the busiest in the world. The particular style of play that we see most often here, of muscular and swift endeavour preferred to more skilful but slower development, brings the goalkeepers tremendously into the game. Elsewhere, particularly in those countries where man-to-man marking is the norm, a goalkeeper may have less to do in a game. But then a good one will do those things just as well when required. British may not be best, but there is no such thing as a bad goalkeeper in the Premier League, and there are not many a division or two lower, or in senior football in Scotland either. The general standard is still astonishingly high, even if the practitioners come from all over the place.

Yet the standard of analysis – the standard, if you will, of sympathetic comprehension – has not really 'trickled down'. For me, the goalkeeper in an averagely busy match is almost by definition the man of the match. He has quite routinely been asked to do the improbable, sometimes the impossible, and has equally routinely gone ahead and done it. He's what Americans call the MVP, the Most Valuable Player, not always, certainly, but a great deal more often than is acknowledged. 'Oh yes,' says a manager on television several times a season, 'our goalkeeper is worth a goal a game to us.' A goal a game! But most teams in most games are separated by only a single goal. A goal a game is the difference between winning and losing, many times a year. A goal a game is something forwards rarely manage for a handful of games in succession, never at all over whole seasons or whole careers. The fans don't see it because they daren't. The administrators continue their relentless barrage of assaults on goalkeeping: free kick if a goalkeeper holds the ball more than five seconds; ban back-passes altogether; outlaw the throw-in by a defender to a goalkeeper. The proposals come along thick and fast. It should be possible to treat them as a series of madcap threats stemming from frustration at one goalkeeper's excellence one day. That would be a testimony to his superiority, a compliment, like asking a boxer to fight an apprentice with one hand behind his back. But it is not so. I no longer think it absurd to imagine a future without goalkeepers; the rate at which changes to their role are proposed is accelerating all the time. And we've barely begun to understand how brilliant what they do can be, and how fundamental to the game.

Alec Whitcher's fond writing about Matthew Reilly is not really that different to what all fans do. Everyone of us has a favourite goalkeeper in the files somewhere. Many are more or less forgotten by the generality of football people, but remembered because they were our men, who provided the reassurance or the amusement we have since found lacking in their successors. How old are you? Are you of the Frank Swift generation? The Peter Bonetti? Did you stand on the terraces behind John

Jackson or Sam Bartram? Or you may have more local memories. Does the name Chick Farr tingle your ear? You learnt your football on the terraces at Bradford Park Avenue. You've never quite trusted a goalkeeper since Cliff Binns? You were brought up in Barnsley and ought to be thinking of retiring. You think things have gone downhill since Peter Downsborough? You come from Swindon, and you think that Downsborough's match, the League Cup Final of 1969 against Arsenal, wrongly thought of as Don Rogers's match, was the high point of your life as a supporter. We all do this. It is a natural condition of sports-following that the earliest memories provide the yardstick, and too bad if the yardstick is time-warped. That side of the appreciation of goal-keeping is nearly private. It is different for each of us, following odd personal circumstances rather than the shared public story of the game. It can take as little as an uncle escorting a six-year-old to a match to start a lifelong but hardly public affection for one particular goalkeeper.

It runs seamlessly into the really private. At school I used to worry about whether I'd ever be as good a goalkeeper as Iain Patrick, but he was nice and taught me a lot of stuff before he became bored by it and got excited by the aerodynamics of racing cars instead. I knew I was a better goalkeeper than Robin Knapp, but how could I make sure everybody else knew it? We all do that kind of thing, too. The curious thing is that there is much less public history of goalkeeping than of the rest of football. People don't sit around in pubs reminiscing nostalgically about Luis Arconada or Renat Dassaev or

Adam Blacklaw or George Farm. (I do, but then, what do you expect? The keeper's a nutter . . .) Great goal-keepers can vanish almost completely. Not just when they played a long time ago, like Ned Doig or Willie Foulke or Albert Iremonger or Happy Jack Hillman. I conducted a microscopic straw-poll the other day, and found people couldn't remember Dino Zoff's name. Zoff, still active and high-profile in football, once the captain of Italy, one of the All-Stars. If Zoff can disappear into oblivion, what hope has a Tony Macedo or a Tommy Lawrence? The reason is that every single time a goal-keeper becomes involved in play, the punters think they're going to be deprived of what they think they hold most dear. A goal.

A while ago Radio 5 Live ran a series of programmes on black footballers in which they examined such things as the persistent racism black players have had to deal with, from the obscenity of racist abuse on the terraces to the persistent myth that black players lacked the courage and stamina of white colleagues.[2] The researchers uncovered much that was fine, on such people as the South African Albert Johanesson, Clyde Best, and Howard Gayle. I, for one, knew nothing of Walter Daniel Tull, a complete hero, who became the first black man to be commissioned an officer in the army and died at the second battle of the Somme. Nor had I heard of Arthur Wharton, apparently the first black player of all in the English League, whose father was Grenadian and whose mother was Scottish. Wharton came from Darlington and played for seven clubs in a fifteen-year career, retiring from Stockport County in

1902. He was a prodigiously gifted goalkeeper, whose 'party trick' was to jump up and swing from the crossbar to catch crosses with his feet. He was an all-rounder at cricket, and apparently a competent or slightly better than competent boxer. But he was also the first person to run one hundred yards in under ten seconds. Now whatever one's feelings about goalkeeping, that is one of those athletic milestones that should never be forgotten. It is surely as important as Roger Bannister's sub-four-minute mile. It seems quite inconceivable to me that an athlete of Wharton's calibre should simply have disappeared from our collective recall, but he has. He should be an athletic hero, a cultural hero. There should be songs about him.

Wharton was something of a Grobbelaar, a clowning and acrobatic goalkeeper. He was mildly disapproved of by the newspapers for that (and routinely referred to at best as 'dusky'), although there is no doubt at all that he was widely respected as a goalkeeper. He rivalled Dr Mills-Roberts as the goalkeeper of Preston North End, in the period immediately after that during which Preston earned the title of 'The Invincibles' by passing through an entire League season undefeated. At that time Preston, who openly paid their players before any other club (and who for that reason were largely responsible for the League being forced to accept professionalism), could afford the very best players in the land. The inference is that Wharton was considered the best by such a fine judge as the great Preston manager, Major Sudell.

Moreover, there is some evidence, as there is with all great goalkeepers, that Wharton invented techniques which dealt admirably with the state of the game as it was then. We know that as a runner he had an eccentric style: 'Sprinting of many kinds has been seen: some sprint bent forward, some with head and shoulders thrown back, but here is a man running away from his field with his body bent forward and running almost on the flat of his foot . . .'[3] As a goalkeeper, we know that he was especially adept at dodging forwards intent upon doing him harm, that he was gymnastic beyond the ordinary run of goalkeepers of the day, and that crowds loved to watch him. 'Tityrus' – J.A.H. Catton of the *Athletic News*, who must have known him well – generally admired his play very much: 'Wharton, although he lost that cigar, can still boast that no goal has been scored past him in the English Cup competition. The darkey *en passant* can give most goalkeepers a good start and a beating . . .'[4] Or again: 'Wharton is indeed a born goal-keeper; he never loses his head, and his hands are always in readiness. His was one of the best exhibitions of goalkeeping I have seen for a very long time.'[5] Wharton is a huge figure in the history of football, who languishes unknown not simply because he played a long time ago, but because he happened to play in a position for which our respect has always been more grudging than it ought. If that is gradually changing, it is high time we rescued figures such as Wharton from an obscurity that is discreditable not to them, but to us.

The odd thing is that little Englanders have long prided themselves on a respect for goalkeeping higher than was found elsewhere. It is as though the perception of goalkeeping corresponded to something central in the national self-perception. And at one level, I suppose it does. Nothing more closely matches the gallant heroism of a doomed square of infantry finally giving way before a vastly superior force than a yellow roll-neck and cloth cap under siege from ten outfield players with a couple of thousand yelling fans behind. The goalkeeper in England is the patron saint of the last ditch and the backs-against-the-wall; no regiment wears a goalkeeper on its cap badge, but they could. We love our goalkeepers for accepting the impossible situations we put them in, at the same time as despising them, in the end, for not always turning those situations around.

It has not always been quite so simple. There are some corners where respect for fine goalkeeping has never been any less than respect for anything else in football. At Liverpool, the Kop acquired over the years a lasting reputation for applauding opposing goalkeepers who had done well before them, and for a veritable connoisseurship of their own. There are lots of descriptions of 'enemy' goalkeepers gratefully receiving ovations from the Kop, even when Liverpool had been beaten as a result. This is not nothing, a public display of sportsmanship that revels in the game itself more than in the result. And it does seem to be true that Liverpool as a club laid more store in making sure they consistently had great goalkeepers than some of their rivals. Of course Liverpool have not had a monopoly, but the honour roll of their goalkeepers is of an incredibly high standard. In the early days, Ned Doig, Sam Hardy, Elisha Scott (of whom was told the story that when he met his great rival, the Everton centre-forward Dixie Dean, in the street one day and Dean nodded his head casually to say hello, Scott flung himself full-length on the pavement to save the swift header he expected to follow) . . . Tommy Lawrence, Ray Clemence, Bruce Grobbelaar. Who knows whether David James will one day have a name as high as these? Incumbents in goal at Liverpool have a lot more than contemporary forwards to contend against. Liverpool's success has been unparalleled, and the conclusion is inescapable. There must be a direct connection between a club that so assiduously collects the finest goalkeepers it can find and then trains them to be still better, and the seemingly endless run of successes that such a club has enjoyed.

Many other clubs have failed to see the lesson. The long caesura in Manchester United's fortunes between the glory days of Sir Matt Busby and the more recent ones under Alex Ferguson can be explained in all sorts of ways, but the salient fact remains that they were a side which didn't seem to pay much attention to goalkeeping. Let the team play the United way (when they could), and surely any goalkeeper would do. They did have goalkeepers capable of brilliance, of course, but no one to match the sustained consistent standard of a Hardy or a Clemence. Even Alex Stepney who, after all, shared in winning the European Cup with Manchester United, falls into that category. Gary Bailey could do quite incredible things, but could not, I think, be *expected* to do them every day, any day. Once Peter Schmeichel arrived – bought for less than half a million pounds, a ludicrous fee by the standards of today, the greatest bargain in modern football – all the so-near-but-so-far stories became championships and FA Cups. It is not a coincidence. Ferguson knew that when he bought him. He expected perfection in goal, and got it. So did Brian Clough with Peter Shilton. It is completely inconceivable that Forest could have won what they did without Shilton; but, and this is where it begins to look hyperbolic, it is perfectly conceivable that another club would have done had he gone to them instead. Any First Division side, I say, could have won the European Cup with Peter Shilton playing in the form he showed in his great final against Hamburg.

The goalkeeper *is* the most important man in the team. Get a weak one, even a fractionally weak one, and he will be exposed in the end. Don Revie's Leeds were so nearly a complete football team. Could they really not have found a more reliably certain goalkeeper than Gary Sprake? Even by scouring the country or the globe, and paying a high fee to get him? They had the money. What might have happened if they had? And so many other clubs. They simply haven't felt it important enough. The directors, the coaches, and the fans simply haven't noticed the plainly self-evident fact: get a good goalkeeper, make him confident of his place in the side, understand the difficulties he labours under, and trust him to improve in time, and the fortunes of the team will race upwards in proportion. Get a great one, and the sky is the limit. It is no coincidence that at Liverpool, in the days before fax machines, the club's telegraphic address was one word: GOALKEEPER.

Then there is the converse position. Great goalkeepers can and do hide the inadequacies of the teams they play for, often for years in succession. Everton have fallen, by their own standards, on hard times of late. (I am aware that writing such a sentence is tempting fate. It is perfectly possible that they may be top of the table as you read these lines. But I will risk a hazarded guess forward.) Neville Southall is coming to the end of a long and very distinguished career in goal. Do you really believe that they will stay up with the big boys if they fail to replace him with somebody of as nearly the same calibre as they can find? I don't. I think that only when they have gone do football clubs notice just how very much they owed to goalkeepers out of the ordinary. Take a team like Coventry, perpetually just managing to stay in the top division year after year, but only just. That is not attributable to 'fighting spirit' or 'character' or any other platitudinous obfuscation. It is the personal triumph of Steve Ogrizovic, their long-serving goal-keeper. Even if, at a conservative estimate, he only turns five or six losses a season into drawn games (and he does a very great deal more), that makes enough difference, in a very marginal equation, to allow a mediocre team to stay in the Premier League. The consequences for the club are huge. Perhaps it would be unreasonable to expect him to be rewarded for a massive contribution to the self-esteem of the club and of its fans. But he is also making possible vastly increased revenues, and football clubs are supposed to be run as businesses now-adays. I have no information, but I am wholly certain that Ogrizovic is not Coventry's highest earning player. He wouldn't be, he's just the goalkeeper. But how

Coventry will regret his departure when they drop down a division the season after he leaves.

Few serious goalkeepers are not somehow missed after they have gone. They become part of the fans' nostalgic baggage, even when they get scant acknowledgement in the official or near-official double-entry ledgers of the game. Once a goalkeeper no longer plays he no longer terrifies the crowd. Accidents can no longer happen then, and it becomes much easier to think of the departed goalkeeper as the genuine hero he never quite was while he played. While points and qualifying and getting one stage further in competitions were at stake, the goalkeeper was routinely loathed – the word is not too strong: the abuse even favoured goalkeepers get just before they make an intervention, when the supporters' terrible hunger for victory, for the avoidance of all that they feel consequent upon defeat, makes them lose any semblance of fairness towards goalkeepers, is really frightening to hear – but once gone it is much easier to pretend that he was respected all along. Fans don't like to be reminded of their own horrible fickleness. They turn, savagely, on players whenever anything important is at stake. Which means, inevitably, that they turn on goalkeepers as often as on anybody. It is easier to be nostalgic, easier to pretend it was not so. For the buck stops with the goalkeeper whether the ball does or not. Goalkeepers are more than the physical last man, the last man on the field. They become the easiest target for the disaffection, the disappointment that runs hand in hand with the euphoria in football.

Goalkeepers, until the recent proliferation of very

long lenses, were always photographed from the rear. Press photographers, like the fans, were there to photograph the high points of the game, which meant the goals. Spread in a shallow V behind the goals, photographers could only hope to see the goalkeeper from the front when he was turned sideways. Normally, what we saw was from the side and the back, while the forwards as often as not came straight towards the camera. We don't easily acknowledge how much of our appreciation of the beauty in sport is due to photography. Until shutter speeds were fast enough to freeze it, nobody had seen a goalkeeper arched and twisting high in the air reaching a ball at the limit of the possible. Now that we all have, they have become standard images of extreme athletic grace, just as the beads of sweaty moisture knocked from the brow of a boxer at the moment of impact are standard images of athletic pain or effort. But even those glorious pictures were from the back. The camera looks beyond the goalkeeper. If the truth were admitted, many pictures of great saves are really frustrated pictures of goals. It would have been more were it not that photographers know that with limited time and an obligation to send to their papers something as spectacular as possible, to beat rivals and get the big picture on the page, they have no better option than to concentrate on the goalkeepers. Rare indeed is the game in which a goalkeeper will not perform the most acrobatic act on the field. We back-page readers have got so used to seeing goalkeeping in this sideways-and-from-behind angle that we no longer really wonder about it. It fits. We barely look goalkeeping in the face.

Even goals conceded, so desperately prayed against at the time, become acceptable when seen backwards. Alec Whitcher, whose books are old-fashioned now, but who was by no means a nostalgia specialist when he wrote, remembered one such goal:

I was told of another such interesting incident which concerned B. Howard-Baker when the Corinthians played at Copenhagen subsequent to the 1914–18 war. As the Corinth team entered the field of play for their first game, stretched right across one of the stands and held in position by a host of spectators, were many yards of broad white canvas, upon which was printed these words: PLEASE, MR BAKER, GIVE US ONE GOAL.

Strange to relate, when the Corinthians were leading 3–0, barely ten minutes from time, Howard-Baker was suddenly brought into action to deal with a long shot which appeared to be going well wide of the post, but as the ball bounced it shot inwards at an acute angle and entered the net. This caused intense merriment, and brought terrific applause from the huge crowd; 'Mr Baker' had, after all, acceded to their long-awaited request. 'H.B.' will, I am sure, thus be fondly remembered by them as the most generous goalkeeper this country has ever sent to Denmark's shores.[6]

Howard-Baker was an all-round athlete, like Arthur Wharton. He won prizes both at water polo and at high-diving, and held the British high-jump record for many years. He was selected for the Stockholm Olympic games in 1912, and again in Antwerp in 1920. He was one of the comparatively few amateur players to have won a full international (as opposed to an amateur international) cap, and one of the very few to have been picked for an English League team. He played for Chelsea for some years and his appearances 'synchronised with a manifest improvement in the form of that club'.[7] He (or his predecessor in the Corinthian goal, W.R. Moon) is a convenient example of the greater gentleness with which we look at goalkeepers in the past because we tend today to see the gentlemanly outlook of the Corinthians as somehow faintly ludicrous. I think we forget how very good for years the Corinthian team was, and confuse their strict amateurism with amateurishness. Remember that the Corinthians twice supplied an entire English international team, in 1894 and again in 1895. Howard-Baker was certainly no gentlemanly joke in goal. He played regularly for the Corinthians from 1921 to 1931, at a time when they were often watched by crowds as big as any side, and the crowds adored him for his agility and for the spectacular long kicks he was able to deliver. The schoolmaster (himself a fine player for them) who wrote the history of the Corinthian club was in no doubt about his status: 'B. Howard-Baker stands supreme among Corinthian goalkeepers since the Great War.'[8]

We are, however, wise to make allowances when reckoning up Corinthian records. For their amateurishness did go so far as to create two peculiar traditions. In the first place, they stopped trying to score once they had nine, and any player on their side who scored a tenth would pay for all the drinks that evening. Secondly, they refused to contest penalties fairly awarded against them. So, for example, in 1920 a Corinthian handled the ball in the penalty area during a match against Crystal Palace and 'true to tradition, the Corinthians did not attempt to defend; and when the kick was taken, the ball was put into the empty goal, with the goalkeeper [in fact the Reverend B.J. Scott] an interested spectator'.[9] This kind of attitude, of course, only works if it is observed on both sides. When the Corinthians played, it seems to have been: in the season 1924/25, the Corinthians played the first games against German opposition since the war, on a tour. They played twice against the Hamburg Sports Verein: 'There was a most interesting feature towards the close of the first game; one of Corinth's men handled in the penalty area, although it was obviously unintentional, but a penalty was awarded. Amidst a hush of excitement, the kick was taken by one of the Hamburg players, who, however, made no attempt to score. This sportsmanlike act made a great impression on the crowd.'[10] Is it absurd to say that a little of that would go a long way in modern football? Crowds love sportsmanship when they think they can afford to. Think only of the way it was always applauded when a team who had a man injured and won a throw-in by the opposition kicking the ball into touch to allow him to receive treatment then returned the ball from the throw. I wonder if a no-attempt-to-save a right, or a no-attempt-to-score a wrong, penalty would still be possible. I want to see it done.

Of course it is easy to be nostalgic about the Corinthians. But my point is that we tend to think that way about goalkeeping in general. I can think of only one goalkeeper who is consistently remembered with real hatred, and that for one single incident. British audiences know nothing about the German goalkeeper Toni Schumacher (his first name was Harald, but he took the name Toni in honour of the great German goalkeeper Toni Turek) except that he once nearly killed Patrick Battiston (of France) in Seville in 1982 in a World Cup semi-final. It was a grotesque foul, hideously violent. Battiston, racing on to a long pass in the middle of the field, was past the German defence when Schumacher charged him down. Battiston had to lie there, unconscious and missing some teeth, for what seemed ages as the medical personnel had been barred from the field, which made his agony seem worse to the spectators. Schumacher should obviously have been sent off, and since less than an hour of the game had been played, this would certainly have given the French a good chance of winning a place in the final. He wasn't even booked. The notoriety of this incident was extraordinary. On the strength of that one moment, Schumacher's run-of-the-mill autobiography became one of the very few sporting books about an athlete with no connection to this country to be translated into English.[11] For a publisher to think it worthwhile gives some idea of the storm Schumacher's foul raised.

Schumacher came across as something less than perfectly sympathetic. An utterly driven man, he doesn't hesitate to whine about team-mates in club and national sides, to make disparaging comments about his predecessor Sepp Maier, for example, or his rival Jean-Marie Pfaff, the great Belgian goalkeeper who earned his living in the German league. He is vengeful in print when he has felt slighted, uptight and savagely competitive for recognition. He mentions a meeting with Lev Yashin, by then long retired and amputated of one leg, a sad figure 'like a burnt-out Formula 1 car without an engine', solely because Yashin paid him a compliment or two.[12] He even claimed to have become friendly with Battiston after the foul, although the form this took was that he offered to pay for the new teeth.

Yet much of what Schumacher has to say about goal-keeping is interesting, the perceptions of a hard, tough man on a hard, tough career. Nostalgia can't really deal with Schumacher: his fifteen minutes of fame, for British fans at least, are simply too brutal. But make no mistake, unsympathetic as he undoubtedly was, he was a very fine goalkeeper. I would say that in the 1982 World Cup Finals, at the time of that foul, he was second in the world only to Renat Dassaev. They can't all be gentle giants after the manner of Pat Jennings or Frank Swift. It takes something of the steel of a Schumacher or a Peter Shilton to become that good. Most manage to conceal the hardness, and not only for reasons of public relations or public presentation. It happens to all goal-keepers to let in goals, of course, and some will inevitably be soft goals. A goalkeeper who makes a big show of toughness and resistance exposes himself to more ridicule when he does let in a bad one than one who has hidden exactly the same qualities under a more agreeable or more sportsmanlike veneer. But they are very hard men all the same. There is nobody more ferociously competi-tive than a world-class goalkeeper, nobody tougher. Gentle old Bert Trautmann, loved by the whole of Manchester? He was a paratrooper, who served on the Russian front, the kind of man with the resources to escape from captivity. You'd be a fool to think him anything less than very tough indeed.

Goalkeepers hate to let in goals. Even in training, even against kids. In the match programme for Pat Jennings's farewell match at Highbury, on 8 May 1985, Glenn Hoddle wrote, 'Pat was brilliant in many games but some of the things he did in training were little short of astonishing. In shooting practice he might let in a few but then he would say, "Right, that's your lot," and you just couldn't score against him after that. He was unbelievable. Pat would unveil his whole repertoire of saves and each carried a hallmark of class. I have no hesitation in describing him as the greatest goalkeeper I have ever seen in the world.'[13] They all hate it, and there is no doubt that some of the greatest saves ever made have been executed on training pitches only in front of team-mates. To be able to say, against professional players of Hoddle's class intent on scoring, 'Right, lads, that's your lot', and then prove it so is incredible. You just can't do that without being tougher than most of us can imagine. The strength of will, the resistance to pain, the determination, the astounding competitiveness that keeps you in there against quite devastating odds. And that was Jennings, the most modest and the least obviously tough goalkeeper there has been. Nostalgia's all very well in its place, but it does no harm to remember things as they were from time to time, too. Not all goalkeepers are as openly tough as Toni Schumacher, and few are anywhere near as good as Jennings. But believe me, all the good ones are very, very hard men indeed. It's not particularly *nice*. But it is one of the ingredients of world-class sport. They have it.

To return to the Corinthian era a moment, with some of the nostalgia washed from our eyes. It was frequently noticed that Corinthian players were physically large, whether from the relative opulence of their gentlemanly diet, or because the selectors looked for bulk, I don't know. They needed to be. Until 1892, when the laws were amended to allow the charging of a goalkeeper only 'in the act of playing the ball or while obstructing an opponent' (still allowing plenty of latitude to forwards), it had been perfectly legal physically to attack the goalkeeper well before the ball reached him. There was often a specialist 'goal-rusher' whose duties were largely confined to disposing of the goalkeeper whenever the ball came anywhere near:

Charging the goalkeeper was a definite form of attack, and was permissible so long as the chargers were onside when the ball was last kicked. In consequence, we learn that 'from a fine middle by Bambridge, Prail got a capital goal, Dewhurst having previously disposed of the goalkeeper'. Some teams, notably Preston North End, made full use of this licence. A half-back, carefully judging the time to pass, would kick the ball in the air in the direction of the goalkeeper who would at once be attacked by two of the inside-forwards, while the third would attempt to slip past the backs and shoot into the empty goal. Corner kicks were even more serious, for the goalkeeper, while side-stepping (and occasionally 'flooring') two forwards, he was still expected to get the ball away. For this reason, many goals were scored from 'scrimmages', and as there were then no nets, many too were the doubtful ones. On one occasion Blackburn Olympic scored a 'classic' goal in that it was palpably offside and did not go between the posts![14]

It's not legal any longer, but it still goes on. Set your video to slow motion and watch what happens to a goalkeeper preparing to receive a corner. You'll see.

Seeing is the beginning. Go to a match, professional or semi-professional or amateur, and concentrate on the goalkeeper for half an hour. You've never done it before. Watch what he does, and try to follow why. He's the captain, arranging his defenders at speed, a general in charge of an orderly retreat. He's busy, all the time, even while standing on the edge of the 'D' staring ahead. There's risk to be evaluated, even then. Things go wrong, an opening presents itself. Then he moves faster than a kingfisher over a stream, but curiously, he's less busy, even though all you see is the blur of his motion. Because then he's only doing one thing, the other options having vanished for the second. Moving, covering that enormous goal. He may not have made it. It doesn't matter. Don't worry about the goal. Work out why not, where he went wrong. Was it the simple failure, the physical failure, of reaction time beaten or the top corner uncovered? Or a misjudgement, a failed gamble or a failure of nerve, a more complex flaw uncovered by a skilful opponent? You won't be halfway there when it happens again, better this time. Something saved, a swinging throw beautifully arcing in the air, biting the turf and spinning neatly into the stride of a team-mate.

Two passes. The other defence beaten for speed. A goal, and the goalkeeper made it. Now you're beginning to see. Keep at it. His left-back is consistently beaten for speed. It makes him creep to cover an area, makes his defending lop-sided. A better forward line would use that. They try it. He knew it was likely, knew where to move as soon as they found it. He's covered something which five minutes ago you wouldn't have noticed. You're getting the swing of it now. What if? Or what if? By God, he's quicker than he looks. He seems to have understood before it had happened. This is sport, all right, not some oddity tacked onto football.

Let's have nostalgia about goalkeeping by all means. One of the things sport can do is provide memories. But let's also have a clear idea of what we ask our goalkeepers to do. The nostalgia too often is a past-tense version of our present incomprehension. All goalkeepers are idiots, crazy as loons, unathletic, and grimly defeated. Ergo, all past goalkeepers were like that, and we remember them fondly because they can't ruin our weekend or our season any more. It doesn't begin to answer the purpose. It is not a punishment to go in goal, a sinecure, or a refuge. It is the place where physical skills of an order unparalleled meet mental demands as frightening as anything in sport. It is a fine thing to be a goalkeeper, any goalkeeper. To be a great one deserves admiration, merits every effort to understand.

I don't care which goalkeeper gets you in the end, which one persuades you that there is a whole vital part of football you had never really noticed before. It might be the sulky one of Simon Armitage's poem:

A man who stubs his reefers on the post
and kicks his heels in the stud-marks and butts,
lighting the next from the last, in one breath
making the save of the year with his legs,
taking a deep drag on the goal-line
in the next; on the one hand throwing out
or snaffling the ball from a high corner,
flicking off loose ash with the other . . .

He is what he is, does whatever suits him,
because he has no highfalutin song
to sing, no neat message for the nation
on the them of genius or dedication;
in his passport, under 'occupation',
no one forced the man to print the word
'custodian' . . .[15]

Or, following the cheery philosophy of its being only a game (which it is, of course; but what the people who try to detract from it by saying that forget to add is that it can matter like hell and still be a game), you might have sympathy with and a laugh from the poor schoolboy goalkeeper, Jupkins:

Joe Jupkins was a goalie,
Resourceful, active, bold,
Yes, admirable wholly;
But, ah, he felt the cold.

So, since a second sweater
Still failed to meet his wants,
Nor was his plight the better

ONLY THE GOALKEEPER TO BEAT

For three thick pairs of pants,

When his side pressed, believing
That danger was there none,
His goal unguarded leaving,
Around it he would run.

A fool to take such chances?
Perhaps; but don't forget,
His school had not finances
to give the goal a net.

So if, the pressure stopping,
The foe did break away,
Back through the goalposts popping,
He'd stand again at bay.

Unconquered to the Final
Joe and his comrades came.
Five minutes left, and nine all!
It was *a thrilling game!*

Down to the far end surging,
his forwards shot and shot;
So, from his lair emerging,
Joe started round to trot.

But – since, I know it well, you
Will not believe my tale,
There was, I ought to tell you,
That day a strongish gale –

By crises still unshaken,
The back (a giant) cleared,

And to that goal forsaken
By Joe, the ball careered.

'Get back, you blighter! Hurry!
Get back!' the warning came;
And with a calm 'Don't worry!'
Joe turned to join the game.

O horror! O disaster!
How could you, Joe, forget
That yesterday your master
Had bought the goal a net?

There, through the meshes peering,
Like some poor chimp caged up,
Helpless he watched doom nearing.

* * *

How Jupkins lost the Cup.[16]

Or, if you prefer your verse a fraction more . . . elevated:

The Ball no Question makes of Ayes and Noes,
But Right or Left as strikes the Player goes;
And He that toss'd thee down the Field,
He knows all about it all – HE knows – HE knows![17]

It really doesn't matter where you start to get the feeling that goalkeeping is more than you'd always thought. It's high time. Some goalless draws are dull, but so are many wins. Sometimes a goalkeeper will lay out before you a feast, a six-course banquet of goalkeeping.

From Albertosi to Zubizareta, from Arconada to Zoff, there's an alphabet out there. All it takes is a little effort to understand.

Just one thing. Please, the next time the commentator's voice rises an octave, as the defence gapes and the forward goes galloping goalwards, when he yells, 'Now! He's got only the goalkeeper to beat!' Just ask yourself: *only*? What's with this *only*?

Notes

Introduction

1. Sam Bartram, *By Himself* (Burke, 1956), p. 77.

Chapter 1

1. James Walvin, 'The People's Game' in *The History of Football Revisited* (Mainstream, 1994 edn), p.36.
2. Philip Stubbes, *The Anatomie of Abuses* (1538), ed. F. J. Furnirall, New Shakespeare Society Series VI, no. 61 (London, 1879), p. 137.
3. Alexander Barclay, *Eclogues V*, quoted by Derek Birley in *Sport and the Making of Britain* (MUP, 1993), p.62.
4. *Calendar of Inquisitions*, Misc. (Chancery) (London, 1916), I, p.599, item 224. This and the following reference are taken from Percy M. Young's *History of British Football* (Sportsman's Book Club edn, 1969), p. 13. Both incidents are referred to in several other histories of football.

5. W.H. Bliss (ed.), *Calendar of Entries in the Papal Registers relating to England and Ireland* (London, 1895), II, p. 162.

6. H.T. Riley (ed.), *Munimenta Gillhalliae Londoniensis* (London, 1859–62), vol. III, app. II, p. 439, cited in F.P. Magoun, *History of Football from the Beginnings to 1871* (Cologne, 1938).

7. See, e.g., Magoun, *History*; Denzil Batchelor, *Soccer, A History of Association Football* (Batsford, 1954); Young, *History* (Stanley Paul, 1968); Geoffrey Green, *Soccer: The World Game* (1953). Quoted verbatim from the minutes of the meeting in the Official History of the Football Association, and often since, e.g. Geoffrey Green, *Soccer: The World Game* (Sportsman's Book Club, 1954), p. 26.

8. Speech by E.C. Morley of the Barnes club.

9. Terence Delaney, *Century of Soccer*, (Sportsman's Book Club, 1963), p. 23.

10. H.C. Benham, *Football at Westminster School.*

Chapter 2

1. Caxton (1960), vol. I, p. 154.

2. Willy Meisl, *Soccer Revolution* (Phoenix Sports Books, 1955).

3. Pete Davies, *All Played Out – The Full Story of Italia '90* (Heinemann, 1990), p. 376.

4. J.A.H. Catton ('Tityrus'), *Wickets and Goals* (Chapman and Hall, London, 1926), p. 159.

5. Simon Inglis, *League Football and the Men Who Made It* (Collins, 1988), p. 392.

6. See, e.g., Nick Hazlewood, *In the Way! Goalkeepers: A Breed Apart?* (Mainstream, 1996), p. 27f. Kinnaird, in goal for the Wanderers in the 1877 Cup Final, had Oxford University's only goal in a 2–1 defeat expunged. The records still show a 2–0 Wanderers win.

7. Gil Merrick, *I See It All* (Museum Press, 1954), p. 129.

8. Charles Buchan, *A Lifetime in Football* (1955).

9. Kenneth Wolstenholme, *Sports Special* (Sportsman's Book Club edn, 1958), p. 149f.

Chapter 3

1. Pat Jennings with Reg Drury, *Pat Jennings – An Autobiography* (Collins Willow, 1983), p. 52f.

2. Eamonn Dunphy, *A Strange Kind of Glory* (Heinemann, 1991), p. 381.

3. Quoted in Bob Wilson, *The Art of Goalkeeping* (London, 1980), p. 33.

4. *Esquire* magazine, October 1996.

5. Bob Wilson, *You've Got to be Crazy*, (Arthur Barker, 1989), p. 245.

6. Frank Swift, *Football from the Goalmouth*, (Sporting Handbooks, 1948), p. 41ff.

7. Stephen F. Kelly, 'Three Liverpool Goalkeepers: Teddy Doig, Sam Hardy, Elisha Scott' in Stephen F. Kelly (ed.), *A Game of Two Halves* (Mandarin, 1993), p. 278.

8. *How to Play Soccer: Association Football* by Four Famous Players [Robert Kelly, Alf Baker, Dicky York and Dick Pym] (Foulsham, 1927), p. 61.

9. Harry Gregg, *Wild About Football* (Souvenir Press, 1961), p. 129.

Chapter 4

1. Ted Ditchburn's contribution in Ralph L. Finn (ed.), *My Greatest Game*, (Saturn, 1951), p. 7.

2. Simon Kuper, *Football Against the Enemy* (Orion, 1994), p. 175. Kuper's remarkable account of the political pressure the Argentine junta exerted to turn the World Cup Finals into a propaganda triumph is both convincing and chilling. He reveals, among a host of sordid details, that the standard urine tests after the final insisted that one of the Argentinian players was pregnant.

3. Gregg, *Wild About Football*, p. 9.

4. Ibid.

5. Peter Shilton with Jason Thomas, *The Magnificent Obsession* (World's Work Ltd, 1982), p. 57.

6. Jennings & Drury, *Pat Jennings – An Autobiography* (Collins Willow, 1983), p. 86.
7. Ibid.
8. Ibid.
9. John Moynihan, 'The World's Greatest Save' in *Football Fever* (Quartet, 1974).
10. Wilson, *You've Got to be Crazy*, pp. 163–7.

Chapter 5

1. 'Law 2: The Ball' in *Laws of Association Football*, as revised July 1995.
2. Gordon Banks, *Banks of England* (Arthur Barker, 1980), p. 26.
3. Reverend P.H. Francis, *Targets in Games* (Mitre, 1951). Francis has a tendency to get carried away with his subject, as, for example, in the passage where he worries tremendously about how draughtsmen are 'huffed' by being passed under the taker, and whether this might be derived from the Roman military habit of passing conquered soldiers under a symbolic yoke made of joined spears. But from time to time he hits upon an analogy that throws more light than darkness: 'There should be no difficulty in understanding that the ball, in football and hockey, represents the players of each side collectively both to themselves and their opponents. Readers of The Pickwick Papers certainly will find

no difficulty in understanding that some object between two rival parties can represent each party both to itself and to the other. They will remember that when Mr. Pickwick rashly intervened in the fight in the inn kitchen between Mr. Pott who was armed with the fire-shovel, and Mr. Slurk who was armed with a carpet-bag, the combatants, "being both acute reasoners", quickly saw certain advantages in having Mr. Pickwick between them. Each combatant saw that Mr. Pickwick's body could conveniently represent him and would receive the blows aimed at him by his opponent. They therefore "with great spirit plied the carpet-bag and the fire-shovel most fearlessly". But there were disadvantages also in having an object between them; for each combatant had to allow his opponent to be represented by Mr. Pickwick's body and had to deny himself the satisfaction of inflicting blows directly on the other. It is not difficult to imagine Mr. Pickwick's body being replaced by a ball . . .'

4. Jack Kelsey with Brian Glanville, *Over the Bar* (Stanley Paul, 1958), p. 124.

5. Frank Swift, *Football from the Goalmouth* (Sporting Handbooks, 1948), p. 159.

6. Montague Shearman (ed.), *Athletics and Football* (Badminton Library series, 1881), p. 351ff.

7. Meisl, *Soccer Revolution*, p. 57.

8. 'Gyula Grosics, the Great Hungarian, Looks at

Goalkeeping the Continental Way' in Gordon Ross (ed.), *The Gillette Book of Football and Cricket* (1963), p. 115.

9. Published in 1905 by Caxton. A wonderful source book for the early history of football, which is very rare. It is missing from the British Library collection, perhaps stolen in the days when security there was not as hot as it is now.
10. Gibson & Pickford, *Association Football*, vol. 1, p. 23.
11. Ibid., p. 177.
12. J. Ashcroft, 'How to Keep Goal' in S. Bloomer *et al, Football Guide, or How to Play 'Soccer'* (Spalding's Athletic Library #14, ed. J.A. McWeeney, 1906).
13. Percy Young, *Football Year* (Sportsman's Book Club, 1958), p. 98.
14. For the best modern account of the careers of both Leigh Richmond Roose and William Foulke, see Hazlewood, *In the Way!*
15. Ralph Waldo Emerson, *English Traits* (1856) in Bohn (ed.), *Works*, II, p. 45.
16. Jennings & Drury, *Pat Jennings – An Autobiography* (Collins Willow, 1983), p. 9.
17. Peter Shilton, *Shilton on Goalkeeping* (Headline, 1992).
18. Kelsey & Glanville, *Over the Bar*, p. 109.

Chapter 6

1. Sir Arthur Quiller-Couch, lecture of 1 May 1913, first published in *On the Art of Writing* (Cassell, 1916).
2. This story is passably well known. Nick Hazlewood (*In the Way!*, p. 19) records that in 1965 the same Brodie once found a hand grenade which had been tossed into his net. His words on that occasion are reported to have been, 'Jesus Christ, eh, Ref!', a succinct and wholly adequate response. The grenade was buried in a bucket of sand, and was later found to have had its firing mechanism removed.
3. Jimmy Greaves and Ian St John, *Football is a Funny Game* ed. Bob Patience (Arrow Books, 1987), p. 44.
4. Jennings & Drury, *Pat Jennings – An Autobiography* (Collins Willow, 1983), p. 94ff.
5. Ibid.
6. Ibid.
7. Ibid.
8. Ibid.
9. Ibid.
10. Alfredo Di Stefano, *For the Love of Football*, reprinted in L. R. Frewin (ed.), *The Saturday Men* (Macdonald, 1967), p. 82.

11. Jennings & Drury, *Pat Jennings – An Autobiography*, p. 168.
12. Ibid., p. 125.
13. Ibid., p. 125.
14. Percy Young, *The Appreciation of Football* (Sportsman's Book Club edn, 1953), p. 28.
15. Reg Moore (ed.), *Football is my Goal* (Phoenix House, London, 1949), p. 16. Contributions by Sam Bartram, Johnny Carey, Ron Burgess, Wilf Mannion, Tom Finney, and Matt Busby.
16. Swift, *Football from the Goalmouth*, p. 117.
17. Merrick, *I See It All*, p. 41.
18. 'Gyula Grosics' in *The Gillette Book of Football and Cricket*, p. 117.
19. Kelsey & Granville, *Over the Bar*, p. 65.
20. Gregg, *Wild About Football*, p. 95.
21. Geoffrey Green, *Soccer: The World Game* (Sportsman's Book Club, 1954), p. 168.
22. Quoted in Dunphy, *A Strange Kind of Glory*, p. 214.
23. Gregg, *Wild About Football*, p. 91.
24. Ibid.

Chapter 7

1. Nick Pitt, 'Tottenham in the 1960s', in Nawrat and Hutchings (eds.), *The Sunday Times Illustrated History of Football*, p. 126.

2. Ian St John and Jimmy Greaves, *Football is a Funny Game*, ed. Bob Patience (Arrow Books, 1987), p. 35.

3. From Arthur Hopcraft and Hugh McIlvanney, *World Cup '70* (Eyre and Spottiswoode), quoted in Willis Hall and Michael Parkinson (eds.), *Football Report, An Anthology of Soccer* (Pelham Books, 1973), p. 154.

4. John Rafferty, in John Arlott (ed.), *The Great Ones* (Pelham, 1968), p. 46.

5. Ibid., p. 45.

6. Quoted in Brian Glanville (ed.), *The Footballer's Companion*.

7. Rafael Alberti, 'Platko, Santander, 20 de Mayo de 1928', collected in *Cal y Canto*, first published 1929.

8. Banks, *Banks of England*, p. 113.

9. Respectively: Joel Bats, Jan Jongbloed, and Antonio Ramallets, the latter the goalkeeper who had so brilliantly defied England in Rio in 1950.

10. Young, *Appreciation of Football*, p. 27.

11. All quotations from Macedo from interview with Clement Freud in the *Observer*, 25 October 1959,

quoted in Tony Pawson (ed.), *The Observer on Soccer*, p. 152ff.

12. Ivan Sharpe, *40 Years in Football*, (Sportsman's Book Club, 1954), p. 153.
13. Hugh McIlvanney, *McIlvanney on Football* (Mainstream, 1994)
14. Batchelor, *Soccer*, p. 56.
15. Finn (ed.), *My Greatest Game*, p. 71.

Chapter 8

1. Brian Glanville, *Goalkeepers are Different* (Hamish Hamilton, 1971).
2. Meisl, *Soccer Revolution*, p. 60.
3. George Orwell, *The Sporting Spirit* from *The Penguin Essays of George Orwell* (Penguin, 1984), p. 321.
4. Sharpe, *40 Years*, p. 66.
5. Ivan Sharpe, in *Fabian and Green* (1960), vol. 3, p. 198.
6. See, for example, the illustration of him on the cover of the first issue of the monthly *Trés Sport*, reproduced in Pierre Delaunay *et al, Cent Ans de Football en France* (Editions Atlas, Paris, 1994).
7. John Macadam, *The Macadam Road*, (Jarrolds, 1955), p. 45.

8. Ibid.

9. Ibid.

10. One of the odder books to reveal a passion for goalkeeping is *The Holy Goalie* (Pentland Press, 1993) by the Rev. Leonard Small, a vastly distinguished Scottish churchman, the Moderator of the General Assembly. He played as an amateur in a professional side (St Bernards, then in the Scottish Second Division) and was awarded an international cap in 1929, and was only persuaded to abandon the goal after preaching with what he calls a 'suitably liturgical cross on my brow' made of sticking-plaster over a wound received at a forward's feet. His office-bearers said, 'We know you got it respectably, but it doesn't look good. We think you had better stop.'

11. *Fun & Games with Alistair Cooke* (Pavilion Books, 1994), p. 7.

12. Vladimir Nabokov, *Speak, Memory* (Gollancz, 1951). Nabokov was surely the only goalkeeper to have had fifty servants as a child (p.33). His passion is fully revealed on p.196: 'I was crazy about goalkeeping. In Russia and the Latin countries, that gallant art had been always surrounded with an aura of singular glamour. Aloof, solitary, impassive, the crack goalie is followed in the streets by entranced small boys. He vies with the matador and the flying-ace as an object of thrilled adulation. His sweater, his peaked cap, his knee-guards, the gloves protruding from the hip-pocket of his shorts, set him

apart from the rest of the team. He is the lone eagle, the man of mystery, the last defender. Photographers reverently bending one knee snap him in the act of making a spectacular dive across the goal-mouth to deflect with his finger-tips a low, lightning-like shot, and the stadium roars with approval as he remains for a moment or two lying full length where he fell, his goal still intact . . .'

13. Hazlewood, *In the Way!*, pp. 130–1.
14. John Motson, *Motty's Diary* (Virgin Books, 1996).
15. *Wisden 1996*, p. 16. See also John Dickson Carr, *Life of Sir Arthur Conan Doyle*, (Carrol & Graf, 1987), p. 54.
16. *Daily Telegraph*, 16.11.96.
17. Ibid., 9.11.96.
18. *Guardian*, 29.11.96.

Chapter 9

1. Shilton & Thomas, *Magnificent Obsession*, p. 77.
2. Ibid., p. 74.
3. Tax Cases Leaflet 3260 (HMSO), p. 8.
4. Banks, *Banks of England*, p. 77.
5. Shilton & Thomas, *Magnificent Obsession*, p. 67.
6. Ibid., p. 73.

7. Reprinted as 'The Streak of Streaks' in Stephen Jay Gould, *Bully for Brontosaurus* (Penguin, 1992), p. 463ff.

8. 'Goalkeepers Claim Sole Right to Real Pressure of Football' in *Daily Telegraph*, 20.1.97.

9. Dan Kavanagh, *Putting the Boot In* in *The Duffy Omnibus* (Penguin, 1991), p. 357.

10. Ibid., p.355.

Chapter 10

1. Alec E. Whitcher, *The Ace of Games*, (Southern, 1945), p. 19.

2. 'Across the White Line', broadcast in February 1996, produced by Hepburn Harrison Graham and presented by Trevor Macdonald.

3. 'A Modern Championship Meeting' (at the London Athletic Club grounds at Stamford Bridge, of all places, 3 July 1886) in Shearman (ed.), *Athletics and Football*, p. 60.

4. *Athletic News*, 18.1.1887, p. 1.

5. Ibid., 25.1.1887, p. 10, reporting a cup tie between Preston North End and Renton.

6. Alec E. Whitcher, *The Voice of Soccer*, (1946), p. 29.

7. Ibid., p. 25.

8. F.N.S. Creek, *History of the Corinthians Football Club* (Longmans, 1933), p. 60.

9. Ibid., p. 50.

10. Whitcher, *Voice of Soccer*, p. 25.

11. Toni Schumacher, trs. by Chris Morris, *Blowing the Whistle* (W. H. Allen, 1988).

12. Ibid., p. 204.

13. Quoted in Wilson, *You've Got to be Crazy*, p. 189.

14. Creek, *Corinthians*, p. 16.

15. Simon Armitage, *Goalkeeper with a Cigarette* (Faber and Faber).

16. J.B. Poynton, 'How Jupkins Lost the Cup', from the *FA Book for Boys, #7*, quoted in *The Footballer's Fireside Book*, compiled by Terence Delaney (Sportsman's Book Club edn, 1963), p. 274.

17. *Rubáiyát of Omar Khayyám*, tr. Edward Fitzgerald. This is stanza 50 in the 1859 edn, stanza 75 in the 2nd edn of 1868.

Books

There seems little point in presenting a complete bibliography on any footballing topic since the publication of Peter J. Seddon's *Football Compendium*, an annotated list of astonishing completeness, and a pleasure in its own right as well as a pleasure to use. My own list of books read, browsed or skimmed in preparing this one runs to some two hundred titles; I have tried to indicate specific references in the text. What follows are no more than a few favourites. There are many, many fine books not included in this list: my apologies to their authors.

A fair sprinkling of fine goalkeepers have written memoirs. I have enjoyed all of them, although not always for their literary qualities. Start with Bert Trautmann's *Steppes To Wembley* (1956).

John Arlott's *Concerning Soccer* (1952) is as nicely written as Arlott made us expect.

J.A.H. Catton, who wrote under the name Tityrus, was a fine late Victorian and Edwardian sportswriter. His style now seems mildly comic, but that is no bad thing.

He was serious about football when that took some courage to do. Try his *Wickets and Goals* (1926).

Herbert Chapman's *On Football* (1934).

The books on tactics I enjoyed most were Willy Meisl's *Soccer Revolution* (1955) and Bernard Joy's *Soccer Tactics* (1959).

Matthew Concanen's *A Match at Football*, a long poem from 1722, is a pleasing oddity, although my top goal-keeping poem remains Rafael Alberti's *Platko* (1929).

F.N.S. Creek's *History of the Corinthan Football Club* is splendidly . . . Corinthian.

There is no shortage of general histories of football: I can read Percy Young with pleasure on almost any subject. A fine musical scholar as well a good sports historian, he was football's equivalent to Neville Cardus. His *History of British Football* (1968) is as good a place to meet him as any, although his lighter books (*The Appreciation of Football* and *Football Facts and Fancies* were published in one volume in 1953) are genuinely funny.

The anthology with the richest goalkeeping section is Brian Glanville's *Footballer's Companion* (1962), and although all anthologies contain something special, it is probably the best of them all. The Aldine Football Novels were meant to be trashy; they are, but almost any of them found in a second-hand store will be money well spent. Good trash entertains just fine.

Pete Davies' *All Played Out* (1990) started the present

boom in football writing, and is often unjustly ignored. Plenty of modern writers (Roddy Doyle, Barry Hines . . .) have included something about football; the most goalkeeperly of them is Dan Kavanagh's louche detective Duffy. Arnold Bennett's *Matador of the Five Towns* (1912) is much older, a fine story including football.

Simon Inglis is known primarily for his work on football stadiums; his history, *League Football and the Men who Made It* (1988) was a great and pleasant surprise to me.

One eccentricity among many that I enjoyed was MacArthur and Kemp's *Elegance Borne of Brutality: an Eclectic History of the Football Boot* (1995).

Peter Shilton's *Magnificent Obsession* (1982) is just that, magnificent, a serious and thoroughly rewarding attack on just what this goalkeeping business is and means.

Bob Wilson has written several good books on goalkeeping, of which the most complete is *You've Got to Be Crazy* (1989), a goldmine of a book.

Among films, the *Arsenal Stadium Mystery* is fun. *The Goalkeeper's Fear of the Penalty* is not.

Among sports newspapers, I like the old *Athletic News*, from Manchester, and the evergreen *l'Equipe* in France.

No such list can close without Alfred Gibson and William Pickford's *Association Football and the Men Who Have Made It* (1905). Four volumes, pretty rare, and magnificent. One day I'll find my own copy. It was well imitated in 1960 by the same publishing company, Caxton, in another four volume set edited by A.H. Fabian and Geoffrey Green: *Association Football*.